Bloom's Modern Critical Views

Bloom's Modern Critical Views

CORMAC McCARTHY
New Edition

Edited and with an introduction by
Harold Bloom
Sterling Professor of the Humanities
Yale University

BLOOM'S
LITERARY CRITICISM
An imprint of Infobase Publishing

3/30/09
WW
$45—

Bloom's Modern Critical Views: Cormac McCarthy, New Edition

Bloom's Literary Criticism
An imprint of Infobase Publishing
132 West 31st Street
New York NY 10001

Library of Congress Cataloging-in-Publication Data

Cormac McCarthy / edited and with an introduction by Harold Bloom. — New ed.
    p. cm. — (Bloom's modern critical views)
  Includes bibliographical references and index.
  ISBN 978-1-60413-395-0 (acid-free paper) 1. McCarthy, Cormac, 1933– —Criticism and interpretation. 2. Mexican-American Border Region—In literature. 3. Tennessee, East—In literature. 4. Southern States—In literature. I. Bloom, Harold. II. Title. III. Series.

  PS3563.C337Z624 2009
  813'.54—dc22
                                    2008040110

Contributing Editor: Pamela Loos
Cover designed by Takeshi Takahashi
Printed in the United States of America
Bang EJB 10 9 8 7 6 5 4 3 2 1

This book is printed on acid-free paper.

All links and Web addresses were checked and verified to be correct at the time of publication. Because of the dynamic nature of the Web, some addresses and links may have changed since publication and may no longer be valid.

Contents

Editor's Note

My introduction analyzes *Blood Meridian* as McCarthy's permanent masterpiece and then proceeds to *All the Pretty Horses* as his best work since, a judgment I do not alter after reading both *No Country for Old Men* and *The Road*.

Steven Shaviro's reading exults in McCarthy's soaring prose, while Terri Witek emphasizes McCarthy's sense that on this earth we live in a place not at all our own.

The Border Trilogy is seen by John Wegner as a map of war and violence, after which Georg Guillemin reads *Suttree* as an "ecopastoral."

Violence is traced in its many Cormacian varieties by Vince Brewton, while Sara L. Spurgeon meditates on the American Religion of *Blood Meridian*.

Earlier novels are the focus of James R. Giles, after which Jay Ellis broods on the Jungian strain in *No Country for Old Men*.

Visions of the wasteland are examined in early McCarthy by Wallis R. Sanborn, while John Cant confronts the ultimate wasteland of *The Road*.

HAROLD BLOOM

Introduction

Blood Meridian (1985) seems to me the authentic American apocalyptic novel, more relevant even in 2010 than it was twenty-five years ago. The fulfilled renown of *Moby-Dick* and of *As I Lay Dying* is augmented by *Blood Meridian*, since Cormac McCarthy is the worthy disciple both of Melville and of Faulkner. I venture that no other living American novelist, not even Pynchon, has given us a book as strong and memorable as *Blood Meridian*, much as I appreciate Don DeLillo's *Underworld*; Philip Roth's *Zuckerman Bound, Sabbath's Theater*, and *American Pastoral*; and Pynchon's *Gravity's Rainbow* and *Mason & Dixon*. McCarthy himself, in his Border Trilogy, commencing with the superb *All the Pretty Horses*, has not matched *Blood Meridian*, but it is the ultimate Western, not to be surpassed.

My concern being the reader, I will begin by confessing that my first two attempts to read through *Blood Meridian* failed, because I flinched from the overwhelming carnage that McCarthy portrays. The violence begins on the novel's second page, when the fifteen-year-old Kid is shot in the back and just below the heart, and continues almost with no respite until the end, thirty years later, when Judge Holden, the most frightening figure in all of American literature, murders the Kid in an outhouse. So appalling are the continuous massacres and mutilations of *Blood Meridian* that one could be reading a United Nations report on the horrors of Kosovo in 1999.

Nevertheless, I urge the reader to persevere, because *Blood Meridian* is a canonical imaginative achievement, both an American and a universal tragedy of blood. Judge Holden is a villain worthy of Shakespeare, Iago-like and demoniac, a theoretician of war everlasting. And the book's magnificence—its

1

language, landscape, persons, conceptions—at last transcends the violence, and convert goriness into terrifying art, an art comparable to Melville's and to Faulkner's. When I teach the book, many of my students resist it initially (as I did, and as some of my friends continue to do). Television saturates us with actual as well as imagined violence, and I turn away, either in shock or in disgust. But I cannot turn away from *Blood Meridian*, now that I know how to read it, and why it has to be read. None of its carnage is gratuitous or redundant; it belonged to the Mexico–Texas borderlands in 1849–50, which is where and when most of the novel is set. I suppose one could call *Blood Meridian* a "historical novel," since it chronicles the actual expedition of the Glanton gang, a murderous paramilitary force sent out both by Mexican and Texan authorities to murder and scalp as many Indians as possible. Yet it does not have the aura of historical fiction, since what it depicts seethes on, in the United States, and nearly everywhere else, well into the third millennium. Judge Holden, the prophet of war, is unlikely to be without honor in our years to come.

Even as you learn to endure the slaughter McCarthy describes, you become accustomed to the book's high style, again as overtly Shakespearean as it is Faulknerian. There are passages of Melvillean-Faulknerian baroque richness and intensity in *The Crying of Lot 49*, and elsewhere in Pynchon, but we can never be sure that they are not parodistic. The prose of *Blood Meridian* soars, yet with its own economy, and its dialogue is always persuasive, particularly when the uncanny Judge Holden speaks (chapter 14):

> The judge placed his hands on the ground. He looked at his inquisitor. This is my claim, he said. And yet everywhere upon it are pockets of autonomous life. Autonomous. In order for it to be mine nothing must be permitted to occur upon it save by my dispensation.
> Toadvine sat with his boots crossed before the fire. No man can acquaint himself with everything on this earth, he said.
> The judge tilted his great head. The man who believes that the secrets of this world are forever hidden lives in mystery and fear. Superstition will drag him down. The rain will erode the deeds of his life. But that man who sets himself the task of singling out the thread of order from the tapestry will by the decision alone have taken charge of the world and it is only by such taking charge that he will effect a way to dictate the terms of his own fate.

Judge Holden is the spiritual leader of Glanton's filibusters, and McCarthy persuasively gives the self-styled judge a mythic status, appropriate for a deep Machiavelli whose "thread of order" recalls Iago's magic web, in which Othello, Desdemona, and Cassio are caught. Though all of the more colorful and murderous raiders are vividly characterized for us, the killing-machine Glanton with the others, the novel turns always upon its two central figures, Judge Holden and the Kid. We first meet the Judge on page 6: an enormous man, bald as a stone, no trace of a beard, and eyes without either brows or lashes. A seven-foot-tall albino, he almost seems to have come from some other world, and we learn to wonder about the Judge, who never sleeps, dances and fiddles with extraordinary art and energy, rapes and murders little children of both sexes, and who says that he will never die. By the book's close, I have come to believe that the Judge is immortal. And yet the Judge, while both more and less than human, is as individuated as Iago or Macbeth, and is quite at home in the Texan–Mexican borderlands where we watch him operate in 1849–50, and then find him again in 1878, not a day older after twenty-eight years, though the Kid, a sixteen-year-old at the start of Glanton's foray, is forty-five when murdered by the Judge at the end.

McCarthy subtly shows us the long, slow development of the Kid from another mindless scalper of Indians to the courageous confronter of the Judge in their final debate in a saloon. But though the Kid's moral maturation is heartening, his personality remains largely a cipher, as anonymous as his lack of a name. The three glories of the book are the Judge, the landscape, and (dreadful to say this) the slaughters, which are aesthetically distanced by McCarthy in a number of complex ways.

What is the reader to make of the Judge? He is immortal as principle, as War Everlasting, but is he a person, or something other? McCarthy will not tell us, which is all the better, since the ambiguity is most stimulating. Melville's Captain Ahab, though a Promethean demigod, is necessarily mortal, and perishes with the *Pequod* and all its crew, except for Ishmael. After he has killed the Kid, *Blood Meridian*'s Ishmael, Judge Holden is the last survivor of Glanton's scalping crusade. Destroying the Native American nations of the Southwest is hardly analogous to the hunt to slay Moby-Dick, and yet McCarthy gives us some curious parallels between the two quests. The most striking is between Melville's chapter 19, where a ragged prophet, who calls himself Elijah, warns Ishmael and Queequeg against sailing on the *Pequod*, and McCarthy's chapter 4, where "an old disordered Mennonite" warns the Kid and his comrades not to join Captain Worth's filibuster, a disaster that preludes the greater catastrophe of Glanton's campaign.

McCarthy's invocation of *Moby-Dick*, while impressive and suggestive, in itself does not do much to illuminate Judge Holden for us. Ahab has his preternatural aspects, including his harpooner Fedellah and Parsee whaleboat crew, and the captain's conversion to their Zoroastrian faith. Elijah tells Ishmael touches of other Ahabian mysteries: a three-day trance off Cape

Horn, slaying a Spaniard in front of a presumably Catholic altar in Santa Ysabel, and a wholly enigmatic spitting into a "silver calabash." Yet all these are transparencies compared to the enigmas of Judge Holden, who seems to judge the entire earth, and whose name suggests a holding, presumably of sway over all he encounters. And yet, the Judge, unlike Ahab, is not wholly fictive; like Glanton, he is a historic filibuster or freebooter. McCarthy tells us most in the Kid's dream visions of Judge Holden, towards the close of the novel (chapter 22):

> In that sleep and in sleep to follow the judge did visit. Who would come other? A great shambling mutant, silent and serene. Whatever his antecedents, he was something wholly other than their sum, nor was there system by which to divide him back into his origins for he would not go. Whoever would seek out his history through what unraveling of loins and ledgerbooks must stand at last darkened and dumb at the shore of a void without terminus or origin and whatever science he might bring to bear upon the dusty primal matter blowing down out of the millennia will discover no trace of ultimate atavistic egg by which to reckon his commencing.

I think that McCarthy is warning his reader that the Judge is Moby-Dick rather than Ahab. As another white enigma, the albino Judge, like the albino whale, cannot be slain. Melville, a professed Gnostic, who believed that some "anarch hand or cosmic blunder" had divided us into two fallen sexes, gives us a Manichean quester in Ahab. McCarthy gives Judge Holden the powers and purposes of the bad angels or demiurges that the Gnostics called archons, but he tells us not to make such an identification (as the critic Leo Daugherty eloquently has). Any "system," including the Gnostic one, will not divide the Judge back into his origins. The "ultimate atavistic egg" will not be found. What can the reader do with the haunting and terrifying Judge?

Let us begin by saying that Judge Holden, though his gladsome prophecy of eternal war is authentically universal, is first and foremost a Western American, no matter how cosmopolitan his background (he speaks all languages, knows all arts and sciences, and can perform magical, shamanistic metamorphoses). The Texan–Mexican border is a superb place for a war-god like the Judge to be. He carries a rifle, mounted in silver, with its name inscribed under the checkpiece: *Et In Arcadia Ego*. In the American Arcadia, death is also always there, incarnated in the Judge's weapon, which never misses. If the American pastoral tradition essentially is the Western film, then the Judge incarnates that tradition, though he would require a director light-years beyond the late Sam Peckinpah, whose *The Wild Bunch* portrays mildness itself when compared to Glanton's paramilitaries. I resort though, as before, to Iago, who transfers war from the camp and the field to every other locale, and is a pyromaniac setting everything and everyone ablaze with the flame of battle. The Judge might be Iago before *Othello* begins, when the war-god Othello was still worshipped by his "honest" color officer, his ancient or ensign. The Judge speaks with an authority that chills me even as Iago leaves me terrified:

> This is the nature of war, whose stake is at once the game and the authority and the justification. Seen so, war is the truest form of divination. It is the testing of one's will and the will of another within that larger will which because it binds them is therefore forced to select. War is the ultimate game because war is at last a forcing of the unity of existence.

If McCarthy does not want us to regard the Judge as a Gnostic archon or supernatural being, the reader may still feel that it hardly seems sufficient to designate Holden as a nineteenth-century Western American Iago. Since *Blood Meridian*, like the much longer *Moby-Dick*, is more prose epic than novel, the Glanton foray can seem a post-Homeric quest, where the various heroes (or thugs) have a disguised god among them, which appears to be the Judge's Herculean role. The Glanton gang passes into a sinister aesthetic glory at the close of chapter 13, when they progress from murdering and scalping Indians to butchering the Mexicans who have hired them:

> They entered the city haggard and filthy and reeking with the blood of the citizenry for whose protection they had contracted. The scalps of the slain villagers were strung from the windows of the governor's house and the partisans were paid out of the all but exhausted coffers and the Sociedad was disbanded and the bounty rescinded. Within a week of their quitting the city there would be a price of eight thousand pesos posted for Glanton's head.

I break into this passage, partly to observe that from this point on the filibusters pursue the way down and out to an apocalyptic conclusion, but also to urge the reader to hear, and admire, the sublime sentence that follows directly, because we are at the visionary center of *Blood Meridian*.

They rode out on the north road as would parties bound for El
Paso but before they were even quite out of sight of the city
they had turned their tragic mounts to the west and they rode
infatuate and half fond toward the red demise of that day, toward
the evening lands and the distant pandemonium of the sun.

Since Cormac McCarthy's language, like Melville's and Faulkner's,
frequently is deliberately archaic, the *meridian* of the title probably means the
zenith or noon position of the sun in the sky. Glanton, the Judge, the Kid,
and their fellows are not described as "tragic"—their long-suffering horses
are— and they are "infatuate" and half-mad ("fond") because they have broken
away from any semblance of order. McCarthy knows, as does the reader, that
an "order" urging the destruction of the entire Native American population
of the Southwest is an obscene idea of order, but he wants the reader to know
also that the Glanton gang is now aware that they are unsponsored and free
to run totally amok. The sentence I have just quoted has a morally ambiguous
greatness to it, but that is the greatness of *Blood Meridian*, and indeed of
Homer and of Shakespeare. McCarthy so contextualizes the sentence that
the amazing contrast between its high gestures and the murderous thugs who
evoke the splendor is not ironic but tragic. The tragedy is ours, as readers, and
not the Glanton gang's, since we are not going to mourn their demise except
for the Kid's, and even there our reaction will be equivocal.

My passion for *Blood Meridian* is so fierce that I want to go on
expounding it, but the courageous reader should now be (I hope) pretty well
into the main movement of the book. I will confine myself here to the final
encounter between the preternatural Judge Holden and the Kid, who had
broken with the insane crusade twenty-eight years before, and now at middle
age must confront the ageless Judge. Their dialogue is the finest achievement
in this book of augmenting wonders, and may move the reader as nothing
else in *Blood Meridian* does. I reread it perpetually and cannot persuade myself
that I have come to the end of it.

The Judge and the Kid drink together, after the avenging Judge tells
the Kid that this night his soul will be demanded of him. Knowing he is no
match for the Judge, the Kid nevertheless defies Holden, with laconic replies
playing against the Judge's rolling grandiloquence. After demanding to know
where their slain comrades are, the Judge asks: "And where is the fiddler and
where the dance?"

I guess you can tell me.
I tell you this. As war becomes dishonored and its nobility called
into question those honorable men who recognize the sanctity of
blood will become excluded from the dance, which is the warrior's

right, and thereby will the dance become a false dance and the dancers false dancers. And yet there will be one there always who is a true dancer and can you guess who that might be?

You aint nothin.

To have known Judge Holden, to have seen him in full operation, and to tell him that he is nothing, is heroic. "You speak truer than you know," the Judge replies, and two pages later murders the Kid, most horribly. *Blood Meridian*, except for a one-paragraph epilogue, ends with the Judge triumphantly dancing and fiddling at once, and proclaiming that he never sleeps and he will never die. But McCarthy does not let Judge Holden have the last word.

The strangest passage in *Blood Meridian*, the epilogue is set at dawn, where a nameless man progresses over a plain by means of holes that he makes in the rocky ground. Employing a two-handled implement, the man strikes "the fire out of the rock which God has put there." Around the man are wanderers searching for bones, and he continues to strike fire in the holes, and then they move on. And that is all.

The subtitle of *Blood Meridian* is *The Evening Redness in the West*, which belongs to the Judge, last survivor of the Glanton gang. Perhaps all that the reader can surmise with some certainty is that the man striking fire in the rock at dawn is an opposing figure in regard to the evening redness in the West. The Judge never sleeps, and perhaps will never die, but a new Prometheus may be rising to go up against him.

ALL THE PRETTY HORSES

If there is a pragmatic tradition of the American Sublime, then Cormac McCarthy's fictions are its culmination. *Moby-Dick* and Faulkner's major, early novels are McCarthy's prime precursors. Melville's Ahab fuses together Shakespeare's tragic protagonists—Hamlet, Lear, Macbeth—and crosses them with a quest both Promethean and American. Even as Montaigne's Plato became Emerson's, so Melville's Shakespeare becomes Cormac McCarthy's. Though critics will go on associating McCarthy with Faulkner, who certainly affected McCarthy's style in *Suttree* (1979), the visionary of *Blood Meridian* (1985) and The Border Trilogy (1992, 1994, 1998) has much less in common with Faulkner, and shares more profoundly in Melville's debt to Shakespeare.

Melville, by giving us Ahab and Ishmael, took care to distance the reader from Ahab, if not from his quest. McCarthy's protagonists tend to be apostles of the will-to-identity, except for the Iago-like Judge Holden of *Blood Meridian*, who is the Will Incarnate. John Grady Cole, who survives

in *All the Pretty Horses* only to be destroyed in *Cities of the Plain*, is replaced
in *The Crossing* by Billy Parham, who is capable of learning what the heroic
Grady Cole evades, the knowledge that Jehovah (Yahweh) holds in his very
name: "Where that is I am not." God will be present where and when he
chooses to be present, and absent more often than present.

The aesthetic achievement of *All the Pretty Horses* surpasses that of *Cities
of the Plain*, if only because McCarthy is too deeply invested in John Grady
Cole to let the young man (really still a boy) die with the proper distancing
of authorial concern. No one will compose a rival to *Blood Meridian*, not even
McCarthy, but *All the Pretty Horses* and *The Crossing* are of the eminence of
Suttree. If I had to choose a narrative by McCarthy that could stand on its own
in relation to *Blood Meridian*, it probably would be *All the Pretty Horses*. John
Grady Cole quests for freedom, and discovers what neither Suttree nor Billy
Parham needs to discover, which is that freedom in an American context is
another name for solitude. The self's freedom, for Cormac McCarthy, has no
social aspect whatsoever.

I speak of McCarthy as visionary novelist, and not necessarily as a
citizen of El Paso, Texas. Emerson identified freedom with power, only
available at the crossing, in the shooting of a gulf, a darting to an aim. Since
we care for Hamlet, even though he cares for none, we have to assume that
Shakespeare also had a considerable investment in Hamlet. The richest aspect
of *All the Pretty Horses* is that we learn to care strongly about the development
of John Grady Cole, and perhaps we can surmise that Cormac McCarthy is
also moved by this most sympathetic of his protagonists.

All the Pretty Horses was published seven years after *Blood Meridian*, and
is set almost a full century later in history. John Grady Cole is about the same
age as McCarthy would have been in 1948. There is no more an identification
between McCarthy and the young Cole, who evidently will not live to see
twenty, than there is between Shakespeare and Prince Hamlet. And yet the
reverberation of an heroic poignance is clearly heard throughout *All the Pretty
Horses*. It may be that McCarthy's hard-won authorial detachment toward
the Kid in *Blood Meridian* had cost the novelist too much, in the emotional
register. Whether my surmise is accurate or not, the reader shares with
McCarthy an affectionate stance toward the heroic youth at the center of *All
the Pretty Horses*.

STEVEN SHAVIRO

"The Very Life of the Darkness": A Reading of Blood Meridian

Your heart's desire is to be told some mystery. The mystery is that there is no mystery.

—Judge Holden (252)

He would look for spiders, and make them fight together, or throw flies into the spider web; and then he watched that battle with so much pleasure, that he would sometimes burst into laughter.

—Colerus, *Life of Spinoza*

Death is a festival, a ceremony, a ritual; but it is not a mystery. *Blood Meridian* sings hymns of violence, its gorgeous language commemorating slaughter in all its sumptuousness and splendor:

> some of the men were moving on foot among the huts with torches and dragging the victims out, slathered and dripping with blood, hacking at the dying and decapitating those who knelt for mercy.... [O]ne of the Delawares emerged from the smoke with a naked infant dangling in each hand and squatted at a ring of midden stones and swung them by the heels each in turn and bashed their heads against the stones so that the brains burst forth through the fontanel in a bloody spew and humans

From *Perspectives on Cormac McCarthy*, edited by Edwin T. Arnold and Dianne C. Luce, 143–155. © 1993 by *The Southern Quarterly*.

on fire came shrieking forth like berserkers and the riders hacked
them down with their enormous knives. . . . (156)

Everywhere in this book, death leaves behind its memorials, its
trophies and its fetishes: the scalps collected by Glanton and his men, the
tree of dead babies (57), the crucified mummy (247), the circle of severed
heads (220), the eviscerated bodies of bearded men with "strange menstrual
wounds between their legs and no man's parts for these had been cut
away and hung dark and strange from out their grinning mouths" (153).
Reading *Blood Meridian* produces a vertiginous, nauseous exhilaration. A
strong compulsion draws us through this text, something beyond either
fascination or horror. "What man would not be a dancer if he could,
said the judge. It's a great thing, the dance" (327). Bloody death is our
monotonously predictable destiny; yet its baroque opulence is attended
with a frighteningly complicitous joy.

Cormac McCarthy, the solitary poet of this exultation, is our greatest
living author: nomadic wanderer, lucid cartographer of an inescapable
delirium. In the entire range of American literature, only *Moby-Dick* bears
comparison to *Blood Meridian*. Both novels are epic in scope, cosmically
resonant, obsessed with open space and with language, exploring vast
uncharted distances with a fanatically patient minuteness. Both manifest
a sublime visionary power that is matched only by a still more ferocious
irony. Both savagely explode the American dream of manifest destiny,
of racial domination and endless imperial expansion. But if anything,
McCarthy writes with a yet more terrible clarity than does Melville. For
he has none of Melville's nostalgia for lost—primitive or uterine—origins.
The "kid" who is McCarthy's nameless protagonist knows nothing of
his mother: she dies giving birth to him (3). And he scarcely knows his
father any better; within the first two pages of the book he has already left
home forever, "divested of all that he has been" (4). We encounter instead
the monstrously charismatic figure of Judge Holden, ironic Ahab to the
kid's unselfconscious Ishmael. Orphanhood is taken for granted in *Blood
Meridian*; the kid, unlike Ishmael, never feels any pathos in this condition.
The judge notes at one point that "it is the death of the father to which
the son is entitled and to which he is heir," so that the "father dead [before
the son was born] has euchered the son out of his patrimony" (145). Such
a double displacement—exile so extreme that we are exiled even from the
possibility, the hope and despair, of exile—characterizes the life of these
wanderers in the desert. The oedipal myth of paradise lost and regained, of
patrimonial inheritance and promised land, has been abolished once and for
all. These travelers will feel different cravings, experience different affects.
The kid's "origins are become remote as is his destiny" (4), and his only

point of reference in "that hallucinatory void" (113) is the unrepresentable extremity in which the judge embraces him "like a son" (306), enfolding him forever in his "immense and terrible flesh" (333).

Blood Meridian is a book, then, not of heights and depths, nor of origins and endings, but of restless, incessant horizontal movements: nomadic wanderings, topographical displacements, variations of weather, skirmishes in the desert. There is only war, there is only the dance. Exile is not deprivation or loss, but our primordial and positive condition. For there can be no alienation when there is no originary state for us to be alienated from. Glanton's riders climb into mountainous regions or descend through narrow canyons, but they always remain in intimate contact with the superficies of the earth, with the elemental forces of ground and sky, snow and hail and lightning, water and wind and barren rock. The journey is limitless, circumscribed only by the infinite vault of "naked and unrectified night" (106), and by the open wound of the horizon, "holocaust" (105) and "distant pandemonium" (185) of the declining sun. This horizon beckons onward to all the "itinerant degenerates bleeding westward like some heliotropic plague" (78). Or it emerges into violent and menacing clarity: "and where the earth drained up into the sky at the edge of creation the top of the sun rose out of nothing like the head of a great red phallus until it cleared the unseen rim and sat squat and pulsing and malevolent behind them" (44–45). In either case, the horizon is a circumference that looms ominously near, lures or threatens, and yet remains forever out of reach. As the judge warns us (thus also explaining the title of the book), "in the affairs of men there is no waning and the noon of his expression signals the onset of night. His spirit is exhausted at the peak of its achievement. His meridian is at once his darkening and the evening of his day" (146–47). Zenith and horizon continually exchange places, without mediation or delay; what is most dim, distant and uncertain abruptly appears as an inescapable fatality. *Blood Meridian* rejects organicist metaphors of growth and decay, in favor of an open topography (what Deleuze and Guattari call "smooth space") in which the endless, unobstructed extension of the desert allows for the sudden, violent and fortuitous irruption of the most heterogeneous forces: "in the convergence of such vectors in such a waste wherein the hearts and enterprise of one small nation have been swallowed up and carried off by another the ex-priest asked if some might not see the hand of a cynical god conducting with what austerity and what mock surprise so lethal a congruence" (153). Yet the entire book consists of nothing but such fatal encounters, lethal congruences of impossible but converging vectors. The riders trace a fractal path upon the surface of the earth; they define an intradimensional space in which the extremities of night and day intersect, a permeable membrane for the incessant transactions of life and death.

They follow the contours of an inverted circle whose circumference is everywhere and whose center is nowhere, "some maelstrom out there in the void, some vortex in that waste apposite to which man's transit and his reckonings alike lay abrogate. As if beyond will or fate he and his beasts and his trappings moved both in card and in substance under consignment to some third and other destiny" (96).

Indeed, we are consigned so utterly and irredeemably to this "third destiny," this elemental desert, that fate and will alike fade into insignificance. We are called to no responsibility, and we may lay claim to no transcendence. *Blood Meridian* is not a salvation narrative; we can be rescued neither by faith nor by works nor by grace. It is useless to look for ulterior, redemptive meanings, useless even to posit the irredeemable gratuitousness of our abandonment in the form of some existential category such as Heideggerian "thrownness" (*Geworfenheit*). We have not fallen here or been "thrown" here, for we have always been here, and always will be. Only the judge seems descended from another world (125). We are never separate from the landscape or from those other voyagers with whom we so disastrously meet and clash, for the same nomadic forces impel us all: "If much in the world were mystery the limits of that world were not, for it was without measure or bound and there were contained within it creatures more horrible yet and men of other colors and beings which no man has looked upon and yet not alien none of it more than were their own hearts alien in them, whatever wilderness contained there and whatever beasts" (138). Nothing inhuman can be alien to me. The world is infinite in novelty and variety, "a trance bepopulate with chimeras having neither analogue nor precedent," and whose "ultimate destination . . . is unspeakable and calamitous beyond reckoning" (245); and yet this world is devoid of final mystery or essential otherness, since all is composed of the one unique Spinozistic substance. We would like to believe that our destiny is lofty and singular—whether it be self-willed or decreed by a transcendent and inexorable fate—but we discover that we are merely "pursuing as all travelers must inversions without end upon other men's journeys" (121). There is finally no mystery, not even in death; if we remain puzzled as to who we are, whence we have come, and whither we are bound, this is only because, the judge explains, "[a]s the dance . . . contains complete within itself its own arrangement and history and finale there is no necessity that the dancers contain these things within themselves as well" (329). Our experience of the world's limits consists precisely in this, that we can never encounter or encompass or transgress those limits. We remain bound in a dance of perpetual immanence.

Western culture has dreamed for centuries of some act of heroic transgression and self-transformation: whether this take the Enlightenment form of rational mastery, or the romantic and mystical one of apocalyptic transfiguration. McCarthy, like Nietzsche, exposes not just the futility of the dream, but—far more troublingly—its inherent *piety*, its ironic dependence upon the very (supposed) mysteries that it claims to violate. What is most disturbing about the orgies of violence that punctuate *Blood Meridian* is that they fail to constitute a pattern, to unveil a mystery or to serve any comprehensible purpose. Instead, the book suggests that "a taste for mindless violence" (3) is as ubiquitous—and as banal—as any other form of "common sense." Scalping has been a common human practice for at least 300,000 years, as one of the epigraphs to the novel suggests. Acts of destruction are as casual, random and unreflective as acts of kindness and civility—which also occur at odd moments in the course of the narrative. The judge demonstrates this point with cynical clarity when he calmly scalps a young child after having rescued it and carried it about and played with it for three days; for all that he and his mates have just destroyed an entire defenseless village, Toadvine is scandalized (164). Toadvine is incapable even of imagining transgression; he robs and kills precisely to the extent that such acts seem to him within the normal order of things. The judge, on the other hand, transgresses only in an ironic mode: by his lights, the perversity of scalping the child after it has come to trust him is no greater than the initial perversity of rescuing it from an otherwise total holocaust. In both cases, actual transgression is impossible. Transgression is an endeavor to exhaust the world, to compel it to reveal itself: as the judge puts it, "Only nature can enslave man and only when the existence of each last entity is routed out and made to stand naked before him will he be properly suzerain of the earth" (198). Such is the self-transcending project of Enlightenment. And we might be tempted to say that whereas all the other characters kill casually and thoughtlessly, out of greed or blood lust or some other trivial cause, only the judge kills out of will and conviction and a deep commitment to the cause and the canons of Western rationality.

But the judge also knows that it is impossible to transgress when there is no Law to violate, and when there is no final accumulation of goods or knowledge to be gathered together and no ultimate boundary to be attained. We cannot deplete the world, we cannot reach the sunset. Beyond the desert, there is only more empty space, the equally daunting infinitude of the ocean, "out there past men's knowing, where the stars are drowning and whales ferry their vast souls through the black and seamless sea" (304). The judge reminds us that "more things exist without our knowledge than with it and the order in creation which you see is that which you have put there, like a string in a maze, so that you shall not lose your way. For existence has its own order and that no man's mind can compass, that mind itself being but a fact among others" (245). *Our* order is never the world's order, not even in the Nietzschean sense of an order that we impose. We mark out paths in the desert or we read the tracks of others, but we cannot thereby master futurity or compel events to our liking. For subjectivity is not a perspective upon or projection into the world, nor even a transcendental condition for our perception of the world; it is just another empirical fact, an inherence within the world like any other. There is no interiority, no intentionality and no transcendence. The radical epistemology of *Blood Meridian* subverts all dualisms of subject and object, inside and outside, will and representation or being and interpretation. We are always exiles within the unlimited phenomenality of the world, for we cannot coincide with the (nonexistent) center of our being: "the history of all is not the history of each nor indeed the sum of those histories and none here can finally comprehend the reason for his presence for he has no way of knowing even in what the event consists. In fact, were he to know he might well absent himself and you can see that that cannot be any part of the plan if plan there be" (329). And so, just as we can never possess the world (since we cannot even possess ourselves), by the same logic we can never transgress the order of the world or estrange ourselves from it—no matter how hard we try.

In the pages of *Blood Meridian*, then, there is room neither for the demonic monomania of an Ahab nor for the self-reflective detachment of an Ishmael. Or better, these types flicker only for a moment, and before we know it they have "passed all into the problematical destruction of darkness" (105). Indeed, there is something of Ahab in Glanton: "He'd long forsworn all weighing of consequence and allowing as he did that men's destinies are given yet he usurped to contain within him all that he would ever be in the world and all that the world would be to him and be his charter written in the urstone itself he claimed agency and said so . . ." (243). Glanton resolves to be equal to his destiny; without the moralistic playacting usually present in such cases, he lays claim to the absurd existential nobility of the tragic hero. Yet there's an enormous difference between what can be called Glanton's stoicism and Ahab's dualistic defiance. Glanton affirms his own agency through an identification with the whole of fate, so that it is as if he has willed even the event that destroys him. Whereas Ahab's will continues to affirm itself against the universe, even at the mortal instant when that universe consumes it into nothingness. Glanton, unlike Ahab, confirms the judge's claim that "war is at last a forcing of the unity of existence" (249). His very aggressiveness and egotism are finally nothing but a means of sacrificing himself to such unity. And his only compensation for this sacrifice is the dubious one of proclaiming his defeat as a higher victory. The judge has little respect for such consolations: "There is room on the stage for one beast and one alone. All others are destined for a night that is eternal and without name. One by one they will step down into the darkness before the footlamps" (331). The play will soon be over, and we fool ourselves if we think that we can derive from it any profits of catharsis or redemption. Glanton's heroic resoluteness does not lend any grandeur to his death; still less does it lead to any tragic recognition or transfiguration: "Hack away you mean red nigger, he said, and the old man raised the axe and split the head of John Joel Glanton to the thrapple" (275).

At the other extreme from Glanton's tragic heroism, there is something of Ishmael in the kid. He drifts from place to place, never taking the initiative, sidestepping mortal engagements and warily refusing the judge's continual seductions. The kid keeps his distance from the claims both of destiny and of agency; he offers to the world only a sort of passive resistance, a silent, obstinate rejection of all finalities and of all melodramatics. Even as he behaves as a good fellow to his comrades, and participates uncomplainingly in the most violent, barbaric actions, he seems to retain the detachment of an observer. His most typical moment is perhaps that when he watches from high in the mountains "the collision of armies remote and silent upon the plain below" (213). The kid's skeptical reserve is analogous to Ishmael's, although it arises from an utter unreflectiveness in the one case and from an exacerbated self-consciousness in the other. For we are never given any insight into the kid's inner life; apart from that manifested in the stubbornness of his refusal to commit himself, he does not appear to have any. I think it is this eerie affectlessness, rather than some more determinate quality, that leads to the kid's hesitation at certain crucial moments: such as when he does not kill Shelby (206–10), or later when he ignores Tobin's advice to launch a preemptive strike against the judge. And this blankness is also what makes the kid into an object of desire for other characters in the book. They lust after him to the precise measure of his own indifference. I am thinking here of strange scenes like that of the old hermit's advances to the kid (20), as well as the judge's disturbing interest in him: "The judge watched him. Was it always your idea, he said, that if you did not speak you would not be recognized?" (328). In fact, it is the kid's very silence and unresponsiveness that the judge singles out in him: "That feeling in the breast that evokes a child's memory of loneliness such as when the others have gone and only the game is left with its solitary participant. A solitary game, without opponent" (329). It is this indifference that irritates the will of the judge, and that he seeks to master and appropriate; this seductive child's loneliness that he needs to baptize and give (re-)birth to, as he does in the parallel case of the idiot (259). The judge reproaches the kid's refusal of tragic knowledge as much as he scorns the futility of Glanton's accession to such knowledge: "You put your own allowances before the judgements of history and you broke with the body of which you were pledged a part and poisoned it in all its enterprise. Hear me, man. I spoke in the desert for you and you only and you turned a deaf ear to me. If war is not holy man is nothing but antic clay" (307). We are left in a no-win situation: the kid's evasive blankness marks a deferral but not an exemption from the all-embracing game of war. He can refuse its communion, but not its claim to be "the truest form of divination" (249). For "[w]hat joins men together, he said, is not the sharing of bread but the sharing of enemies. . . . Our animosities were formed and waiting before ever we two met" (307). There is no retreat, no separation. The kid cannot refuse the judge's election, any more than he can live up to it. This Ishmael will not be thrown free, and will not survive the wreck.

Glanton and the kid may represent opposite poles of a dialectic, but it is a stalled dialectic, one that fails ever to advance. All these heroic or evasive stances only bring us back by circuitous routes to the immanence of the landscape and the imminence of death, that "wry and grinning tradesman good to follow every campaign or hound men from their holes in just those whited regions where they've gone to hide from God" (44). We cannot run and hide in the desert, for the desert's vastness already enfolds the shape of our destiny. "You wouldn't think that a man would run plumb out of country out here, would ye?" (285), Toadvine complains. Death stalks these vast expanses of space and time, as inevitable and unforeseen as the uncanny bolts of lightning flashing out in the darkness that repeatedly punctuate the book. There is no reserve of potentiality in *Blood Meridian*; everything is cruelly, splendidly actual. There is no transcendence, and no possibility of standing out from Being. There is no stance by which subjectivity might fold back upon itself, thereby affirming and preserving itself, or at least attenuating the shock of those multiple, fatal encounters that mark its inherence in the world: as the judge warns, "Any man who could discover his own fate and elect therefore some opposite course could only come at last to that selfsame reckoning at the same appointed time, for each man's destiny is as large as the world he inhabits and contains within it all opposites as well" (330).

This "third destiny," exceeding both will and fate, is an immanent function of the landscape itself, which means that it is also a function of writing. McCarthy's sublime prose style resonates with those of Faulkner, of Melville and of the King James Bible. And by any criterion, McCarthy's writing is as great as any of these. But still more important, I think, is the way in which the language of *Blood Meridian* caresses the harsh desert landscape, slides amorously over its surfaces. The language of *Blood Meridian* is not primarily mimetic, as in classical models of the novel; but neither is it turned inward to thought or back upon itself, as is canonically the case with modernist texts. It is rather continually outside itself, in intimate contact with the world in a powerfully nonrepresentational way. McCarthy's writing is so closely intertwined with the surfaces of the earth and the depths of the cosmos that it cannot be disentangled from them. "Books lie," says the judge, referring to the salvational fables of scripture; but the actual, material words of God—who "speaks in stones and trees, the bones of things"—these do not lie (116). The writing of *Blood Meridian* composes such an immanent, material language, a speaking inscribed in the rocks and in the sky, in the very physical body of the world: "In the neuter austerity of that terrain all phenomena were bequeathed a strange equality and no one thing nor spider nor stone nor blade of grass could put forth claim to precedence. The very clarity of these articles belied their familiarity, for the eye predicates the whole on some feature or part and here was nothing more luminous than another and nothing more enshadowed and in the optical democracy of such landscapes all preference is made whimsical and a man and a rock become endowed with unguessed kinships" (247).

In a passage such as this one, the effect of the language is the same as the effect of the light. Minute details and impalpable qualities are registered with such precision that the prejudices of anthropocentric perceptions are disqualified. The eye no longer constitutes the axis of vision. We are given instead a kind of perception before or beyond the human. This is not a perspective *upon* the world, and not a vision that *intends* its objects: but an immanent perspective that already *is* the world, and a primordial visibility, a luminescence, that is indifferent to our acts of vision because it is always passively at work in whatever objects we may or may not happen to look at. McCarthy's narrative follows the progress of the kid, and to a lesser extent of other of Glanton's men; but it is never really written from their points of view. The prose enacts not a symbolization or a hermeneutics but *an erotics of landscape*, moving easily between the degree zero of "desert absolute" (295) and the specific articulations of water, mud, sand, sky and mountains. It leaps from the concrete to the abstract and back again, often in the space of a single sentence. It observes a fractal symmetry of scale, describing without hierarchical distinction and with the same attentive complexity the most minute phenomena and the most cosmic. And its observations cannot be attributed to any fixed center of enunciation, neither to an authorial presence nor to a narrating voice nor to the consciousness of any of the characters. There is only an incessant fluid displacement, a flux of words and of visions and palpations, indifferent to our usual distinctions between subjective and objective, between literal and figurative or between empirical description and speculative reflection. The book is written "[a]s if the very sediment of things contained yet some residue of sentience. As if in the transit of those riders were a thing so profoundly terrible as to register even to the uttermost granulation of reality" (247).

Blood Meridian thus refuses to acknowledge any gap or opposition between words and things. It insists that there can be no fissure or discontinuity in the real. But if this be the case, then there can also be no separate order of signification, and questions about the adequacy or inadequacy of language to what it describes cannot even arise. Speaking of "representations and things" (136), the judge remarks, "What is to be deviates no jot from the book wherein it's writ. How could it? It would be a false book and a false book is no book at all" (141). This is not to argue (like the philosophers decried in Plato's *Sophist*) that it is impossible to lie or to speak what is not—though as far as I can tell, everything the judge says throughout the book is in some sense true, even if the pragmatic effect of his ironies and sarcastic insinuations is to deceive his listeners. Nor is it to say that the book fatally determines the course of what happens, or conversely that it faithfully reproduces that course. It is rather to insist, in the manner of Spinoza, that the order of words and images is literally the same as the order of actions and events. The judge affirms an ontological parallelism between thing and representation, between 'being' and 'witness': "Whether in my book or not, every man is tabernacled in every other and he in exchange and so on in an endless complexity of being and witness to the uttermost edge of the world" (141). Language no less than the desert floor is a space which comprehends everything, but in which the complex intrication of heterogeneous forces fatally leads to unwelcome encounters and deadly confrontations. Words and images are inherently dangerous; they participate, just as do bodies, in the "ultimate game" of war, the "testing of one's will and the will of another within that larger will which because it binds them is therefore forced to select" (249). Mimesis is not an imitation of the real so much as an aggressive and provocative solicitation of the real. The judge recalls that "he'd once drawn an old Hueco's portrait and unwittingly chained the man to his own likeness. For he could not sleep for fear an enemy might take it and deface it . . ." (141). The making of images and words is not a tranquil process of recollection and perpetuation, but a continual movement of accretion that also implies the cruelty of triage or selection. The judge duplicates the world by obsessively copying all that he encounters into his notebooks; his simulations of various objects allow him to dispense with or even destroy the originals, "to expunge them from the memory of man" (140). He complains, "Whatever in creation exists without my knowledge exists without my consent" (198). But the more that is drawn or written and that hence becomes known, the more that is thereby subjected, not to human agency or adjudication, but to "war, whose stake is at once the game and the authority and the justification" (249). The writing of *Blood Meridian* is a catastrophic act of witness, embracing the real by tracing it in gore. McCarthy's previous novel, *Suttree* (1979), ends with the admonition to flee the cruel huntsman and his hounds, "slaverous and wild and their eyes crazed with ravening for souls in this world" (471). *Blood Meridian* ignores this advice, and instead conjures the presence of those hounds, tracks them as closely as possible. For McCarthy as for the judge, writing is inevitably an act of war: deracination, divinatory affirmation, the composition and conduction of dangerous forces, and the production of an active counter-memory.

Writing, like war, is a ceremonial and sacrificial act; and *Blood Meridian* is a novel written in blood, awash in blood. Yet for all its lucidity in the face of horror, this is not a book that sets a high value upon self-consciousness. And for all its exacerbated sense of fatality, its tenor is profoundly anticlimactic and anticathartic. *Blood Meridian* places the reader in the position of one "who has offered up himself entire to the blood of war, who has been to the floor of the pit and seen horror in the round and learned at last that it speaks to his inmost heart . . ." (331). But there is no purgation or release in this recognition, no curative discharge of fear and pity. We are rather swamped by emotions which can find no outlet; we too are implicated in this savage spectacle. We perform acts of sacrifice—"the slaying of a large bear" (329), or of many men—not to propitiate alien gods and not to ward off distant calamities, but to confirm our own complicity with the forces that crush and annihilate us. "Is not blood the tempering agent in the mortar which bonds?" (329). The scariest thing about *Blood Meridian* is that it is a euphoric and exhilarating book, rather than a tragically alienated one, or a gloomy, depressing one. Our pulses quicken as "considerations of equity and rectitude and moral right [are] rendered void and without warrant" (250), subsumed in the trials of war. Once we have started to dance, once we have been swept up in the game, there is no pulling back.

The judge states categorically that "[a] ritual includes the letting of blood. Rituals which fail in this requirement are but mock rituals" (329). All the devastations chronicled in *Blood Meridian* occur in a ritual space and time, an Outside that helps to enforce, yet stands apart from, the social bond: "Here beyond men's judgements all covenants were brittle" (106). Glanton and his men exist only to disrupt the orderly procedures of production, conservation and trade; they "carried no tantamount goods and the disposition to exchange was foreign to them" (121). They ravage the very order upon which they parasitically feed. Their actions all fall under the rubric of what Georges Bataille calls *nonproductive expenditure*: prodigality, play, waste, recklessness, empty display and unmotivated violence. Beneath the mask of a Darwinian struggle for survival, or a Hobbesian war of all against all, or even a lust for wealth and power and honor, they sumptuously, gratuitously squander their own lives—together, of course, with those of many others—at every turn. They have no spirit of seriousness or of enterprise; they unwittingly pursue self-ruin rather than advantage. All these men—and not just the kid—are childlike in their unconsciousness, or indifference, as to motivations and consequences. According to the judge, "Men are born for games. Nothing else. Every child knows that play is nobler than work. He knows too that the worth or merit of a game is not inherent in the game itself but rather in the value of that which is put at hazard. . . . All games aspire to the condition of war" (249). Glanton and his men give themselves over to the game of war wholeheartedly, playing without taking care to preserve their stakes. Their lack of awareness is more than a match for the judge's extreme lucidity, if it is a question of reaching the point where "that which is wagered swallows up game, player, all" (249). For the clash and testing of wills in which the judge exults must end, not in the victory of one, but in the sacrificial consumption of everyone and everything. And such is finally our inmost, most secret and most horrific desire.

Blood Meridian performs the violent, sacrificial, self-consuming ritual upon which our civilization is founded. Or better, it traumatically re-enacts this ritual, for foundations are never set in place once and for all. More blood is always needed to seal and renew the pact. The American dream of manifest destiny must be repeated over and over again, ravaging the indifferent landscape in the course of its lemmings' march to the sea. Our terrible progress is "*less the pursuit of some continuance than the verification of a principle*" (337), an obsessive reiteration without advancement, for we build only to destroy. There is no escaping this ritual, no avoiding the point at which we are compelled to assume the fate we have assigned to others, by putting up our own lives as the ultimate stake. But there is also no power or knowledge to which participation in the ritual gives us access, no occult secret unveiled before an elite of initiates. We sacrifice in vain, we sacrifice to nothing. There is nothing mysterious or transfiguring or even surprising about the ritual: "The evening's progress will not appear strange or unusual even to those who question the rightness of the events so ordered. . . . We are not speaking in mysteries" (329). We all end up like the kid, violated and smothered in the shithouse; but how can we dare attach a unique significance even to this? For we are granted no marks of distinction, no special dispensation, but only the ever-renewed immanence of the dance, embodied in the grotesquely pirouetting figure of the judge, "huge and pale and hairless, like an enormous infant," who "never sleeps" and who "says that he will never die" (335). In the "light and nimble" feet of this perpetually smiling, Zarathustrian child, we may perhaps see the reason for this book's shocking *cheerfulness*. Everything in *Blood Meridian* is violence and blood, dying and destruction. But even darkness and death have their own proper vitality. As the second of the book's three epigraphs, taken from Jacob Boehme, reminds us: "It is not to be thought that the life of darkness is sunk in misery and lost as if in sorrowing. There is no sorrowing. For sorrow is a thing that is swallowed up in death, and death and dying are the very life of the darkness."

Works Cited

McCarthy, Cormac. *Blood Meridian or the Evening Redness in the West*. New York: Random, 1985.
———. *Suttree*. 1979. New York: Vintage, 1986.

TERRI WITEK

Reeds and Hides:
Cormac McCarthy's Domestic Spaces

Nearly all the protagonists in Cormac McCarthy novels flee from or
lose their homes. Kenneth Rattner lights out from the cabin he shares with
Mildred and his young son (*The Orchard Keeper*), Lester Ballard's family farm
is sold out from under him (*Child of God*) as is John Grady's ranch house (*All
the Pretty Horses*), Culla and Rinthy Holme strike out from the perverse Eden
of their incestual home (*Outer Dark*), Suttree trades in his family's substantial
housing for a houseboat (*Suttree*), and "the kid" leaves his alcoholic father's
cabin to wander the practically trackless Southwest (*Blood Meridian*).

Such flight patterns, perhaps a cultural memory from restless immigrant
ancestors, are central to our country's literature. But if, as this literature
suggests, Americans are committed to flight, they remain equally bound to
an idea of home. The painful dilemma occasioned by these twin desires is
explored without sentimentality in Cormac McCarthy's six novels.

No one would claim that Cormac McCarthy is a domestic writer: in
a June 24, 1993 review of *All the Pretty Horses* published in *The New York
Review of Books*, Denis Donoghue complains succinctly: "He is not good with
village Romeos and Juliets or indeed with any lives that have entered upon
communities, cultural interests, attended by customs, proprieties, and laws."
McCarthy's imagination "refuses to give credence to the world as it has come
to be in its personal, social, and political forms." I think McCarthy's quarrel

From *The Southern Review* 30, no. 1 (January 1994): 136–142. © 1994 by Louisiana State
University.

is that the metaphors we construct about our existence don't match up with the brutal realities they should rightfully represent and are therefore only a shared delusion. Bent on exposing the chimera by which communities live and lie to themselves, and himself a firm proponent of flight, McCarthy is therefore at his most fierce and convincing when taking on such conventional images of community life as the spaces we choose to call home.

From the first, Americans have made metaphors of a collective identity, and dwelling places have always been fashioned as emblems of the family. Historically, these images have been powerfully ideological. In *The American Family Home: 1800–1960*, Clifford Edward Clark argues that by the end of the eighteenth century, for example, the rhetoric of family life was that families should work as a balanced combination of mutually independent parts, as hierarchical and as orderly as the Greek Revival architecture so beloved of early colonists, representing as it did the imagined reversal of that perceived chaos which greeted the first European immigrants. For the Victorians the house was a moral edifice, a cornerstone of society which combined the careful display of beauty with the sanctuary aspects of church, both presided over by the house's guiding angel, Mother. For post–World War II suburbanites, the house was one of thousands which tried to express simultaneously both the individuality and the conformity of its family, a task as paradoxical as the balance of majority rule and individual freedom which has always been the core dilemma of democracy. No matter how ideas of the family change, the American dwelling place acts out its inhabitants' deep beliefs about the way individuals go about living together.

Cormac McCarthy's first move in challenging such morally freighted metaphors as the American home is to present dwelling places, and therefore the communities they represent, as impermanent. From Suttree's houseboats to the clapboard houses of the earlier books to the makeshift digs of Harrogate or Ballard (caves are an exception, and will be discussed later), most of the places people live in in McCarthy's novels seem one step away from returning to the flotsam and jetsam from which they are, often enough, literally constructed. Houseboats, tenuously connected to the ground, are poised for flight. While Suttree is in Gatlinburg his moored one almost sinks, and Reese's, like the Reese family itself, appears on the scene and then vanishes in the novel's upriver. As homes which are also modes of transit, houseboats act out literally the impermanence of community life which is McCarthy's continual subtext. Ground dwellings are not necessarily more lasting. Gene Harrogate's below-bridge accommodations, which he regards as both luxurious and private, are so weakly constructed that nearly any community agency would classify him as homeless.

The houses which claim more for themselves in McCarthy's books are shown to be just as impermanent as Gene Harrogate's rigged-up dwelling.

Like Knoxville's aging apartment buildings, all are subject to McCarthy's wrecking ball. If characters' houses aren't taken from them outright, they are liable to invasion—either by wild animals or by angry citizens whose rules about such things are different from the owners'. In *The Orchard Keeper*, for example, old Uncle Arthur's house is disturbed by both the law and large cats, elements of civilization and its opposite, neither of whom have much regard for the individual within. This double force, a type of lawless law which decides against the permanence of buildings and the communities they house, is even more evident in *Blood Meridian*, in which the townspeople invite Glanton's men into what they think of as their stable communities, only to have them virtually destroyed: the book's moveable Indian encampments are wiped out without the accompanying illusions.

Even the hacienda of *All the Pretty Horses*, perhaps McCarthy's most enduring house, is endangered. The economic vigor of that beautiful home and its family depends on the bunkhouse, which is finally too close for comfort. When an inmate of the bunkhouse undertakes an affair with the daughter of the big house, he must be brutally expelled in an effort to save the house and family, which have been altered forever, as if by encroaching rot. McCarthy engineers this so that our sympathies are with the lower-class outsider John Grady, and of course this is a standard romantic ploy. It is worth considering, however, that John Grady is a more sympathetic cousin to other, more fatal McCarthy outsiders. His effect on the established community of the hacienda is not so different from that of Glanton's men, who ride into *Blood Meridian*'s towns to a warm welcome and then turn into community wreckers, wild animals in the living room.

Even the grandest house is only an illusion or two ahead of shared community spaces like the wonderful inn in *The Orchard Keeper* which collapses and later burns, both times spilling its occupants into the night. All spaces in which people live together in McCarthy's novels seem to be elaborations of the campfires which dot *Blood Meridian*. Perverse versions of Boy Scout wiener roasts, these shared sites demonstrate the fragile underpinnings of all community life: people disappear from them, reappear, and are occasionally disposed of on the spot. The campfires themselves are dismantled and remade nightly in different places, an emblem of the endlessly repeated patterns of impermanence which drive the characters' lives.

And yet McCarthy's characters seem compelled toward imitations of domesticity: think of Lester Ballard's underground home, complete with dead wives. But domesticity rarely works for them, a fact which is often enough demonstrated in gender terms so that we may see that domestic spaces are emblematic not only of family, but of a family's women. When powerful women inhabit Cormac McCarthy's texts, they often act as catalysts for destruction: ensconced at home, they become inadvertent homewreckers.

A dark reversal of the Victorian era's Angel in the House, such a woman is often, as Suttree thinks of his former wife, a "mater dolorosa," a sorrowing mother. Mildred Rattner is a sorrowing mother, as is Gene Harrogate's sick, offstage one, her words carried out into the world by a daughter who is in the process of becoming the same thing. One of the reasons men so early and guiltily leave home in McCarthy books is because of these women's power, derived from a pain so great that it becomes too much for the men who are implicated in their grief. The consequences of having such women at home expand to include the larger community. The successful butter farm in *Outer Dark*, for example, has as its center a fruitful woman whose children have all died; we are not surprised to find out in a later scene that even if the butter has been made, the farmer has failed to deliver it to the local store. One of the bleak jokes of *Outer Dark* is that the extension of this particular maternal grief across the landscape echoes the plight of Rinthy Holme, filled with milk that goes unused as she searches for her banished baby.

Rinthy is Cormac McCarthy's premier example of the *mater dolorosa*, but even the kinless Joyce, Suttree's whore/girlfriend, shows how the Dark Angels of McCarthy's households are implicated in their downfall. Suttree and Joyce seem to have a workable adult relationship until they begin to get specifically domestic: Suttree leaves his houseboat to move in with her, they get an apartment, eventually they even buy a car. What looks like social and domestic prosperity in American terms is their ruin. Soon Joyce doesn't want to go whoring: when she becomes a drunken caricature of a bored housewife, Suttree leaves her. The better their dwelling, the more impermanent it gets, in other words, and the Knoxville apartment buildings which are torn open for our inspection merely reinforce the point. Joyce also goes to show that you don't have to be a biological mother to become a sorrowing woman: all you need to do is attempt to resist the transience of all things by establishing yourself in a self-deluding version of home.

For the women of McCarthy novels, the only alternative is to die, as Lester Ballard's women do, as Wanda Reese does during a rainfall which reveals to her lover Suttree the matriarchal structure of her family. Only in this way can McCarthy's women avoid the sorrow of their involvement with men who are bound to flee them. Yet neither type of woman really wins out in McCarthy's books the way some of the male characters do, and if both types inhabit the same domestic space we eventually see them as versions of each other. *All the Pretty Horses'* Alejandra starts as a tempestuous virgin like Wanda Reese and beds John Grady in the bunkhouse, or in the great outdoors they share with their horses in a tangle of downy fetlocks. But no matter what the setting, their brief domesticity is doomed. Alejandra ends up a sorrowing woman like her aunt; both finally select against John Grady in order to preserve their brother and father's house (literally, his law-abiding and patrician lineage). John Grady and Alejandra sleep together for the last time at a hotel near a train station in a town which is home to neither of them; the symbols of impermanence are ranged around them and they know it.

Rinthy Holme's grieving motherhood offers a twist on McCarthy's usual scenario in that Rinthy leaves home before her brother Culla does. But this is a narrative sleight-of-hand, because the true catalyst for the action is that Rinthy's brother disappears with their baby. Though Culla returns, the male child's forced exodus has the same effect on their little family as any male's flight: it breaks up the only home they know. When Rinthy leaves, she is trying to trade her brother's house for her son's. She doesn't recognize what she finds, however; when she unknowingly beds down near a "little calcined ribcage," the phrase suggests a birdcage, some dwelling for a small animal who has vanished. Rinthy cannot fit within such a space all that is left of her child; she is disqualified from living with either her brother or her son. McCarthy leaves *Outer Dark's mater dolorosa* sleeping at a communal site where the major male characters have convened just shortly before. In typical McCarthy fashion, they have gathered, worked out the final consequences of their sins without her, and then vanished.

As such stories illustrate, adult men and women do not inhabit the same dwelling places very easily in any of McCarthy's books. What usually happens is that the domestic spaces, of which the prototypical examples are the campsites in *Outer Dark, Blood Meridian,* and *All the Pretty Horses,* are composed of men without women. These men, as their all-male communal spaces suggest, are frontiersmen—whether they are living in the southwestern plains or in a southern city. And yet, unlike traditional frontiersmen, they are hardly preparing the way for more permanent dwellings. In *Material Life in America 1600–1860,* a group of scholars claims that homesteading was traditionally a stable pattern of the same three steps performed over and over: "one, two, three—hovel, house, home." But this process is if anything reversed for McCarthy's pioneering souls, who must resist building structures which would eventually house women whom they would most certainly grieve and then flee.

McCarthy's insistence on the impermanence of domestic spaces lets his protagonists do more than avoid their women, however. McCarthy characters seem to understand implicitly that with such things as cash crops and permanent buildings comes not freedom but alienation: think of our suburbs, each family locked into an individual but similar house, a cliché which is the furthest reach, in house terms, of the American dream. According to material culturists, impermanent dwellings have the advantage of enforcing a particular type of community, despite their appearance; such structures are so high-maintenance they actually force their inhabitants to depend on each other, and to venture out into the larger world. Consider a freezing, racist Gene Harrogate warming himself over black Knoxvillians' stoves and bottles, Lester Ballard negotiating for an ax-handle, Culla Holme trying to find cocoa for Rinthy. Despite the acknowledged impermanence of their ties, a frail community of need is established anyway. And the further question McCarthy asks us to consider is why, given the benefits of impermanence and the transience of all things, should we create anything that outlasts us anyway? The first dwellings of American settlers were earthfast, pegged to the ground as if to dramatize the mortal equation between them, and McCarthy demands that we should be equally precise in our definition of human communities.

Tellingly, the most permanent dwelling places in McCarthy's books lie within the earth itself. The judge in *Blood Meridian* makes the distinction between them as images of the human condition:

> For whoever makes a shelter of reeds and hides has joined his spirit to the common destiny of creatures and he will subside back into the mud with scarcely a cry. But who builds in stone seeks to alter the structure of the universe and so it was with these masons however primitive their works may seem to us.

By this definition, most of Cormac McCarthy's characters are hide-and-reed dwellers: the description is true of the human body as well as of constructed homes. But Lester Ballard (and Gene Harrogate makes a brief comic version of the attempt) decides at the last to live in stone, like those ancients the judge describes. Like many McCarthy protagonists, he operates first according to a backwards form of frontiersmanship, progressing from home to hovel. While his move into the caves can be thought of as a further undoing, at that point the process seems to be the reverse of itself as well, for in the caves Ballard is lord of a mansion far more permanent than any plantation house. He also has, perversely, figured out how to share domestic space with women, first by accruing dead paramours and then by becoming a macabre version of those he has killed. At the height of his powers he transforms himself into the Angel of the House who controls both its style and its display: he has truly become his home's moral center. Of course, to have made this sort of domestic space beneath towns of reed and hide is to have attempted to alter the universe, and this is forbidden. Like Culla and Rinthy's baby, who violated the oldest taboo with his birth, he must be exiled from the place that expresses his truest condition.

It would be reassuring to think that, despite the impossibility of living in stone and despite the transience of those shelters of reeds and hides which matches the brevity of our lives, we might still call the earth our home. But the world seems largely indifferent to its inhabitants in Cormac McCarthy's books, whether they dwell in boats, lean-tos, caves, or two-story houses. We are reminded that these characters are without the benefit of those mythologies which describe the earth as a mother. If such myths held true in McCarthy novels, the earth would be the ultimate sorrowing mother her creatures both yearn toward and flee. But McCarthy won't let us make the metaphor more comfortable when he expands it. In his books the earth is no grieving woman but merely itself, trackless and yet filled with signs that refuse to yield up their significance. And unlike the houses we build, the world is not a metaphor for us: we have not constructed it, it has constructed us. We are therefore its metaphor, its fragile dwellings whose patterns of impermanence finally display, despite the efforts of McCarthy's characters, an endurance of their own. As the judge exhorts his listeners: "This you see here, these ruins wondered at by tribes of savages, do you not think this will be again? Aye. And again. With other people, with other sons."

What last, then, are human patterns of impermanence written on the earth's hard walls. The patterns themselves, McCarthy's work argues, are the only dwelling place we have: they are quite literally the one home truth permitted. Cormac McCarthy does not deny that the spaces we inhabit are metaphors for our collective identity. On the contrary: they match precisely and mercilessly to teach us that no place in the world is home, that everywhere is a potential campsite, that every boy must be the frontiersman of what will turn out to be a grave-sized chunk of earth. Therein lies the ferocious power of McCarthy's treatment of domestic space in his novels. Of course, unlike the doomed inhabitants of some sleepy Mexican town, we never expected him to bring good news. At his best and least comforting, the hard logic of Cormac McCarthy's position and the beauty of his writing become the lawless law against which the usual metaphors of home will not prevail. That is when, homebodies all, we let him in.

JOHN WEGNER

"Wars and Rumors of Wars" in Cormac McCarthy's Border Trilogy

Evenin Mr Johnson, he said.

Evenin son.

What's the news?

The old man shook his head. He leaned across the table to the windowsill where the radio sat and turned it off. It aint news no more, he said. Wars and rumors of wars.

—*Cities of the Plain*

The Modern Era has nurtured a dream in which mankind, divided into its separate civilizations, would someday come together in unity and everlasting peace. Today, the history of the planet has finally become one indivisible whole, but it is war, ambulant and everlasting war, that embodies and guarantees this long-desired unity of mankind. Unity of mankind means: No escape for anyone anywhere.

—Kundera, *The Art of the Novel*

War is the central thesis to McCarthy's southwestern works. *The Crossing* begins between World War I and World War II with America on the verge of the Depression, and *Cities of the Plain* essentially ends in 1952 as America's presence in Korea grows. John Grady Cole's father returns from a World War II POW camp sick and dying; *The Crossing* ends with Billy's witness

---

From *Southern Quarterly* 38, no. 3 (Spring 2000): 59–71. © 2000 by *Southern Quarterly*.

31

of the "strange false sunrise . . . of the Trinity Test" (Hunt 31); and *Cities of the Plain* begins with John Grady's drinking with Troy, a war veteran. Even more pervasive are the accounts of the Mexican Revolution that become integral parts of the trilogy's narrative: Dueña Alfonsa's story to John Grady about Francisco I. Madero; Billy's encounters with the blind revolutionary and the patriot in the bar late in *The Crossing*; and Travis's story in *Cities of the Plain* of crossing the border after the fighting in Juárez. The two wars that form the backdrop of the trilogy represent opposite ends of the spectrum. The Mexican Revolution was fought on horseback and train track by peasants and ill-equipped soldiers. The war's most popular figure was a barbaric, illiterate guerilla warrior, Pancho Villa. World War II, on the other hand, was the first great technological war, fought from the air and ended with arguably the twentieth century's most significant and deadly discovery, the atomic bomb. In McCarthy's *Border Trilogy*, these two wars act as historical frames for the novels, defining and mapping the world in which these characters must live and survive.

The journey of *Blood Meridian*'s kid prefigures both the importance of war and the multiple international crossings of John Grady Cole and Billy Parham in the *Border Trilogy*.[1] His movement from Tennessee to Texas begins directly after the Mexican-American War (1846–1848), and he participates in various filibustering gangs whose goals are to rid the earth of the heathen tribes below the newly formed border and make a little money while doing it. The kid flits in and out of the lives of the famous and infamous, known and unknown figures of the West and other fictional characters based closely upon historical persons. In essence, the kid actively participates in American expansion West and South.[2] Concomitantly, the epilogue to *Blood Meridian* seems to foreshadow *All the Pretty Horses*, *The Crossing*, and *Cities of the Plain*.[3] While there are many philosophical implications of the man "progressing over the plain by means of holes" (*BM* 337), he is quite literally digging fence posts, fence posts John Grady Cole and Lacey Rawlins wish did not exist and fence posts Billy and Boyd Parham will burn for firewood on their first trip to Mexico. John Grady and Billy's nostalgia for a time before the man digging post holes, the time of the kid's youth, is a product of naïveté, Hollywood, picture books, and youthful exuberance—a romanticizing of pre–World War I America.

McCarthy's *Blood Meridian*, however, is not necessarily part one of a border tetralogy. Ostensibly (and perhaps paradoxically), his first southwestern novel offers a counter-argument to the trilogy's almost wistful and romantic look at the pre-industrial Southwest. In a type of midrash on his own work, McCarthy offers a pre-revisionary comment on his own nostalgic western novels, revealing "the impossibility of separating ourselves from the events of our past that we now find to be morally objectionable" and that "American history [is] a series of violent cultural transformations, a history of slaughtered selves and strange, incongruous births" (Parrish and Spiller 463). John Grady, in particular, would have done well to read *Blood Meridian* before setting out across the border searching for his Big Rock Candy Mountain. McCarthy's novels are bound by their region, just as the Southwest remains bound to itself and its history. It is a region redefined from the Mexican North to the American Southwest by war, and it is a region where some areas still have more in common with Mexico City than New York City.

The kid enters Texas and the Southwest shortly after the American defeat of Mexico and during the negotiations regarding the Treaty of Guadalupe Hidalgo. At this pivotal moment in history America creates the border that John Grady and Billy will later cross.[4] The kid's life of isolation and degradation spans both the American Civil War and Mexico's war with Spain. When he meets Elrod on the plains and the judge in the jakes, Porfirio Díaz has recently gained the Presidency in Mexico, superseding Benito Juárez, who successfully defended Mexico against Maximilian and Spain's attempts to reassert its colonial power in Mexico. During the war, Juárez's "capital city" was El Paso del Norte, a city vital for supplying weapons and American money. Juárez's victory was crucial to the United States' and Mexico's relations because his fierce Mexican pride created an anti-American sentiment that persists even today.[5] When Díaz wrested control from Juárez (an Indian peasant who rose to power), he opened Mexico's border to rich US investors who appropriated the land and resources, oppressing the Mexican population with foreign economic interests. The northern Mexico and southwestern United States in which McCarthy sets his four southwestern novels exist in the aftermath of 110 years of revolution and war. Mexico's revolving door began with Miguel Hidalgo y Costillo's cry for Mexican independence from Spain (1810) and continued for the next 100 years: Agustin de Iturbide (1821); Santa Anna (1823–1855); Benito Juárez and Melchor Ocamp Ignacio Comonfort (1855–1872); Porfirio Díaz (1876–1910). A hundred years after the Hidalgo-led revolution, Mexico was still in turmoil with a revolution led by Francisco I. Madero (1910), who was joined (at first) by Emiliano Zapata and Pancho Villa. Madero gave way to Victoriano Huerta (1913), who quickly lost the presidency to Venustiano Carranza (1914). The next three years were marked by violent civil war and interim presidents. In 1917 under Carranza's leadership, Mexico crafted its constitution (a constitution still in use today), but Carranza was assassinated in 1920 and Alvaro Obregón became President. Obregón's election effectively marked the end of the revolution. Despite sporadic revolutionary violence in Mexico, Obregón was a strong leader who served a four-year presidency that helped stabilize the Mexican government after ten years of revolution.

In the midst of this bloodshed below the border, McCarthy's characters live both in the historical moment and in its aftermath. Glanton's gang lays the groundwork for men like William Randolph Hearst to enter into the Mexican economy and buy La Babícora, a purchase that occurred only six years after the kid meets the judge in the jakes. Unlike the kid, who rides with historical men, the boys from the *Border Trilogy* simply live in the historical aftermath of bloodshed in Mexico. The anti-American sentiment, Magdalena's difficult (and fatal) attempt to cross the border, and Eduardo's hatred for the leprous paradise north of the border in *Cities of the Plain* are all products of history, but they are not part of an archived historical moment in that history. They are, in other words, the stuff of fiction. From the exact dates and weather patterns of *Blood Meridian* to the vague location of the White Lake brothel, McCarthy's southwestern works grow less historically and geographically specific. It is this distinction that separates the completed *Border Trilogy* from *Blood Meridian*. History, an important, viable character in *Blood Meridian*, becomes an influence—a secondary, subtle motivator—in the trilogy, where it is the human responses to that historical influence that take center stage. John Grady Cole may believe "in individualism, free will, volition . . . [and that] every man born on this planet is an Adam, free of memory and external constraint, able to shape his illimitable 'self' in any way he chooses" (Pilkington 320). However, the history lesson John Grady learns from Dueña Alfonsa contradicts that American ideal. Instead, he learns, as Quijada tells Billy, that the "soul of Mexico is very old" (*C* 385); the past influences and controls the present. The scalping, filibustering gangs like Captain White's and Glanton's prefigured the economic filibustering gangs led by Hearst. This continual and oppressive American presence fueled the 1910 Mexican Revolution that tightened the border restrictions the Treaty of Guadalupe Hidalgo had created. John Grady and Billy travel to a Mexico controlled by the PRI, the Partido Revolucionario Institucional, a political party created in 1938. Creating a political party that institutionalizes the revolution, in effect, implies that the government represents the revolution and its ideas for reform. By the same token, the government eliminates the need for any new revolutions, implying that Mexico is in a constant state of controlled revolution and change. For Mexico, then, the revolution is continual and ongoing, hence the past is a significant part of the present.

Whether history or myth, McCarthy's trilogy seems to contend that "the past that was differs little from the past that was not" (*BM* 330). When Billy Parham talks to the traveler in the epilogue to *Cities of the Plain*, the narrator tells him that "This story like all stories has its beginnings in a question" (277). The traveler's story, a story within a story "in what we must imagine to be some unknown infinitude of alternate being and likeness," is a retold narrative explaining why the Mexican narrator drew a map of his life (275). His tale of a dreamer and a group of men engaging in a "blood ceremony that was then and is now an affront to God" blurs boundaries between dreams and reality and contends that there is a common history among all men, hence a common history among cities, among nations (280). The narrator's discussion of "common histories" and his story about his dreamt dreamer's dream, with all of its inherent philosophical complexities, seem to deconstruct boundaries that separate men and generations: "Two worlds touch here" within the traveler's story (276, 285). That point of contact mirrors the lives of John Grady Cole and Billy Parham. Ostensibly, the question that begins the story of the two protagonists of the trilogy asks whether "His history is the same as yours or mine" (*COP* 285). This duality reflects the opening of the trilogy just as the "candleflame and the image of the candleflame caught in the pierglass" introduce us to John Grady (*APH* 3). If we treat these as one, then it is necessarily true that history is a shared experience and boundaries themselves do little to separate the effects of events where two worlds touch. The image and the reality (the myth and the history) are not two distinct objects; both become "twisted and righted" when the wind blows (*APH* 3).

Much of what is twisted and righted historically is war. McCarthy's southwestern fiction consistently provides historical reminders of the "wars and rumors of wars" (*COP* 61) that Mr. Johnson hears on the radio, and these rumors constantly remind us that history and all the events of history revolve around war and revolution. The constant of McCarthy's southwestern fiction is the effect of war on men and women. The dominant historical event of the Southwest has been the revolutions in Mexico that created a new border between the wealthy United States and the poverty-stricken Mexican people. The battles south of the border influenced America's readiness for World War I, and the United States returned to the Southwest to perfect its ability to end world wars by building and testing the atomic bomb. Yet, even that capability does not stop the military intrusion on the land and its people as the government plans to buy Mac McGovern's ranch to extend the White Sands Missile Range.[6] McCarthy's southwestern fiction rejects the judge's admonition that "If war is not holy man is nothing but antic clay" (*BM* 307). Rather, these novels cry out against the meaninglessness of war and the repetitive historical patterns that create war, arguing that war will simply bury man in the clay that much faster. *The Border Trilogy* rejects the clichéd hope that to know history is to avoid repeating it. It argues that "The war changed everything" (*COP* 78), but McCarthy does NOT SPECIFY WHICH war because they are all the same, caused by the same types of events. The change is constantly revolving, violently and inevitably, and "wars and rumors of war" dominate the discourse of the twentieth century.

The two wars that dominate the trilogy are the Mexican Revolution and World War II, and America's involvements in both of these conflicts are defining moments in American history. Both Don Héctor and Dueña Alfonsa speak "of the revolution and of the history of Mexico . . . and of Francisco Madero" (*APH* 144).[7] Madero's revolution was intended to recreate Mexico and end the dictatorships that oppressed the worker and peasant. While it is true that the revolutionary party claimed victory after 1917, the poverty in Mexico that John Grady and Billy see subverts the rhetoric of change. The revolution offered hope to the masses that free elections could create equality. Even though Don Héctor correctly dismisses Madero and his revolution as quixotic (146), the revolution "was one of the last old-fashioned, pre-industrial wars, in which modern techniques and machinery had only an occasional role to play. It was a war of epic battles and mythical warrior-heroes, two of whom—Pancho Villa and Emiliano Zapata—have achieved fame throughout the world" (Rutherford 213).

In McCarthy's *Border Trilogy* the revolution comes to represent the peasant's kindness in the face of continued oppression. The foreign ownership of places like La Babícora by men like William Randolph Hearst and the corruption of Captain Raúl, who imprisons the old man Orlando at Encantada, are continually opposed by the basic human kindness of the workers, those very people the revolution should have freed from oppression. It is a country, Travis tells Billy and the other cowboys, where the goodness of the people contrasts with the reality of the historical moment:

> I was a cattlebuyer for Spurlocks. . . . I rode all over northern Mexico. Hell, there wasnt no cattle. Not to speak of. Mostly I just visited. . . . I liked the country and I liked the people in it. I rode all over Chihuahua and a good part of Coahuila and some of Sonora. I'd be gone weeks at a time and not have hardly so much as a peso in my pocket but it didnt make no difference. Those people would take you in and put you up and feed you and feed your horse and cry when you left. You could of stayed forever. They didnt have nothin. . . . You could see that the revolution hadnt done them no good. A lot of em had lost boys out of the family. Fathers or sons or both. Nearly all of em, I expect. They didnt have no reason to be hospitable to anybody. Least of all a gringo kid. That plateful of beans they set in front of you was hard come by. But I was never turned away. Not a time. (*COP* 90)

As I have shown elsewhere, the Mexican Revolution is an overt presence in each book of the trilogy.[8] It appears in *All the Pretty Horses* with

Luis's story of Huerta, and Luis and Antonio's continued subjection to Don Héctor reveals the failure of the revolution to effect social reform or increased independence for the peasants. The failure of Madero's revolution is a prominent theme in both Dueña Alfonsa's and Don Héctor's conversation. The revolution is even more prominent in *The Crossing*, historically the earliest of the novels with its beginning in 1939 during Cardenas's presidency. In his travels, Billy encounters such characters as the young female revolutionary and her mother-in-law and the blind revolutionary who tells him his story. The corrido about "El güerito" that Billy hears on his return from the US seems to cast Boyd as a hero for the oppressed, a revolutionary fighting against the "patrón's men" (381). But, more importantly, as Dirk Raat has said, "corridos function as barometers of the Mexican's attitudes towards events. The corrido is a kind of collective diary, an ethnohistorical document containing facts about society and history. Most corridos depict the Mexican as either victim or hero and often have themes of intercultural conflict. Many express frustration and anger over Anglo and North American dominance, and are, at times, a call to action" (48). Even Quijada admits the corrido "tells about him. . . . The corrido is the poor man's history" (*C* 386). The corrido allows those not in power to lament their oppression and to rail against that oppression. In essence, then, the corrido offers hope. The Mexican people needed a hero because they lacked power.[9] They may have gained certain agrarian reforms, but absentee landowners still dominated Mexico. The living circumstances of the Muñoz family and of the indian Quijada, who works for Hearst's La Babícora, reiterate the failure of the revolution, land reform, and the continued presence of foreign ownership of Mexican resources.

The revolution may have had little effect on the distribution of power and income in Mexico, but America's reaction to it helped reshape fundamental aspects of the American military and attitudes about war. While the United States never officially entered the Mexican Revolution, America invaded Vera Cruz in 1914, and after Pancho Villa's attack on Columbus, New Mexico, the government mobilized 40,000 National Guardsmen on the border near El Paso by 18 June 1916 (Vanderwood and Samponaro 10, 12). Even though America technically maintained its neutrality, the mobilization of so many troops gave the army a chance "to test new equipment and to train personnel, to hone its command structure and modernize its supply and support services. . . . Because of its Mexican venture, the U.S. Army finally became a twentieth-century fighting force, in large part due to Pancho Villa" (Vanderwood and Samponaro 186). Pershing's foray into Mexico chasing Pancho Villa specifically helped the army develop tank warfare and redefine troop supply from mule and train dependencies to vehicular supply. In essence, America's training along the border helped the troops' preparedness for World War I.[10]

Perhaps most importantly, though, the army's pre–World War I presence in the Southwest influenced its return to the Southwest to prepare for World War II. If the first World War showed America's willingness to involve itself in Europe's problems, the second World War created the American superpower mystique. The atomic bomb, a creation with its heart in the Southwest, fundamentally changed the face of war in the modern world. No longer would two opponents meet on the field and battle trench to trench. The technological wizardry that eliminated human contact with the enemy heightened the brutality of war. Glanton's gang is animalistic, but they see the value of human life. Modern warfare removes the human(ity) from war, creating apathy and devaluing the warrior's knowledge of his enemy's life, hence his own. In essence, the atomic bomb made it easier to kill both from a technological standpoint and from a psychological standpoint. The effects extend beyond the battlefield. As Robert L. Holmes asserts in *On War and Morality*, the "paradox of contemporary civilization is that beyond a certain point the individual's security begins to vary inversely with the power embodied in the systems meant to ensure that security" (3).

Mr. Johnson's "wars and rumors of wars" hold in them not just the history of civilization, a contention that would agree with Judge Holden's theories on war; these wars he hears on the radio (probably Korea and possibly the Egyptian Revolution) carry with them the threat of total annihilation of all countries because of the destructive power of the atomic bomb. War is nothing new, as Mr. Johnson says,[11] and that war dominates the discourse is nothing new to McCarthy readers. The epigraphs that open *Blood Meridian* point to the violence inherent in mankind. However, the *Border Trilogy* is not just about violence; it is about the inevitability of war, the inability to survive peacefully. At times, war seems god, or at least (as Kundera claims), war offers unity. Holmes argues that

> Since originating an estimated forty thousand years ago, war has consumed more wealth, demanded greater sacrifice, and caused more suffering than any other human activity. In shaping history it has eclipsed even religion, in whose service it has so often been enlisted. But although war has brought out the worst in man, it has also brought out the best. While it cannot be said to have done much for music, it has inspired literature and poetry and brought advances in science, medicine, and technology that otherwise might have been long in coming. Ruskin claims that it has been essential to art as well. It has sometimes been the cohesive force that has brought together divided peoples to form strong and durable societies. (12)[12]

This would seem to be the case in the Mexico of the *Border Trilogy*. Travis's account of his trips to Mexico as a cattle buyer mirrors moments both John Grady and Billy experience in their trips to Mexico. John Grady, on his way back to the Hacienda de Nuestra Señora de la Purísima Concepción, gets a ride with some farmworkers "[a]nd after and for a long time to come he'd have reason to evoke the recollection of those smiles and to reflect upon the good will" of the men in the truck (*APH* 219). Similarly, Billy and Boyd both receive assistance from the peasants and workers in *The Crossing*. The kindness of the Mexican people is contrasted and perhaps fostered by the oppressive world in which they live. The hombres del país who take the handcuffed captain are men of the country, not men of the government (*APH* 281). They instinctively know that John Grady is telling the truth about his horses and require no retribution for his actions in kidnapping a man of the government. Boyd's immediate popularity after "kill[ing] the manco in a gunfight" and the worker's shout that "hay justicia en el mundo" (*C* 317–18; there's justice in the world) also signal the underlying dissatisfaction of the Mexican populace. Billy's later encounter with the drunk patriot further subverts the docility of the populace and points to the potentially violent anti-American sentiment in the country (*C* 356). McCarthy's continual references to the Madero revolution accentuate the dichotomy between the revolution's goals and its achievements. These are people who have no reason to offer kindness, especially to gringo kids, but who do so despite the false hope created by a revolution eventually institutionalized and adopted by the dominant political machine of the country.

Much like the revolution in Mexico, World War II created false hopes in America. When Billy returns to America, he tries to enlist because "I dont have anyplace to go" (*C* 341), but the army will not take him because of his heart. Dianne C. Luce contends that "Billy's attempts to enlist in the armed services come to stand for his only sustained effort to live among men in *The Crossing*, and this enterprise is doomed, too" (211–12).[13] However, Billy's desire to join the community by entering the army is ironic: the institution he tries to join is a primary cause of the increased alienation and isolation he and John Grady feel. These are boys "disinherited by war and war's machinery" (*COP* 204). After trying to enlist multiple times, Billy works on a line camp, and, in a scene that mirrors his later encounter with the Mexican patriot, he goes to a bar in Winslow and orders a beer. In a second bar, where he meets a soldier and a bartender, his reticent stoicism causes problems. The bartender claims the "uniform dont mean nothin to him" (*C* 349). He follows this accusation with a bit of patriotic fear-mongering, telling the soldier that Billy would care if a uniform with "that risin sun on the collar . . . was comin down Second Street" (*C* 349). The patriotism is tempered by the location of the patriot: an empty bar in Winslow, Arizona, where a soldier drinks alone.

Billy later drifts across the Southwest where "[b]y the spring of the third year of the war there was hardly a ranch house in all of that country that did not have a gold star in the window" (*C* 350). The Southwest has "had it pretty rough. . . . Pretty rough," Mr. Sanders tells Billy (*C* 351). There is little talk of the glory of war on Billy's wanderings.

Nevertheless, the war was a boon for the Southwest. Despite the gold stars and rough times for the families, war transformed the West economically.[14] However, the economic benefits did not match the loss of life and hope that McCarthy infuses into his World War II veterans. Billy's encounter with the American patriot takes place in an empty bar. John Grady's father returns from war a broken, dying man. As John Grady and Billy are talking about their respective trips to Mexico, Billy tells John Grady "this country aint the same. Nor anything in it. The war changed everything. I dont think people even know it yet" (*COP* 78). World War II was a war that robbed America of joy in victory. Unlike in previous, imperialistic wars, America gained no land; and unlike World War I, this was not the war to end all wars. After World War I, Americans listened

> to network radio shows. . . . [S]educed by the imagery of advertising and the cinema, encouraged to ride out of familiar, stable locations in search of the unfamiliar or for the sheer experience of movement, Americans became a part of a distinctively modern, discontinuous and anonymous culture: a culture that was, and is, not specifically tied down to any individual locality, state, region—or, indeed, to any particular nation. (Gray 50)

This seduction by technology became less pleasurable after World War II and Hiroshima. America suffered heavy losses and inflicted even greater losses by dropping the bomb, a move that stunned the world. More obvious, though, was the effect on servicemen returning to America. John Grady's father, a former POW and survivor of the Bataan Death March, returns not "the same" despite his son's assertion that he is the same "inside" (*APH* 12). On their last ride, he looks "over the country with those sunken eyes as if the world out there had been altered or made suspect by what he'd seen of it elsewhere. As if he might never see it right again. Or worse did see it right at last" (*APH* 23). John Grady's father may be wracked by pneumonia (many Bataan survivors returned with fatal pneumonia or other deadly infectious diseases), or he may have cancer or emphysema promoted by the cigarettes and lighters distributed to American soldiers.

Much like John Grady's father, Troy returns from the war isolated. After his discharge from the army, he "wandered all over this country" (*COP* 22), he tells Billy—right after telling him about a driving trip to Amarillo with

Gene Edmonds, when the "front of the car . . . was just packed completely full of jackrabbit heads . . . all lookin out, eyes all crazy lookin" (*COP* 22). Troy's story highlights the post-war industrial world. While it is still possible to hit jackrabbits driving in West Texas at night, the likelihood has diminished somewhat as the rabbits have grown used to cars. Gene Edmonds's "brand new Olds Eighty-eight" (21) roaring down the highway is America in the twentieth century. The trip from El Paso to Amarillo (around 418 miles) in ten hours is a modern miracle in 1949. (Compare Troy's trip to that of John Grady and Lacey Rawlins, who ride from San Angelo to Eldorado, 43 miles, in one day, in *All the Pretty Horses*.) The speed of the trip, however, is countered by the hellish grill "covered with blood and rabbit guts" (22). The death and ghoulish appearance of these rabbits is classic McCarthy; it is also a classic confrontation between technology and nature. America's new-found love affair with the American automobile, with dynamic movement, creates gothic images of morbidity.

Shortly after John Grady and his father discuss the selling of the ranch, poker, and John Grady's grandfather, his father sees a newspaper and wonders, "How can Shirley Temple be getting divorced?" (*APH* 13).[15] Shirley Temple's divorce signifies the passage of time and the loss of innocence. To John Grady's father, the death of the grandfather and Shirley Temple's divorce both represent the death of pre–World War II values and life; in some respects, the divorce symbolizes the failure of World War II to fulfill the promise of peace, prosperity, and worldwide democracy. The end of the war in

> 1945 brought both euphoria and a rush to fulfill the promise of the myth of return. . . . The nation that emerged from the war, and to which the veterans returned, was not the place they had left. . . . But the most profound gap between the expectation and the reality of victory was opened by the breakdown of the wartime alliance between the United States and the soviet [sic] Union. Whatever else victory was supposed to mean, the establishment of permanent peace and a rational world order was the irreducible minimum. (Slotkin 329, 332)[16]

Shirley Temple's divorce, the grandfather's death, and the loss of the ranch do not exactly offer order. Paradoxically, according to Alex Hunt, the splitting of the atom, a moment of supreme Cartesian physics, created disunity and "challenges our anthropocentric view of the relationship between humanity and the natural world" (31). As Hunt says, Billy's tears at the end of *The Crossing* "mourn the violence of humanity and humanity's ultimate alienation from nature through its appropriation of nature's power" (37).

Isolation and alienation seem at the heart of McCarthy's novels; however, the alienation of the individuals comes at a time when America has exponentially increased its worldwide involvement in other countries' affairs. The very creation and use of the atomic bomb virtually forced America into a universal role as a Big Brother peacekeeper, making isolation impossible to maintain. Wars and rumors of wars will always intrude; the technology of the twentieth century delimits John Grady's desire to live on "a little spread up in the hills" where he can kill his own meat and remove himself from the world below (*COP* 77). What John Grady and Billy learn is that "each of us has a secret frontier within him, and that is the most difficult frontier to cross because each of us hopes to find himself alone there, but finds only that he is more than ever in the company of others" (Fuentes 161). Essentially, isolation and alienation are never complete because technology subverts the ability to remain alone. World War II acts as a moment of aporia for these boys: the alienation and isolation of the individual is deconstructed by the ever-growing communal responsibility and intrusion.

The governmental intrusion upon the lives of the ranchers in the Southwest signifies this communal growth. Lurking in the background of *Cities of the Plain* are the army surveyors sent to "find the sorriest land they could find" (11). This land will become part of the militarized Southwest that includes Ft. Bliss and the White Sands Missile Range. Increased military presence began during the Mexican Revolution and continued as America created its nuclear arsenal. The transition from privately owned land did not always go smoothly, though. While McGovern recognizes that "the army's" goin to take this place," the only way Mr. Prather will "leave [is] in a box" (264, 62). When John Grady interrupts Mr. Johnson as he listens to the radio, we get a short history of New Mexico. Mr. Johnson tells John Grady that "Oliver Lee always said he come out here because the country was so sorry nobody else would have it and he'd be left alone. Of course he was wrong. At least about bein left alone" (61). The army will "take the whole Tularosa basin. . . . Folks will piss and moan about it. But they dont have a choice. They ought to be glad to get shut of it" (62). Oliver Lee was wrong on both accounts, it seems. Not only would he not be left alone, something John Grady must also learn, but he has moved to land that people do want. The army's takeover was just another in a long history of land wars that includes the Mexican Revolution, the Lincoln County Wars, and the expansion of White Sands Missile Range.[17] Even before the military takeover of the land, Lee was involved in the Lincoln County wars in New Mexico. This battle over land and water rights "attracted desperados from all parts of New Mexico, Texas, Colorado, and south of the Rio Grande" ("White Sands" sect. 3). The most famous participant was, of course, Billy the Kid.

When Mr. Johnson tells John Grady he is listening to "wars and rumors of wars," he echoes our experience reading McCarthy's *Border Trilogy*. These three novels are replete with allusions and direct references to the wars that dominate the American Southwest and northern Mexico's past. Even those who fail to participate directly in the wars are affected, and the wars themselves are products of earlier wars. This constant revolution of war and violence sits at the heart of the trilogy. More importantly, though, that history affects everyone, without distinction. John Grady and Billy cannot reverse the world by running to Mexico or returning the wolf to her natural habitat. Instead, these conflicts hold within them the sense that what "is constant in history is greed and foolishness and a love of blood and this is a thing that even God—who knows all that can be known—seems powerless to change" (*APH* 239). John Grady and Billy are left "disinherited by war and war's machinery" (*COP* 204); yet "[t]he world of our fathers resides within us" (*COP* 281). The paradoxical country whose technology both alienates and unifies becomes a world within which John Grady Cole cannot survive. His knife fight with Eduardo, the challenge made by honking a car horn, is emblematic of the dichotomy of the modern world after World War II.

The kindness Billy encounters as the trilogy ends is subverted by the circular nature of the novel. Billy's room off Betty's kitchen returns us to the opening of *The Crossing*. In a sort of postmodern looping, we are returned to the time of Billy's childhood before he leaves to return the wolf to Mexico. In essence, we return to the Parham family's move out of Grant County (named for Ulysses S. Grant) to Hidalgo County (named for Guadalupe Hidalgo, the father of Mexican independence). It is this looping back to war and war's referents that defines McCarthy's *Border Trilogy*. The history of the region and those who live there is shrouded in war. John Grady and Billy become men unified by war and violence, and this war creates a map of existence for each person, a map both distinct and overlapped with the maps of others.

NOTES

1. Leo Daugherty sees in *Blood Meridian* (1985) the "warrior judge's work to achieve dominion—to be the realized ... archon of this Anaretic planet" (164), and Rick Wallach makes an apt comparison between the martial codes of *Beowulf* and *Blood Meridian*, contending that the "structured social systems that justify and promulgate conflict, represent violence as craft, and conventionalize destructive activity in a craftsmanly way" (113). Robert L. Jarrett, in his *Cormac McCarthy*, argues that the judge "articulates an ideology of conquest that defends unlimited war as the supreme arbiter of the conflict between ... wills (81), and that *Blood Meridian* "forces its readers ... to confront the history of violence and the unicultural rhetoric of the antebellum period of Manifest Destiny" (93). War and *Blood Meridian* seem to go hand in hand (or perhaps hand to hand), and while we cannot necessarily call Judge Holden the novel's spokesman, he does do the most speaking about war:

This is the nature of war, whose stake is at once the game and the authority and the justification. Seen so, war is the truest form of divination. It is the testing of one's will and the will of another within that larger will which because it binds them is therefore forced to select. War is the ultimate game because war is at last a forcing of the unity of existence. War is god. (249)

2. For discussions of history in *Blood Meridian*, see John Sepich, *Notes on Blood Meridian* (Louisville: Bellarmine College P, 1993); and Dana Phillips, "History and the Ugly Facts of Cormac McCarthy's *Blood Meridian*," *American Literature* 68.2 (1996): 433–60.

3. Edwin T. Arnold, in "The Mosaic of McCarthy's Fiction," contends that "the ending of *Blood Meridian* looks forward, the beginning of *Pretty Horses* looks backward, and they meet at a point where text joins text" (19).

4. See Américo Paredes, *"With His Pistol in His Hand": A Border Ballad and its Hero*. Paredes contends, "It was the Treaty of Guadalupe that added the final element to Rio Grande society, a border. The river, which had been a focal point, became a dividing line. Men were expected to consider their relatives and closest neighbors, the people just across the river, as foreigners in a foreign land" (15).

5. Juárez's victory represented "a triumph of anti-colonialism in an age of dominant empires. As such, it anticipated the struggles of the mid-twentieth century in an exemplary manner" (Hamnett xii). The Treaty of Guadalupe Hidalgo separated El Paso del Norte between the two countries. Named after Benito Juárez in 1888, Juárez gained its notoriety during the Revolution of 1910–1920. The city was crucial to Francisco Madero's early volley to overthrow Díaz, providing access to American arms and other goods. See my forthcoming article, "Mexico's Revolutionary History and Cormac McCarthy's *Border Trilogy*," in *Myth, Legend, Dust: Critical Responses to Cormac McCarthy*, ed. Rick Wallach (Manchester: Manchester UP, 2000) for a more complete discussion of Juárez and the *Border Trilogy*. See Hamnett's *Juárez* for biographical information on Benito Juárez and his fight for Mexican autonomy from France.

6. There is, of course, historical precedent for the army's purchase of McGovern's ranch. In 1941–42, when the government began the Los Alamos project (the atomic bomb), they intended to lease the land from ranchers. After testing the bombs, fearing radiation fallout, the government offered to buy the ranches or extend the leases. If ranchers did not agree to either of those terms, the army would file a "condemnation suit" ("White Sands" sect. 4). As late as 1982, the Dave McDonald family was still protesting the army's rancher payment program. McDonald contended that the army did not follow the lease agreement. For more information about land issues, see "White Sands Missile Range—A Regional History," and Ferenc M. Szasz, *The Day the Sun Rose Twice: The Story of the Trinity Site Nuclear Explosion, July 16, 1945* (Albuquerque: U of New Mexico P, 1984).

7. Gail Moore Morrison argued in 1999 (before the completion of the trilogy) that the revolutionary tales put John Grady's disappointments in perspective and transform him into a man of action (191). I would agree that the tales are important, but John Grady seems already a man of action in *All the Pretty Horses*. In fact, he would do well to be less action oriented and more thoughtful. These tales also do not, it is revealed in *Cities of the Plain*, teach John Grady much about Mexico. Even after his trip to Mexico in *All the Pretty Horses*, he still asks Billy, "Dont you think if there's anything left of this life it's down there?" (*COP* 218). Unlike Billy, who seems to understand that Mexico does not provide an answer ("I concluded my business down there a long time ago"), John Grady still sees Mexico as a panacea for the dying ranch life.

8. For extended discussion of the historical Madero and his presence in the trilogy, see my "Whose Story Is It? History and Fiction in Cormac McCarthy's *All the Pretty Horses*," *Southern Quarterly* 36.2 (1998) 103–10. For more comprehensive historical explication of the trilogy's many references to the Mexican Revolution, see my forthcoming article, "Mexico's Revolutionary History and Cormac McCarthy's *Border Trilogy*."

9. See Américo Paredes, With a Pistol in His Hand for the best discussion of corridos. See also Merle E. Simmons, *The Mexican Corrido as a Source for Interpretive Study of Modern Mexico* (Bloomington: Indiana UP, 1957), for an impressive collection of corridos arranged by subject.

10. Michael D. Carman writes that "[t]he Army's chief of staff and inspector general reported that the entire Army had benefited from the mobilization" (48). See also Clarence C. Clendenen, *Blood on the Border: The United States Army and the Mexican Irregulars* (London: Macmillan, 1969), for a discussion of Pershing's pursuit of Villa and American preparation for World War I. Vanderwood and Samponaro also contend that the US Army was ranked behind Germany and Japan at the turn of the century. The American Air Force was in worse shape. Because the government moved the training ground to the Southwest border and trained pilots in Mexico (188), the plane the gypsies move in *The Crossing* (401–02) could be an American Air Force plane used during training.

11. Two of John Grady Cole's uncles "were killed in Puerto Rico in eighteen ninety-eight" (*APH* 7). Most likely, they were killed in the Spanish-American War.

12. I should point out that Holmes's work focuses on the inherent immorality of any war, arguing against philosophers like Augustine who contend that war can be just (morally correct). Holmes quotes those who support war as useful to art and science, including an interesting passage from Adolf Hitler's *Mein Kampf:* "Mankind has grown great in eternal struggle ... and only in eternal peace does it perish" (qtd. in Holmes 13). Hitler's claim sounds similar to something Judge Holden would say.

13. Luce writes that Billy's damaged heart suggests "his shortcoming is more in courage than in the capacity for understanding" (212). I would add a secondary reading of the scene as a commentary on the absurdity of the army and war. Billy's own logical observation "If I'm goin to die anyways why not use me" (*C* 341) shows both the subtle humor in McCarthy and the silliness of an army that recognizes "You aint got noplace else to go" (*C* 337) but refuses to allow him to enlist.

14. See Gerald D. Nash, *The American West Transformed: The Impact of the Second World War* (Bloomington: Indiana UP, 1985), for a discussion of World War II's impact on the American economy. Obviously, World War I changed the American economy as well: "from a debtor nation [the United States] had been transformed into a creditor nation, with loans to Europe worth $13,000,000,000" (Gray 50).

15. Temple's divorce was reported on page one of the *San Angelo Daily Standard* on 5 December 1949.

16. Slotkin's *Gunfighter Nation* is an excellent look at the myth of the West and its development in film and politics. The passages quoted above discuss John Ford's *Fort Apache* (1948), a film in which an adult Shirley Temple appears. Interestingly enough, Slotkin points out that between 1947 and 1949 Hollywood produced approximately 150 Westerns, many of them either propaganda/patriotic films or anti-war films detailing transgressions by American armed forces.

17. While Mr. Johnson's story of Oliver Lee and Colonel Fountain seems odd intermixed with army intrusion, his story reinforces the violence of the Southwest, representing "one of the last old-West killings" in the region ("White Sands" sect. 3). Lee, along with William NcNew, was accused of "defacing" a brand on a steer belonging to W. A. Irwin of El Paso.

Albert J. Fountain served as a Special Prosecutor for the case. On 31 January 1896, Fountain and his eight-year-old son disappeared while returning home from Las Cruces. The bodies were never recovered. See William Keleher, *The Fabulous Frontier: Twelve New Mexico Items* (Sante Fe, NM: Rydal P, 1945), for a more comprehensive discussion of Lee and Fountain. Interestingly, Fountain fought with Benito Juárez at one time.

Works Cited

Arnold, Edwin T. "The Mosaic of McCarthy's Fiction." Hall and Wallach 17–23.

Arnold, Edwin T., and Dianne C. Luce, eds. *Perspectives on Cormac McCarthy*. Rev. ed. Jackson: UP of Mississippi, 1999.

Bingham, Arthur. "Syntactic Complexity and Iconicity in Cormac McCarthy's *Blood Meridian*." *Language and Literature* 20 (1995): 19–33.

Carman, Michael Dennis. *United States Customs and the Madero Revolution*. El Paso: Texas Western P, 1976.

Daugherty, Leo. "Gravers False and True: *Blood Meridian* as Gnostic Tragedy." Arnold and Luce 159–74.

Fuentes, Carlos. *The Old Gringo*. Trans. Margaret Sayers Peden and Carlos Fuentes. New York: Farrar, 1985.

Gray, Richard. *American Poetry of the Twentieth Century*. Longman Literature in English Series. Ed. David Carroll and Michael Wheeler. New York: Longman, 1990.

Hall, Wade, and Rick Wallach. *Sacred Violence: A Reader's Companion to Cormac McCarthy*. El Paso: Texas Western P, 1995.

Hamnett, Brian. *Juárez*. New York: Longman, 1994.

Holmes, Robert L. *On War and Morality*. Princeton: Princeton UP, 1989.

Hunt, Alex. "Right and False Suns: Cormac McCarthy's *The Crossing*, and the Advent of the Atomic Age." *Southwestern American Literature* 23.2 (1998): 31–37.

Jarrett, Robert L. *Cormac McCarthy*. New York: Twayne, 1997.

Kundera, Milan. *The Art of the Novel*. Trans. Linda Asher. New York: Grove, 1987.

Luce, Dianne C. "The Road and the Matrix: The World as Tale in *The Crossing*." Arnold and Luce 195–219.

McCarthy, Cormac. *All the Pretty Horses*. New York: Vintage, 1993.

McCarthy, Cormac. *Blood Meridian or The Evening Redness in the West*. New York: Vintage, 1992.

McCarthy, Cormac. *Cities of the Plain*. New York: Vintage, 1999.

McCarthy, Cormac. *The Crossing*. New York: Vintage, 1995.

Morrison, Gail Moore. "*All the Pretty Horses*: John Grady Cole's Expulsion from Paradise." Arnold and Luce 175–94.

Paredes, Américo. *"With His Pistol in His Hand": A Border Ballad and its Hero*. Austin: U of Texas P, 1958.

Parrish, Tim, and Elizabeth A. Spiller. "A Flute Made of Human Bone: *Blood Meridian* and the Survivors of American History." *Prospects* 23 (1998): 461–81.

Pilkington, Tom. "Fate and Free Will on the American Frontier: Cormac McCarthy's Western Fiction." *Western American Literature* 27.4 (1993): 311–22.

"Porfirio Díaz, Remarkable President of Mexican Republic." *San Angelo Daily Standard* 7 Mar. 1911: A2.

Raat, W. Dirk. "The Mexican Pet and Other Stories: Folklore and History." *Twentieth-Century Mexico*. Ed. W. Dirk Raat and William H. Beezley. Lincoln: U of Nebraska P, 1986. 44–54.

Rutherford, John. "The Novel of the Mexican Revolution." *The Cambridge History of Latin American Literature*. Vol. 2. *The Twentieth Century*. Ed. Roberto González Echevarría and Enrique Pupo-Walker. Cambridge: Cambridge UP, 1996. 213–25.

Slotkin, Richard. *Gunfighter Nation: The Myth of the Frontier in Twentieth-Century America*. New York: Atheneum, 1992.

Vanderwood, Paul J., and Frank N. Samponaro. *Border Fury: A Picture Postcard Record of Mexico's Revolution and U.S. War Preparedness, 1910–1917*. Albuquerque: U of New Mexico P, 1988.

Wallach, Rick. "From *Beowulf* to *Blood Meridian*: Cormac McCarthy's Demystification of the Martial Code." *Southern Quarterly* 36.4 (1998): 113–20.

"White Sands Missile Range—Regional History." Public Affairs Office White Sands Missile Range. 8 May 1998. <http://www.army.mil/paopage/Pages/reghis.htm>.

GEORG GUILLEMIN

Introduction:
The Prototypical Suttree

The more we learn about nature, the more its reiterative meaninglessness
will appall us. Ultimate horror lies not in the heart of darkness but in the
heart of enlightened understanding of nature.
>   —Karl Kroeber, *Ecological Literary Criticism*

The most intriguing literary aspect of McCarthy's fiction is that his
narrative voice is increasingly at odds with his narrative vision. McCarthy
pitches a highly stylized, wholly man-made literary practice against his
evolving ecopastoral universe, until a stalemate between humanist discourse
and post-humanist idea invests his fiction with a narrative melancholia that is
actually very common in pastoral fiction. Out of the dialectic tension between
narrative voice and narrative vision, however, evolves a version of pastoral
without equal in the American literature of the latter half of the twentieth
century. The subject of this comprehensive study will be the evolution of
McCarthy's work: the shift from traditional pastoralism in *The Orchard
Keeper* (1965) to the wilderness turn in *Child of God* (1973), and from the
anti-pastoralism of *Outer Dark* (1968) to the negative biocentrism of *Blood
Meridian* (1985) and finally to the ecopastoralism of the *Border Trilogy*.[1]

The study is based on the assumption that a compositional triangle is
at play throughout McCarthy's work. One side of the triangle is formed by a
pervasive spirit of melancholia, used—in keeping with a tradition going back

From *The Pastoral Vision of Cormac McCarthy*, 3–17. © 2004 by Georg Guillemin.

to baroque times (or even biblical times)—as a literary device for creating narrative distance. In a way, melancholia itself seems to narrate the novels. Another side of the triangle is allegoresis, the encryption of narrative contents in parabolic images and story lines in the manner of fables. On the third side of the triangle we find the pastoral theme, understood as the principal quest for harmony in a better world. All the novels mentioned above are defined by the interaction of melancholy mood, allegorical style, and pastoral theme.

The one novel not mentioned, *Suttree* (1979), does not invite inclusion into a pastoral review of McCarthy's work. It stands out because of its urban setting, and therefore contains few nature scenes that would validate a pastoral reading. It may, however, be used as the perfect introduction to McCarthy's style, being, as it were, McCarthy's longest novel and the most complex. *Suttree* marks a halfway point in McCarthy's fiction, not just because it was the fourth novel published but also because it concludes the cycle of Southern novels. In some respects *Suttree* might count as his most Southern work (due to the tall tales, banter, and local color), while in other respects it seems barely American (due to its use of stream of consciousness and its Old World iconography).

Actually, *Suttree* is less a pivotal than a prototypical work. McCarthy began to work on the novel in the early 1960s (before he wrote *The Orchard Keeper*), and it reads like a debut novel: Dense description alternates with the lean prose of the plot action; loquacious monologues with idiomatic dialogue; isolated episodes with a vaguely linear story line; autobiographical hints with intertextual links. Then again, the book draws on the writing experience of the three foregoing novels. Like these it uses expository tableaux, scenes of violence, and episodic tangents to describe the protagonist's psyche.

In the context of discussing McCarthy's pastoralism, the singularity of *Suttree* constitutes not so much a challenge as a windfall. As a prototypical work, the novel contains all the compositional elements that will be essential for the individual interpretations of the novels. A selective discussion of these elements will introduce the intended critical approach without preempting the discussion of the larger context. This critical sleight of hand—involving *Suttree* in precisely the kind of reading it does not accommodate—will serve to define three compositional mainstays in McCarthy's writings: the above-mentioned elements of pastoral genre, allegorical style, and melancholy perspective. In each of McCarthy's novels these elements interact to form a tripartite structure that showcases the author's aesthetic order. The combination makes sense, for melancholy subject matter generally favors allegorical parables either of self-deprecation or self-empowerment, while pastoral narratives generally favor utopian parables of escape into a better, simpler world. And as he acknowledges the futility of his escapism, the pastoral narrator tends to succumb to melancholia.

Suttree is set in the Knoxville of the early 1950s, or, more precisely, in the urban wasteland of McAnally Flats, a depressed neighborhood adjacent to the Tennessee River and part of downtown Knoxville. The novel's wealth of authentic detail reflects the fact that McCarthy grew up and went to college in that town.[2] The text introduces the district as "a world within the world" (4), a microcosm of speakeasies, black shantytowns, and houseboats (one of which the protagonist Cornelius Suttree inhabits). The stark representation of this "terra damnata" (306) from Suttree's point of view recalls the literary tradition of the gentleman observer mingling with the poorest of the poor.

Coming from a bourgeois family background, this "reprobate scion of doomed Saxon clans" (136) has renounced his Catholic faith, social status, and career prospects to become a fisherman. Among Suttree's pariah friends is young Gene Harrogate, one of McCarthy's likable but never-do-well picaro figures. At their first encounter in the workhouse, Harrogate is incarcerated for sexually abusing watermelons. All his schemes reveal similar maturity and resourcefulness, such as his plan to dynamite his way into a bank vault that results in his breaching a sewer main instead. Along with the idiomatic banter, roughhousing, and tall tales, the humor of this picaresque story line constitutes a counter-discourse to the existential gloom of the novel's bulk. After two abortive romances, a pilgrimage into the Appalachians, and the discovery of a dead man in his own bed (suggesting he had survived his own death) Suttree eventually leaves the city and takes to the road. The novel ends with an image reminiscent of Dante's "The Wood of the Suicides," in which black hounds terrorize the souls.[3] The narrator addresses the reader directly in seeming abdication of both urban civilization and agrarian pastoralism:

> An enormous lank hound had come out of the meadow by the river like a hound from the depths and was sniffing at the spot where Suttree had stood.
> Somewhere in the gray wood by the river is the huntsman and in the brooming corn and in the castellated press of the cities. His work lies all wheres and his hounds tire not. (471)

This conclusion connects directly to a passage in the prologue in which, analogously, death is said to besiege the city; the references here are again to Dante, to Poe's "The Masque of the Red Death," and to Melville's weaver god in *Moby Dick* (446): "The city beset by a thing unknown and will it come from forest or sea? The murengers have walled the pale, the gates are shut, but to the thing's inside and can you guess his shape? Where he's kept and what's the counter of his face? Is he a weaver, bloody shuttle shot *through* a timewarp, a carder of souls from the world's nap? Or a hunter with hounds or do bone horses draw his deadcart through the streets and does he call his trade to each?" (*Suttree* 4–5) The liberal use of intertextuality here suggests not so much a postmodern pastiche with indeterminate meaning but rather, creates a passage that reads like the back-reference typical of allegorical writing, the implied threat being death.

In short, *Suttree* combines a picaresque quest for survival with a modernist quest for truth, a baroque style with existentialist despair. The novel sustains comparisons to Eliot's "Waste Land" and Camus's *Myth of Sisyphus* (1942), to Joyce's *Ulysses* (1918) and Selby's *Last Exit to Brooklyn* (1957), and to Twain's *Huckleberry Finn* and Dante's *The Divine Comedy*.[4] It invites a close reading of its iconography as much as it invites psychoanalysis. But in spite of its complexity, the novel manifests a unified composition.

In discussing McCarthy's aesthetic, it is essential to note that the melancholia underlying the narrative process does not originate in pastoral nostalgia. On the contrary, the pastoral theme of loss seems chosen as a suitable articulation of melancholia as such. Melancholia appears in McCarthy's writings in the form of an obsession with death or mortality, as well as in a consistent maintenance of narrative distance. Such melancholy distancing, understood as a time-honored literary device, originates in the biblical image of the agonized prophet on the hill who watches the world from afar on its course toward ruin. In the novel at hand, this conceit is used, for instance, when Suttree associates the rubble of a riverside lot with the emblem used by the Puritans to invoke the divine sanction of their mission: "[A]ll this detritus slid from the city on the hill" (411). Here, the narrative melancholia is translated into the protagonist's despondency as well as into his inability or unwillingness to assume any form of civic responsibility.

Suttree's self-chosen outcast status is never fully explained beyond a deep-seated resentment of the bourgeois pattern of domesticity, prosperity, and morality. He has abandoned his wife but continues to be traumatized by losing first her and later his child, "choked with a sorrow he had never known" (153). Yet his primitive life revolves around nothing at all, and its meaninglessness horrifies him just as much. In a scene reminiscent of mad King Lear on the heath, his quest for meaning takes a suicidal turn: "Suttree stood among the screaming leaves and called the lightning down. It cracked and boomed about and he pointed out the darkened heart within him and cried for light. If there be any art in the weathers of this earth. Or char these bones to coal. If you can, if you can. A blackened rag in the rain" (366).

In the sense that plot and exposition are organized around the search for the meaning of life and death, *Suttree* parallels the part of Quentin Compson in Faulkner's *The Sound and the Fury* (1929). Both characters have an academic background; both are haunted by their families' past. Here, as there, suicidal neuroses articulate themselves in obsessions with time and the chiaroscuro of light.[5] Among the relevant passages counts a childhood memory of a horse race in which Suttree's grandfather offers

> that simple comparison of rotary motions and in the oratory to which he was prone that they had witnessed a thing against which time would not prevail.
>
> He meant a thing to be remembered, but the young apostate by the rail at his elbow had already begun to sicken at the slow seeping of life. He could see the shape of the skull through the old man's flesh. Hear sand in the glass. Lives running out like something foul, nightsoil from a cesspipe, a measured dripping in the dark. The clock has run, the horse has run, and which has measured which? (136)

On a personal level, then, the novel reads like a psychological profile of its main character. From among the sermons of evangelists Suttree picks the jeremiads, a family photo album resembles a "picturebook of the afflicted" (130), a snake under a rock is hailed as "little brother death" (284), and his hard-drinking uncle has a "smell of death at the edges" (16). Suttree's sensory spectrum is fine-tuned to aspects of mortality. He provokes life-threatening experiences as if to seek death, involving himself in brawls, contracting typhoid, sustaining severe injury, and starving himself during his hike into the Gatlinburg wilderness. With the reclusive rag-picker he converses about God and dying. The ragman admits, "I always figured they was a God" but "I just never did like him" (147), and Suttree feels the same way. His skepticism and a longing for death inform his idea that "Death is what the living carry with them. A state of dread, like some uncanny foretaste of a bitter memory. But the dead do not remember and nothingness is not a curse. Far from it" (153).

Upon closer scrutiny, the melancholia apparent in Suttree and in the narrator of *Suttree* loses some of its mournful aspect and is in fact drained of any emotion whatsoever. Its intrinsic nature is the catatonic state described in William James's lecture on the "sick soul."[6] What James says about Tolstoy could be applied to Suttree, namely that the perceived meaninglessness of life "was like those first discomforts of a sick man, to which he pays but little attention till they run into one continuous suffering, and then he realizes that what he took for a passing disorder means the most momentous thing in the world for him, means his death" (153). James suggests that sentiments of such emotionally deadened melancholia do not originate in the subject's physical or social reality, but "have their source in another sphere of existence altogether, in the animal and spiritual region of the subject's being. Conceive yourself, if possible, suddenly stripped of all the emotion with which your world now inspires you, and try to imagine it as *it exists*, purely by itself, without your favorable or unfavorable, hopeful or apprehensive comment. It will be almost impossible for you to realize such a condition of negativity and deadness" (150). The state of mind James describes essentially captures not only the meaninglessness that perturbs Suttree, but, moreover, the narrative perspective governing McCarthy's writings in general. It is precisely this melancholy equanimity that conditions the pastoral vision of McCarthy. If optimistically interpreted, its pessimistic indifference bestows an egalitarian existential status on all terrestrial phenomena alike. James's words support this line of argument as he arrives at the following conclusion: "No one portion of the universe would then have importance beyond another; and the whole collection of its things and series of its events would be without significance, character, expression, or perspective" (150).

What is most important, then, about the death-centeredness of *Suttree* is that death assumes a leveling function. The narrative form transporting the egalitarian aspect of death in effect simulates the folkloric emblem of Death personified, which comes for each and every person regardless of status. Relevant images include dreams of the dead: "In a dream I walked with my grandfather by a dark lake and the old man's talk was filled with incertitude. I saw how all things false fall from the dead. We spoke easily and I was humbly honored to walk with him deep in that world where he was a man like all men" (14). Toward the end of *Suttree*, after "[t]he wilderness has treated him with a sublime indifference" (Longley 87) and after the typhoid fever has failed to carry him off, melancholia gives way to the affirmative insight "I know all souls are one and all souls lonely" (459). Elsewhere, this notion is rephrased in a way that calls to mind transcendentalist writing or Whitman's[7] poetry: "It is not alone in the dark of death that all souls are one soul" (414). In the course of the same soliloquy, Suttree comes to renounce his modernist quest for a stable sense of self, though no post-humanist implication reveals itself yet: "I spoke with bitterness about my life and I said that I would take my own part against the slander of oblivion and against the monstrous facelessness of it and that I would stand a stone in the very void where all would read my name. Of that vanity I recant all" (414).[8] On the plot level of the text, this moment of epiphany provides the novel's theme of suicide with "a resolution to the very problem central to 'The Myth of Sisyphus,' and one presented with elements strikingly in common with that work. While many readers of *Suttree* have felt that the novel simply stops, it does resolve itself and does so in the same way as Camus's work: in an act of will rather than an act of rational thought" (Shelton 72).

On the meta-narrative level, however, the cause and resolution of Suttree's crisis matter less than the fact that his fixation on death creates a protagonist with a melancholy point of view. Among McCarthy's novels,

Suttree is the only one with an intellectually active protagonist, while in all his novels the narrative perspective coincides with the protagonists' points of view. In a prototypical manner, *Suttree* shows how the protagonist's melancholia is indistinguishable from that of the narrative consciousness. In other words, although character and narrator are distinct entities, they virtually share a point of view. Since he channels the narrative perspective, Suttree's focus on death creates the cognitive condition for subjecting all that is seen and all that is told to the death-centered vision of the melancholy narrator. Analogously, the protagonists of all the other novels function as vessels for the narrative gaze even as the narrators remain amorphous, and even if most of McCarthy's figures come across as curiously lifeless. In book after book, these unreflective nomads represent a melancholia that they do not contain within themselves.

The uneasy reception with which McCarthy's writings have occasionally been met may be due not so much to the author's penchant for violent action, but to his rhetoric and iconography. McCarthy is a storyteller in a parabolic sense. The secret of his symbolism is that it works not symbolically but allegorically at a time when allegoresis has just begun to regain respect as a literary mode. Its semantic single-mindedness renders allegory alien to the romantic, realist, or modernist schools of literature. Some postmodern writing has rehabilitated allegoresis through its use of parable, and typological structure through its use of intertextuality. But McCarthy can hardly be considered a postmodern writer. Any de-centering intention he may share with postmodernism owes less to the influence of fashionable theory than to the subversive energy of the grotesque. His allegorical iconography partakes of the realism Mikhail Bakhtin has defined as carnivalesque. A case in point, Suttree's hallucination during his wilderness quest calls to mind Shakespeare's *Midsummer Night's Dream*, Goethe's *Faust II*, or the tableaux of Hieronymous Bosch. The use of the grotesque is as typical of McCarthy's style as the mannerism of the run-on sentences: "And along the little ways in the rain and lightning came a troupe of squalid merrymakers bearing a caged wivern on shoulderpoles and other alchemical game, chimeras and cacodemons skewered up on boarspears and a pharmacopoeia of hellish condiments adorning a trestle and toted by trolls with an eldern gnome for guidon who shouted foul oaths from his mouth-hole and a piper who piped a pipe of cloverbone and wore on his hip a glass flasket of some foul smoking fuel that yawed within viscid as quicksilver" (287–88). The problem of allegorical discourse is that it retards its own interpretation. It fails to signify anything beyond the finite meaning it confers through parable or type. The following emblem easily translates into the Ophelia motif, but what to make of it? "In an old grandfather time a ballad transpired here, some love gone wrong and a sabletressed girl drowned in an icegreen pool where she was

found with her hair spreading like ink on the cold and cobbled river floor"
(283). No context is given; the image presents itself without preparation and
comment and is dropped again. Emblems like this one abound in *Suttree* and
in McCarthy's novels generally. The insertion of these emblems must seem
arbitrary if the text is approached with realistic criteria, and critics who have
so approached it tend to write themselves into a rage.[9]

Actually, McCarthy's craftsmanship does not suggest that anything is
left to chance or escapes narrative control even if his novels are not laid out
to foreground plot progression, denouement, or character development. The
plots progress, and the characters develop, to the degree that they serve to
accumulate, rather than order, installments of a certain story as if to complete
a mosaic of stills rather than to scroll a film in linear sequence. McCarthy's
texts may therefore repeat intratextual stories or emblems and connect to
stories told elsewhere by McCarthy or by other writers. They often affect
a retold quality that is indigenous to oral storytelling and overrides the
concerns of dramatic structure and mimetic exposition. In order not to end in
a diagnosis of structural paucity, critical studies of McCarthy would do well
to focus on the allegorical composition that gathers the emblems, banter, tall
tales, and monotonous syntax into a unified aesthetic.

The effects of allegoresis in *Suttree* are impossible to overlook. The
novel's prologue is all parable, explicitly establishing the textual setting as
a stage. The baroque idea that the world represents a stage fronting for a
higher form of being, and, inversely, that text and stage represent the world
in microcosm, is the very presupposition of McCarthy's aesthetic.

> The rest indeed is silence. It has begun to rain. Light summer
> rain, you can see it falling slant in the town lights. The river lies in
> a grail of quietude. Here from the bridge the world below seems
> a gift of simplicity. Curious, no more.
> [...] A curtain is rising on the western world. A fine rain of
> soot, dead beetles, anonymous small bones. The audience sits
> webbed in dust. Within the gutted sockets of the interlocutor's
> skull a spider sleeps and the jointed ruins of the hanged fool
> dangle from the flies, bone pendulum in motley. Fourfooted
> shapes go to and fro over the boards. Ruder forms survive. (5)

Apart from its allegorical quality, the excerpt contains emblematic allusions
to melancholia (the skull, the dust-covered audience, the watcher on the
bridge) and the hope of survival. The narrative tension between the prologue's
descriptions of urban squalor and the concluding emblem does not seem
intended to qualify a Dickensian scenery with a sense of irony. Rather, it
places in typological sequence two images of the world, one describing it

as a pest house and the other describing it as a stage. The latter represents the very image underlying the passage from *Macbeth* from which Faulkner also took his title *The Sound and the Fury*.[10] What is added to the familiar image is that the theater seems decommissioned, bypassed by time, while "ruder forms" than audience, actors, and interlocutor—that is, creatures less refined—"survive." The survivalist notion, while originating in the retrospective melancholia of the text, implies a narrative indifference toward these cultural artifacts. At the same time, it invests life forms with existential privileges that do not share in the high drama of life. Thus, a sense of rivalry between a tragic view of life and a comic one surfaces, and this aspect ushers in the essence of McCarthy's pastoral vision.

What few pastoral aspects are found in *Suttree* manage to run the whole gamut of American pastoralism. For one thing, *Suttree* describes a ruined mansion, "which might have been lifted from the pages of any southern pastoral lament," while the novel remains free of pastoral nostalgia. The reader will look "in vain for the great theme of 'the past in the present,' for the burden of southern history, for . . . the conflict between tradition and modernity" (Grammer 30). A daydream occurring as Suttree walks the crumbling halls of the mansion and "through the ruined garden" contains the words "something more than time has passed here" (136). The scene obviously refers to Southern pastoralism in the emblem of the ruined mansion and ruined garden as something so anachronistic that it has ceased to be an object even of nostalgia. In this sense the scene reduces literary back-references, such as to Sutpen's mansion in Faulkner's *Absalom, Absalom!* (1936), to the function of stage props and discourages any elegiac or tragic reading of the novel. To read it in an anti-pastoral sense would equally miss the point, because pastoral escapism as a lifestyle choice is clearly still available to Suttree, as his wilderness trip demonstrates. The mansion, then, functions like a prop representing an anachronistic pastoral nostalgia and helps create a setting against which a new pastoralism defines itself. The same narrative function is inscribed in the following reflection on the *Westward-Ho!* version of pastoral escapism: "[T]he country rolls away to the south and the mountains. Where hunters and woodcutters once slept in their boots by the dying light of their thousand fires and went on, old teutonic forebears with eyes incandesced by the visionary light of a massive rapacity, wave on wave of the violent and the insane, their brains stoked with spoorless analogues of all that was, lean aryans with their abrogate semitic chapbook reenacting the dramas and parables therein and mindless and pale with a longing that nothing save dark's total restitution could appease" (4). The passage alludes to the ideas of the Puritan errand into the wilderness, of Manifest Destiny, and of white supremacy. This legacy is identified not just as obsolete but also as pathogenic.

What presents itself in answer to traditional versions of pastoral and in contrast to the gnostic materialism of the city is not a unified ecopastoral alternative. One of several alternative approaches is suggested by Suttree's immersion in nature, and this approach takes its cue from transcendentalism, even in regard to Suttree's failure to become one with the cosmos: Rather than the sublime, he experiences the trivial and the grotesque. Another approach is personified in the Native American Michael who, like Suttree, is a fisherman, and who shares advice, food, secret bait, and a talisman. "As it turns out, Suttree—however he may aspire to it—proves incapable of the kind of oneness with the river which Michael has attained" (Young 105). In a sense, Suttree's mystification over Michael's teachings reflects the role of the Native American worldview as an ecological utopia. A third alternative to traditional pastoral vision is suggested in the treatment of wilderness, and it is the ecopastoral vision that subsumes the other two.

McCarthy's pastoralism is ecopastoral not just because it respects the ecological equality of all creatures and favors undomesticated nature over agricultural land, but, moreover, because it equates the external wilderness of nature with the social wilderness of the city and the internal wilderness of the human mind. As they ignore the distinction that is commonly made between these realms, McCarthy's texts themselves come to function as a narrative wilderness of images and scenes and reflections. In this sense, the interaction of the several modes of wilderness also makes it possible to discuss *Suttree* as if it were in fact a pastoral novel.

Moreover, the equivalence of the several modes of wilderness in the text integrates the picaresque into the pastoral. Without exception, McCarthy's novels contain picaro figures, that is, deracinated protagonists preoccupied with survival more than with lofty quests, and gifted with a comic resourcefulness. Harrogate evidently reveals the trickster-like attributes of the picaro and, in a less comic way, so does Suttree. What matters here is less their identification with this generic role model than the fact that the type of the picaro is allegorically conceived (unlike a realistic character); that the picaresque genre is comic (as opposed to tragic); and that Suttree's quest for survival in an alien cityscape parallels his quest for survival in the Appalachians. Both environments are wild; in neither environment does he care to dominate; and survival in either is equally hard. As if Suttree were in part a "Doomed Huck" (Charyn 14), in part as grandiloquent as Whitman, the novel's ecopastoralism and its picaresque aspects subscribe to the same wilderness ethos.

The egalitarian treatment of society and nature in *Suttree* is two-sided insofar as everything that initially seems meaningless and alien to Suttree later becomes meaningful and inclusive. As if to evoke the proverbial glass of water looking no longer half empty but half full, an angelic boy offers

Suttree a drink of water in the final scene. The moment contrasts favorably with Suttree's earlier, grotesque vision of his Saxon forebears who "wait for the water-bearer to come but he does not come, and does not come" (136). Suttree affirms his kinship with the land when he "was struck by the fidelity of this earth he inhabited and he bore it a sudden love" (354).[11] The positive sense of self and place he regains is obviously an extension of his integration into the human environment of his friends, qualifying the trauma of individualized death with the prospect of collective survival. As Vereen Bell argues in regard to the "common cause against the rule of death" in *Suttree*, "This commonality within, which may and should arise from the universality of suffering, is the quid pro quo in human life, brought into life, ironically by death" (*Achievement* 110).

In a way, the survivalist reversal of Suttree's view of life at the novel's end suggests a need to reinterpret the novel's grotesque imagery. For the grotesque, too, is of an egalitarian quality insofar as it is designed to level hierarchies and join incompatible aspects together and to be, above all, infinite, depersonalized, and dynamic. Suttree's dictum "Nothing ever stops moving" (461) captures the anarchic flux at the heart of the grotesque. The grotesque imagery in *Suttree* becomes emblematic of the kind of survivalism that Bakhtin identifies in the grotesque realism of the Renaissance: "The last thing one can say of the real grotesque is that it is static; on the contrary it seeks to grasp in its imagery the very act of becoming and growth, the eternal incomplete unfinished nature of being. Its images present simultaneously the two poles of becoming: that which is receding and dying, and that which is being born; they show two bodies in one, the budding and the division of the living cell. At the summit of grotesque and folklore realism, as in the death of one-cell organisms, no dead body remains" (*Rabelais* 52).

McCarthy's ecopastoralism bespeaks a worldview whose egalitarian underpinnings logically transcend the preference of the pastoral imagination for natural landscape settings. It embraces various modes of narrative discourse, from the loftiest abstraction to the most proletarian idiom. It places philosophical meditations side by side with the most mundane detail. If man is a relative to all living things and is on an existential par with them then civilization represents but one ecosystem among many, and literary discourse yet another. In this sense, every episode and every description in *Suttree* assumes its carefully calculated part in the novel's cosmology. Once McCarthy's aesthetic order is understood, all other aspects begin to fall into place. On this view, all of McCarthy's novels, including *Suttree*, are intrinsically ecopastoral and call for ecocritical readings.

McCarthy's pastoralism defies traditional pastoral approaches because these tend to reduce the pastoral theme to a surface function against which other concerns are played out. McCarthy's pastoralism, however, is inclusive and holistic. The subsequent passage in *Suttree*, for instance, contains the machine-in-the-garden motif, but in a manner that subjects the symbol of intruding industrialism itself to destruction, as if to suggest a shared tendency to entropy while integrating it into the dominant theme of natural beauty. "Wasn't two minutes the whole car was afire. I run to the door and got it open and we was goin up this grade through the mountains in the snow with the moon on it and it was just blue lookin and dead quiet out there and them big old black pine trees going by. I jumped for it and lit in a snowbank and what I'm going to tell you you'll think peculiar but it's the god's truth. That was in nineteen and thirty-one and if I live to be a hunnerd year old I don't think I'll ever see anything as pretty as that train on fire goin up that mountain and around the bend and them flames lightin up the snow and the trees and the night" (182). The slight shifts in focus (from boxcar to door to moonlit snow to pines and back to the receding train), which are effected not through differentiation but through concatenation, result in a nonhierarchical structure that highlights nothing so much as the fact that nothing is highlighted. Man, machine, and nature seem to be in perfect harmony in an aesthetic that is based on the relatedness of things, and not on the incongruity of the machine in the garden. Nowhere in this scene does the train signify industrial intrusion or even contrast with the setting. Instead, the whole scene becomes an emblem of the paradoxical harmony of destruction that informs the savage tableaux of *Outer Dark* and *Blood Meridian* as much as Lester's dream of his last ride in *Child of God* (170–71) or the "miracles of destruction" that the Mormon seeks in *The Crossing* (142).

The parable of the train suggests a pastoral truth that goes beyond the realm of nature to include mankind in shared mortality. Taking the place of the romantic sublime, this vision introduces a metaphysical component in McCarthy's ecopastoralism. The chapters to come will use the term "nature mysticism" to describe this sense of a deeper truth in nature and the integrative function of this mysticism for the texts' sense of pastoral. Whatever is mystical about McCarthy's ecopastoralism ought to be understood as a reference to the experience of the egalitarian essence of the universe, such as described by Whitman in *Specimen Days* as "an intuition of the absolute balance, in time and space, of the whole of this multifarious, mad chaos of fraud, frivolity, hoggishness—this revel of fools, and incredible make-believe and general unsettledness, we call *the world*; a soul-sight of that divine clue and unseen thread which holds the whole congeries of things, all history and time, and all events, however trivial, however momentous, like a leash'd dog in the hand of the hunter" (894). Whitman's dog-and-hunter simile hints at the need for figurative language to describe an essentially ineffable observation. The meaning of the term *animism* in this study—wherever it is applied to describe the ecopastoral ethos in McCarthy's novels—is attendant on this reductive concept of mystical perception, and is in turn to be understood as the conviction that all things animate and inanimate share in existential equality. In short, it is arrived at by way of nature mysticism more than by ecological argument.

The inclusion of an ecocritical angle has become established procedure in McCarthy criticism. The chapters to follow will go a step further and undertake close readings designed to show that McCarthy's work as a whole is crafted according to a unified ecopastoral aesthetic. McCarthy's novels themselves, in their emphasis on multifaceted structure and semantic interrelationships, affect the complexity of ecosystems. Each textual aspect interrelates with any number of other aspects, and so the analysis of their egalitarianism becomes the most pressing and rewarding task of the McCarthy critic.

NOTES

1. Not discussed, then, are McCarthy's two short stories, "A Wake for Susan" (1957) and "A Drowning Incident" (1958); the TV drama *The Gardener's Son* (1977); and the drama *The Stonemason* (1998).

2. Arnold writes that *Suttree* contains more than 150 named characters, many of whom are based on historic personae ("Naming" 57). Incidentally, McAnally is already mentioned in *The Orchard Keeper* as the destination of Sylder's whiskey runs (29). McCarthy's father, a lawyer, served on the legal board of the Tennessee Valley Authority, so the novel's rebellious undertones suggest autobiographical motives. Also, the fact that, like McCarthy, Suttree spent time at the local university explains the protagonist's prolixity.

3. *The Divine Comedy*, Canto XIII. The parallel is pointed out by Arnold ("Naming" 68, n. 21).

4. For the parallels between *Suttree* and works by Camus and Eliot, see Shelton's essay; for the parallels to Dante, see Arnold's essay "Naming, Knowing and Nothingness."

5. The intertextuality is made explicit when Suttree dreams of stopping in front of a watchmaker's shop and watching the timepieces arrest themselves in his presence (453–54). The fact that Quentin drowns himself finds a meaningful analogy in Suttree's fear of drowning and his mortification when a suicide is pulled from the river and he perceives that "the dead man's watch was still running" (10).

6. McCarthy's knowledge of James is mentioned in Garry Wallace's problematic but nonetheless useful article "Meeting McCarthy" (138). This information suggests that McCarthy carefully calculates the narrative effect of his narrators' melancholia, rather than drawing on any personal sense of disenchantment.

7. Suttree's realizations that "there is one Suttree and one Suttree only" (461) and "[a] man is all men" (422) are compared by Bell to "Walt Whitman speaking in a new idiom and time" (*Achievement* 110).

8. The quote reconnects to "The Waste Land" in which Eliot speaks of "these fragments I have shored against my ruins" (504). The intertextuality confirms that Suttree's quest for meaning and self is informed more by a modernist crisis of meaning than by the postmodernist contestation of all hegemonic structures of meaning.

9. Sullivan's critique of *Suttree* is a case in point: "The shape of the novel is amorphous, even for McCarthy, whose long suit has never been dramatic structure. One gets the impression that McCarthy walks through the world cramming his brain with experience both actual and vicarious and then goes to work and gives everything back, scene upon scene, the devil take the hindmost" ("Citizens" 341).

10. Macbeth's words are these: "Life's but walking shadow; a poor player / That struts and frets his hour upon the stage, / And then is heard no more: it is a tale / Told by an idiot, full of sound and fury, / Signifying nothing" (act 5, scene 5). The lines are so familiar that McCarthy could hardly have created the image without having intended the reader's inference of the intertextuality and the attendant melancholia.

11. The context is Suttree's love affair with Wanda; his feeling of cosmic harmony recalls *Leaves of Grass* in which Whitman writes: "And I know [. . .] that all the men ever born are also my brothers . . . and the women my sisters and lovers, / And that a kelson of the creation is love" (31).

VINCE BREWTON

The Changing Landscape of Violence in Cormac McCarthy's Early Novels and the Border Trilogy

Cormac McCarthy's appearance on the national literary radar with the successful publication of *All the Pretty Horses*, after years of largely "academic" interest in his work, also inaugurated on a substantive level a clearly defined second phase in his career as a writer. Chronology alone would mark McCarthy's first phase as a novelist as the two decades between 1965 and 1985 that saw the publication of *The Orchard Keeper, Outer Dark, Child of God, Suttree,* and *Blood Meridian*, while the Border Trilogy spans the 90s, including *All the Pretty Horses* (1992), *The Crossing* (1994), and his latest, *Cities of the Plain* (1998). A historicist approach to McCarthy's fiction, however, corroborates the chronological separation in that it reveals the correlations between the work of McCarthy's two major periods on the one hand and the cultural moments, popular and otherwise, with which their conception and composition coincided.

A clear and discernible correlation exists between the novels of McCarthy's first period and the era of American history defined by the military involvement in Vietnam, while the novels of the Border Trilogy exhibit a similar imaginative and thematic debt to the changing political and cultural landscape of America beginning in the 1980s, a landscape best evoked by the Reagan presidency and the Gulf War with Iraq in 1991. The correspondences between McCarthy's work and his times are part of a

From *Southern Literary Journal* 37, no. 1 (Fall 2004): 121–43. © 2004 by University of North Carolina Press.

larger cultural equation whereby contemporary historical events influenced prevailing cultural attitudes on the one hand, and cultural production on the other, a form of influence manifested in film and literature generally, but felt with equal force in the arena of national media culture, in the campaigns for president in 1980 and 1984, and in the political discourse of the 1980s. Perhaps all cultural artifacts are a product of their times, but the novels of McCarthy's first phase are recognizably so in ways worth exploring, as is the case with the Border Trilogy. To understand how the works display this influence, in some cases a covert influence, requires situating McCarthy's novels afresh in their historical contexts.

The two separate cases of correspondence between McCarthy's work and his cultural milieu are united primarily by the representation of violence and issues closely related to violence in the novels, a circumstance not surprising given that two wars have had a major impact on the cultural terrain of McCarthy's career. Between the novels of the early phase and the work of the Trilogy, a major shift occurs in McCarthy's storytelling and that shift is directly a product of a changing aesthetic of violence in his work. The transformation of McCarthy's aesthetic of violence takes shape as a movement from the serial event to the symbolic drama: the former representing conflicts always contingent and soon to be superseded by fresh eruptions of violence; in the latter, a central act of violence is the single event itself toward which the narrative proceeds and which regularly contains the work's larger thematic conflicts if not in every case their resolution. McCarthy's transition between the serial and the symbolic returns him to the tradition of southern literary violence that relies on violence as the site where divergent interests converge for dramatic effect.

While all literary violence can be viewed as formal in the sense that it has achieved literary form, normally we make a distinction between formal violence on the one hand—violence governed by rules, agreements, and cultural assumptions, typified by the formal duel—and informal violence on the other hand—violence that is fragmentary, unconsidered, "random," or "senseless," as public discourse of our time denotes it. Southern literature—from which Cormac McCarthy emerges in terms of our understanding of his work, especially in his early, Tennessee-centered vision—favors a narrative strategy in which violence represents a climax of tensions and stress with the literary text. For McCarthy, the conflict between an older order and the newer one replacing it persists from *The Orchard Keeper* to *Cities of the Plain*, a novel in which the closing of the western range ultimately brings about the displacement and final alienation of his surviving hero. Thus McCarthy's return in the Border Trilogy to the symbolic violence familiar to southern literary genealogy marks a repetition worthy of our attention, for it is a return that reinforces our sense of his participation in the southern literary tradition he had seemingly relinquished in his turn to a new subject and place, the American Southwest.

The Vietnam experience, while never appearing directly in McCarthy's novels, has nevertheless left a deep imprint on his early work. Three novels in particular, *Child of God*, *Suttree*, and *Blood Meridian*, show the influence of imagery and ideas issuing from the military-political experience of Vietnam. While *Child of God* and *Suttree* contain repressed traces of the Vietnam experience, *Blood Meridian* comes close to being a novel whose true subject is Vietnam, a kind of allegory of American involvement in Southeast Asia and of the reverberations of that history in the American psyche. Although the date of publication puts *Blood Meridian* forward into the second cultural moment that in turn left its mark on the Border Trilogy, the novel of 1985 is significantly an artifact of McCarthy's two-decade working through of the war and the mediation of that war by American popular culture. Critical thought on McCarthy has certainly hinted at such a connection. John Emil Sepich, in a footnote to his essay on the historical sources of *Blood Meridian*, writes, "The literature of 'atrocities' in Vietnam seems consistent, in its language, with that of Glanton's 'atrocities'" (138). Sepich, however, does not draw any inferences from the similarity (138). Andrew Nelson refers to *Blood Meridian* as "a book which finally dislocates the reader from the adventure of Manifest Destiny," an interesting observation when we consider that Michael Herr made a similar point in his classic *Dispatches* (1977) about our involvement in Vietnam. In a work whose influence on *Blood Meridian* seems significant, Herr surmises that we "might as well say that Vietnam was where the Trail of Tears was headed all along, the turnaround point where it would touch and come back to form a containing perimeter" (49). Herr uses the familiar imagery of Native American dispossession to suggest that the disastrous American involvement in Vietnam was the logical conclusion of the ideology of Manifest Destiny. Along these same lines, Richard Slotkin has pointed out that Sam Peckinpah's famous western *The Wild Bunch* mirrors contemporary history in its depiction of a struggle between democracy and tyranny that miscarries and becomes instead an orgy of bloodshed directly suggestive of the carnage in Vietnam (880). Similarly, reviewers of *Blood Meridian* have compared it to Peckinpah's films (Tatum 479). But the full significance of the link between the historical event of Vietnam and the artistic vision of McCarthy's first phase as a novelist remains to be explored. One persistent theme in McCarthy's early work is the loss of the American myth of innocence. American mythology has long woven together John Winthrop's imagery of the "city on the hill" with the older notion of the New World as an earthly paradise that generated a national self-conception of righteousness. The literary myth of the new American Adam similarly depends on the framing metaphor of America as a relocated garden, while

the Puritan vision of a sanctified national mission in an Edenic paradise
added a crucial component of virtue/innocence to the national identity, even
if that innocence is no more than a disassociation from the dubious legacy
of Old World social arrangements. Innocence so conceived is the tangible
quantity expunged from the American self-definition as a direct result of the
military intervention in Vietnam and the soiled spectacle of our support for
corrupt regimes, the pervasive loss of faith in authority, and the appalling
images and stories of that war. In Dog Soldiers, Robert Stone sums up
this loss of innocence, or ignorance, in Vietnam: "You can't blame us too
much. We didn't know who we were till we got here. We thought we were
something else." (57)

National mythology thus has linked purpose (mission) with place
(paradise metaphors), a process that associates innocence with possession
—McCarthy's work charts the dissolution of both. *Child of God* chronicles
the sad and sordid history of Lester Ballard's dispossession and alienation
in rural Sevier County, Tennessee. Lester's mythic exile takes the narrative
form of his eviction from the family farm in the novel's opening scene. From
this point on in the novel, Lester occupies a series of downwardly mobile
dwellings, from rented shacks, to jail cells, to caves in the bowels of the earth,
and at last an asylum for the criminally insane. His crimes conversely rise to
a crescendo of horror, from voyeurism and petty theft, to arson, attempted
rape, murder, mutilation, and necrophilia. Lester's dispossession obliquely
represents the national loss of innocence while also allegorizing the expulsion
of the American psyche from the sheltering myth of "city on the hill" virtue,
an expulsion that exposed the national consciousness to a two-decade ordeal
of bad conscience.

Although Ballard's existence may be confined to the margins of the
social order, storytelling reinserts him, or his legend, into the heart of the
community. His cross-dressing presence on the outskirts of the civilization
corresponds directly with his behavior: where law and taboo are remote,
everything is permitted. The falling away of social restraint also reveals
itself in the dumpkeeper, Ballard's confrere of the margins, who slides from
outraged parent to incestuous father in the heat of a wrestling match in the
weeds. The space of the margins is like the traditional space of war, located
on the periphery, but one nevertheless generated by the cultural center.
Ballard's dispossession places him on the civic limits, just as the organized
apparatus of the state creates the scene of war where frequently, despite the
well-intentioned rules of warfare, nothing is forbidden. The two sites are
comparable in another way familiar to postmodern thought: as marginal
spaces, both the scene of Ballard's depravity and the scene of war have the
uncanny ability to become central. In this respect, our national stock of lore
concerning Vietnam mirrors the legend of Lester in the hollows. Part of

our narrative compulsion concerning Vietnam involves its function as a sign of the expansion of our capacity as a nation to misstep, the furthest point down the road of civic dishonor we have traveled in the twentieth century. Whether American ideals and conduct were at their worst between 1959 and 1973 has become in some ways beside the point. What matters is that public discourse on Vietnam acts as a nether limit for American civilization and serves as a boundary for American behavior within the bigger story of our history in the last century.

The ballad of Lester Ballard plays a comparable role in Sevier County to the national obsession with Vietnam. Ballard's catalogue of misdeeds transacted on the margins yields for the community a reinforced conviction of the existence of those margins that their own lesser meannesses and misdemeanors approach but never transgress. Lester's ghoulish crusade transforms him over time into the hobgoblin of Sevier County mythmaking while his narrative provides the county's inhabitants with a representative means for containing the story of communal deviance within the larger narrative of the community as a whole. Lester establishes the necessary boundary marker—like the cultural sign of Vietnam—and in this he has a function similar to a taboo, which, as Bataille reminds us in *Erotism*, directs us away from the prohibited action while in the same movement fixating our interest.

The gruesome quality of Lester's practices has heretofore been considered within the theoretical framework of the grotesque in southern literature. While the theory of the grotesque opens up *Child of God* in interesting ways, Ballard's obsession with corpses (bodies) and his purloining of trophies from the dead transcend the ordinary pilfering of a criminal. Having been symbolically expelled from the community, Lester feeds on the edges of communal space. Out on the margins, Ballard recreates the world from which he has been estranged, and the corpses, clothes, and ultimately the "fright-wig" itself have the talismanic quality of the souvenired trophy. Ballard's trophies allow him to incorporate the community that has unincorporated him, thus providing him with potent totems to shelter him existentially from what Vereen M. Bell describes as "more abasement than most humans could imagine" (Achievement 55). Every emblem Lester strips from the dead performs the function of the war trophy for the soldier still in combat, for whom the sliced-ear or thumb marks an overcoming of death dread through a symbolic overcoming of the foe. Like the soldier, Lester's metaphorical consumption of objects and human remains confirms the Bakhtinian idea that to consume the world is to tame our fear of it (296).

The retrieval of Lester Ballard's collection of corpses at novel's end bears an eerie resemblance to the return of dead servicemen from Vietnam, a cultural sign deeply intertwined with the consciousness of the period in which Child of God was composed. McCarthy seems to be invoking the pathos of a sign already present in the psyche of his readers to charge this scene in his novel with the emotional freight of the dead soldier and the corresponding national trauma of that image. Sevier County's dead, wrapped in "muslin shrouds on which was stenciled Property of the State of Tennessee," are repatriated in a movement that mimics the return of servicemen during the war years in official body bags (196). Lester Ballard's victims now share in the cultural mourning experienced by a nation for the casualties of war, deaths that seemed to many then and now as lives "wasted," to use the soldier's slang, in an expenditure of life not sufficiently sustained by a meaningful purpose as in previous wars. For Sevier County's collective memory, the murdered victims occupy a place of unassigned meaning: the myth-making surrounding their murderer is unable to establish that they were killed for any sensible reason—not even as a product of the powerful but inchoate "meanness" with which they identify their own history of violence. Lester's enigmatic career of murder and necrophilia can offer no closure or final understanding, a fact signaled by the mute narration of the gruesome homecoming.

While Child of God has an obvious political subtext, Suttree, a Joycean epic of the days and nights of Cornelius Suttree, down and out in Knoxville, Tennessee, would appear to bear less resemblance to a clandestine novel of Vietnam. Yet, the narrative of Suttree's daily life resonates with both the experience of war generally and Vietnam in particular. Ballard's serial enactment of murder, by comparison, moves forward without a readily apparent object: even vengeance is absorbed into the series, for Greer's death is only one more murder, neither the first nor the last. Violence in the life of Cornelius Suttree follows a similar sequence in which encounters have neither a cumulative effect nor contribute to a narrative movement toward one central or conclusive moment of violence. Rather, the bar fights of Suttree and his cronies and the titanic struggle of Ab Jones against the police, to cite the main arteries of violence in the sprawling novel, are inherently provisional. Partly for this reason, Suttree and Child of God have struck some critics as bereft of plot, or as Bell puts it, "innocent of theme and of ethical reference and plot" ("Nihilism" 31). The episodic quality of these novels, however, is neither an artistic failing nor lack of a sustained vision on McCarthy's part, but on the contrary marks an importation of an aesthetic of violence from the heavily televised and reported war in Southeast Asia.

Bell's commentary on Suttree unintentionally reinforces the idea that the novel contains disguised references to Vietnam. Of the reckless quality to Suttree's life, Bell writes: "The consequence of Suttree's removing himself from normal society is that it removes him from ordinary amenities of the modern world and thus in a sense displaces him in time. He is therefore in the presence of death daily in the way a citizen of an earlier century would be" (Achievement 92). One need not look to an earlier century as a source for Suttree's daily experience. Bell's assertion rings particularly true for the soldier who is removed from "ordinary amenities" and lives in "in the presence of death daily." McCarthy inscribes the experiential reality of war into the novel not, I think, to tell elliptically the ongoing story of Vietnam but to impart to his narrative the wholly contingent and provisional nature of the daily life of an individual outside the normally sustaining entities of family, work, and religion. In the unsheltering existential sky of McCarthy's early work, human beings face reality in unrelentingly gritty episodes of pain and pleasure, a kind of life Bell characterizes as where "the world itself is always insisting upon its own reality; it is then to be dealt with as itself and not at the subordinated service of ideas" (Achievement 77). Ideas, particularly those pertaining to the conventionally ordered life bounded by family, conventional politics, and commerce, cannot resist the reality of Suttree's world that always "insists" more powerfully than any attempts to organize it. These attempts to frame and arrange the uncontainable truth of our being find expression in the reproach of Suttree's father, who argues to his son that "The world is run by those willing to take the responsibility for the running of it. If it is life you feel that you are missing I can tell you where to find it. In the law courts, in business, in government" (13–14). Cornelius Suttree's difficulties hardly stem from missing out on life. Quite the contrary, McCarthy demonstrates that for the son life is really quite like war and has an awesome and unsettling immediacy the law courts, business, and government cannot match.

Bell describes Suttree's companions as "an odd little band of ragtag existential heroes" (81). A primary convention of the war genre in literature and film is the handful of soldiers who constitute a microcosm of the conflict, or of humanity in general. Crane, Remarque, O'Brien, James Jones, Hasford, Kubrick, and Oliver Stone all make use of the organizing principle of small-unit soldiery in their works. Suttree's companions—"By nine oclock that night they were twelve or more, all good hearts from McAnally"—carouse with the kind of intensity and abandon of those who live entirely for the moment—"Who the fuck are we fighting? said Suttree. Who the fuck cares, if he aint from McAnally bust him" (184–186). McCarthy's dubious heroes serve as a chorus for the conflict at the core of the novel, that between Suttree and his world. Arnold and Luce remind us that McCarthy labored over this voluminous novel during a twenty-year period that almost perfectly coincides with the Vietnam years. Like the television series M*A*S*H, McCarthy situates the novel's action entirely in the 50s, so that although direct representation of Vietnam is formally denied, many of the text's associations and other points of reference with Vietnam work in service of the novel's primary conflicts (8).

Bell concludes his assessment of the Suttrean odyssey with this perceptive remark: "Suttree's hard lessons harden him and eventually free him from sentimental regret, leaving him with perspective, which is at least like transcendence" (101). Bell's insight could be inserted seamlessly into a discussion of the hero of war literature, whose ordeal in the crucible of war transforms him from the naive recruit and does confer something like transcendence, or at least an unsentimental perspective, as a result. When Bell contends that McCarthy never allows us a "readerly station" above the action of Suttree, that "we are solidly in it," we recognize that McCarthy wants us to experience the vertiginous and visceral quality of Suttree's daily struggle for survival, for redemption, a struggle comparable to the soldier's day to day combat with fear, deprivation, and suffering.

The narration of Suttree's nearly fatal illness and subsequent recovery calls to mind Frederick Henry's wounding and recuperation in *A Farewell to Arms*. For Suttree, the experience forms the final act in the drama of his transformation. The novel had begun with a simile of war: "The night is quiet. Like a camp before battle. The city beset by a thing unknown and will it come from forest or sea?" (4). His health restored, McCarthy's hero stands beside the road with new clothes and suitcase, like "someone just out of the army or jail" (470). Suttree's hard-won perspective invokes finally a farewell to arms that seems more permanent than any before. In the end, Suttree appears to bid farewell to some of his relentlessly uncompromising resistance to the organizing principles of his world, a stance he had long maintained out of some authentic alienation that refuses spurious consolation—the distinctive apartness common to McCarthy's characters as the price of maintaining their original humanity.

Blood Meridian takes us further historically from our time than any of McCarthy's other novels while ironically carrying us closest to the heart of darkness that was the American experience in Vietnam. McCarthy tips his hand as to his intentions in the Captain's recruiting speech that has as its direct referent the war with Mexico over Texas in 1846 and the ill-conceived military expedition that initiates the kid's bloody sojourn in Mexico. The subject of the speech doubles as a muted commentary, at times cryptic, at times direct, on various aspects of the Vietnam conflict:

> We fought for it. Lost friends and brothers down there. And then
> by god if we didnt give it back. Back to a bunch of barbarians
> that even the most biased in their favor will admit have no least
> notion in Gods earth of honor or justice or the meaning of
> republican government.... Did you know that when Colonel
> Doniphan took Chihuahua City he inflicted over a thousand

casualties on the enemy and lost only one man and him all but a suicide? . . . We are to be the instruments of liberation in a dark and troubled land. . . . Unless Americans act, people like you and me who take their country seriously while those mollycoddles in Washington sit on their hindsides, unless we act, Mexico—and I mean the whole of the country—will one day fly a European flag. Monroe Doctrine or no. (33–35)

Replace the European flag with the banner of Communism to complete the analogy.

The irony of the Captain's rhetoric—"Colonel Carrasco is asking for American intervention"—when viewed in light of his expedition's imminent slaughter, links this intervention with our own in Southeast Asia. The Captain's military disingenuousness matches that of American policy makers and Pentagon planners who seriously miscalculated the potential for American casualties in the war. The Captain's worldview has the almost self-parodying mixture of idealism and self-interest of American rhetoric of the war era. Explicit in the Captain's appeal to the kid is the understanding that their mission will be conducted on behalf of civilization—and just as explicitly he appeals to the kid's baser nature: "we will be the ones to divide the spoils" (34). Innocence mingles with a denial of greed here, anticipating the loss of the one and the wholesale embrace of the other.

What begins as an appeal to join a crusade, however bungled in its execution and morally dubious, degenerates further still with the kid's second recruitment into Glanton's band of scalphunters, a collection of rogues about whom Herr might have been writing when he described the "common pool" of soldiers on leave in Saigon: "redundant mutilators, heavy rapers, eye-shooters, widow-makers, nametakers, classic essential American types; point men, isolatos and outriders like they were programmed in their genes to do it" (35). Glanton's band of outriders was initially welcomed by the citizenry of Chihuahua City and officially commissioned by the governor and a private society to end Apache depredations on the populace. This relationship dissolves in chaos when the band begins to prey on the populace itself, a souring comparable to what became of the relationship between the Vietnamese people and their would-be protectors. Motivated ostensibly by greed and a bounty on Apache scalps, Glanton's band soon abandons the troublesome distinction between Apaches and other Indians, collecting those scalps most easily culled. In this collapse of the separation between friend and foe, the novel illustrates a parallel with one of the common myths of Vietnam, that soldiers were at times unable, or perhaps unwilling, to discriminate between friendly villager and Viet Cong, further eroding the American relationship with the South Vietnamese.

The connection between the band's scalphunting and the military policy of the "body count" in Vietnam was first made by Sepich, who does so only to propose a comparison in kind of atrocities. Glanton and his men lay claim to nominal success in the reckoning of scalps, but their conflict, as in Vietnam, is endless, the dogs of war not to be appeased with the offering of a few hundred scalps. For many Americans, Vietnam was a nightmare that seemed to have no end. In *Blood Meridian*, McCarthy expands this idea into one of the work's most powerful themes, and Judge Holden figures as the living embodiment and oracle of an ontology of war: "War endures. . . . War was always here. Before man was, war waited for him" (248).

The war waged by Holden and his associates is by its nature endless and in its essence less the pursuit of an object than the practice of a trade, "the ultimate trade," as Holden calls it (248). Steven Shaviro describes *Blood Meridian* as a book of "restless, incessant horizontal movements: nomadic wanderings, topographical displacements, variations of weather, skirmishes in the desert" (145). While McCarthy supplies particulars of geography, the reader experiences a collapse of time and space so that only the ceaseless repetition of violence remains foregrounded, enacted in a kind of no-place of desolation. The novel depicts the scalphunters as the ultimate practitioners of their trade, warriors for whom war is no longer waged as an instrument of policy or even for gain, but for its own sake, and generative of its own radical state of being: "wholly at venture, primal, provisional, devoid of order" (172).

If *Blood Meridian* serves as McCarthy's epic treatment of war in Vietnam, the reactions of one commentator on the novel are interesting when juxtaposed with the observations of a commentator on the war itself. About the ambiguous experience of reading *Blood Meridian*, Shaviro writes "Bloody death is our monotonously predictable destiny; yet its baroque opulence is attended with a frighteningly complicitous joy," and he goes on to contend that

> The scariest thing about *Blood Meridian* is that it is a euphoric and exhilarating book, rather than a tragically alienated one, or a gloomy, depressing one. Our pulses quicken as "considerations of equity and rectitude and moral right [are] rendered void and without warrant" (250), subsumed in the trials of war. Once we have started to dance, once we have been swept up in the game, there is no pulling back. (154)

Michael Herr's observations on his own relationship to the soldiers and experience of war are remarkably similar to Shaviro's:

> But of course we were intimate, I'll tell you how intimate. . . . We covered each other, an exchange of services that worked all

right until one night when I slid over to the wrong end of the story, propped up behind some sandbags at an airstrip in Can Tho with a .30-caliber automatic in my hands, firing for a four-man reaction team trying to get back ... until the whole night had passed and I was looking at the empty clips around my feet behind the berm, telling myself that there would never be any way to know for sure. I couldn't remember ever feeling so tired, so changed, so happy. (67–68)

The likeness revealed here goes beyond the critical hypothesis that McCarthy's chronicle of nineteenth-century border history was influenced by his conscious or unconscious immersion in the cultural discourses of Vietnam. Certainly the subject matter is the same. One can argue with justice for the existence of a parallel between the trade of war as practiced by the scalphunters and the conflict in Vietnam—by eschewing territorial conquest as its goal, the United States doomed itself to a war of attrition that came to resemble, finally, the dark night of war primordial against an enemy of seemingly infinite numbers and boundless will. But one can and should go further to say that *Blood Meridian* insists upon a meditation on the darkness of our violent natures and the full range of scarcely imaginable, scarcely representable consequences that follow when human nature gives free play to the death drive.

While McCarthy's initial series of novels owes an unacknowledged debt to the Vietnam experience, the Trilogy shares significant associations and images with the Gulf War of 1991. The desert landscape had not been a prominent part of the American imagination since the Second World War, but the Iraqi invasion of Kuwait in 1990, the American military build-up in Saudi Arabia, and most importantly, the around-the-clock media coverage of events in the Gulf thrust the sensibility of the desert back into the American consciousness.

The western landscape, including the desert, is ground commonly associated with the literary and film genre of the western. Richard Slotkin has argued that the revival of the western in the 1980s was "motivated in part by nostalgia for old movie forms and styles," and that it "owed something to the popular mood of the Reagan presidency" (881). The influence of the popular mood in some form is visible in McCarthy's Border Trilogy that, though spanning the 90s in terms of publication, shows significant traces of both popular cultural discourse in the 1980s as well as the imaginative legacy of the 1991 Gulf War. In McCarthy's hands, however, the cultural discourse of the 1980s—with everything that that implies for us politically and socially—remains undeniably McCarthean, which is to say that it is fundamentally characterized by ambiguity rather than certitude.

The Trilogy marks a sea-change in McCarthy's fiction in his treatment of the hero. In contrast to Lester Ballard, or the kid, or even Suttree, the protagonists of the Trilogy are unambiguously heroic. In this connection we should recall that the reconstitution of the hero was a central part of the cultural rhetoric of the 1980s. Gail Moore Morrison points out that one reviewer of *All the Pretty Horses* finds John Grady Cole "simply too good at everything" (190). A similar charge could be leveled against the sixteen-year-old Billy Parham in *The Crossing*, who adeptly captures and transports a wolf on horseback to Mexico, and with his younger brother Boyd vanquishes would-be rapists and a posse of agents working for "Senor [Randolph?] Hearst." Despite an untimely death, Boyd also falls into this class of larger-than-life teenagers, about whom Billy remembers: "There aint but one life worth livin and I was born to it. That's worth all the rest. My bud was better at it than me. He was a born natural. He was smarter than me too. Not just about horses. About everything. Daddy knew it too. He knew it and he knew I knew it and that's all there was to say about it" (The Crossing 420). The heroic is not a part of McCathy's vision before *All the Pretty Horses*, and to cite commercial ambition as the cause of this shift would be a disservice to the seriousness of his work, and in any case is unfounded given the noncommercial, metafictional structuring of the narrative in *The Crossing*.

In the Border Trilogy, McCarthy has undertaken to tell authentic westerns using the basic formulas of the genre while avoiding the false sentimentality, uncritical nostalgia, and unearned happy endings that often characterize the genre in its popular forms. Slotkin identifies seven oppositions or conflicts that serve as hallmarks of the western, all of which in some form can be found in the Trilogy:

> Between white civilization and redskin savagery; between a corrupt metropolitan "East" and a rough but virtuous "West;" between tyrannical old proprietors (big ranchers) and new, progressive entrepreneur (homesteaders); between the engorged wealth of industrial monopolies (railroads) and the hard-earned property of citizens (farmers); between old technologies (stagecoaches) and new (railroads); between the undisciplined rapacity of frontier criminals and the lawman's determination to establish order ... between the violent culture of men and the Christian culture associated with women. (874)

It may be that some or all of these conflicts find their way inevitably into narrative when the genre of the western is employed. It seems more likely that the presence of all seven in McCarthy's Trilogy indicates a self-conscious effort by a postmodern writer interested in telling a western and interested in a genre that lends itself to storytelling about storytelling.

Much in the same way that the genre of the western was employed by John Ford in *The Searchers*, and later Clint Eastwood in *Unforgiven*, to tell morally sophisticated stories using the "simple"—and thus familiar—vocabulary of the western, so too McCarthy uses the western to explore the most permanent concerns of literature: the profound relationships between being and witness, between truth and desire, and the persistent proximity of violence to narrative. Each of the novels of the Border Trilogy relies on a version of the traditional western's conflict between right and wrong. As heroes, John Grady Cole and Billy Parham both are deeply moral in a conventional sense and are guided by a code of principled conduct, though still susceptible to internal conflict concerning their own actions and motives. When we see Cole and Parham a decade or so older in the final volume, in fact, though Billy's ardor for the austerities of cowboy life has waned, their core values remain unchanged. At critical moments in the narratives, the heroes find themselves pitted against clear injustice, or what seems the deliberate presentation of evil, and McCarthy's eschatology mirrors the rhetoric of good and evil that underscored the U.S.-led war of public opinion that made the Gulf War possible. While it would be unwarranted to posit a direct connection between these novels and any series of contemporary events, a significant cultural yearning to be able to distinguish clearly between good and evil made itself felt in the early 90s, and McCarthy's work seems to reflect that desire. To have arrived at this moral destination from the "ambiguous nihilism"—to use Bell's phrase—of McCarthy's first phase is a remarkable development.

Both *The Crossing* and *Cities of the Plain* make use of a familiar Hollywood motif from the post-Vietnam era of the 1980s—the rescue mission. Film and television rescue dramas involving Vietnam POWs have continued to meet our psychic and entertainment needs well into the mid-90s, and, while McCarthy foregrounds this motif in the Trilogy, the effect on the narrative as a whole is far more complex than the use to which it is put in films like *Uncommon Valor*, or the Rambo saga, in which the Vietnam conflict is restaged in order to be won "this time." The rescue plot of *All the Pretty Horses* is a function of McCarthy's emergent interest in the love story during his second phase, and for the rescue plot to succeed, Alejandra must be "rescued" from her world in order to live with John Grady in his. The preamble to this rescue involves yet another plot standard from the 1970s—the unjustly accused hero—in which the ringing phrase "for a crime he did not commit" gives credentials to the central character as an anti-establishment hero. John Grady's love for Alejandra being inadmissible in caste-bound Mexico, her father arranges Cole's false arrest and imprisonment. As in classical tragedy, the false accusation and its tragic outcome flow ultimately out of the best, most essential elements of John Grady's character. Against Rawlins's will and John Grady's own better judgment he had helped Blevins recover (steal) his horse, and thus stands wrongly accused of the very serious crime of horse theft. This act among others emphasizes the "mixed" quality necessary to the hero of the western, the capacity to cross the line in pursuit of good. As Slotkin puts it: "the action of the narrative requires that borders be crossed by a hero whose character is so mixed that he can operate effectively on both sides of the line" (874). Blevins's horse is a magnificent example of its breed, and this fact in itself tunes up Cole's sense of justice, as if conscience makes a stronger than usual demand in the case of so fine an animal. In this juncture, McCarthy links Cole's passion for horses, a passion that lies at the very heart of his character, with the narrative circumstances that separate him from Alejandra and place him in prison.

The main action of *All the Pretty Horses* functions as a variation on one of Slotkin's basic conflicts, that "between tyrannical old proprietors (big ranchers) and new, progressive entrepreneurs (homesteaders)" (xxx). Cole is an entrepreneur in the most basic sense of the word, and what he undertakes is the impossibility of love with Alejandra: "He told her that he could make a living and that they could go to live in his country and make their life there and no harm would come to them" (252). The failure of this romance in *All the Pretty Horses* reinscribes John Grady Cole in the myth of the stoic American of the frontier: "He saw very clearly how all his life led only to this moment and all after led nowhere at all. He felt something cold and soulless enter him like another being and he imagined that it smiled malignly and he had no reason to believe it would ever leave" (254). Cole accepts this psychologically withering condition, however, without surrendering his fundamental will to live. Christina Bold's definition of the protagonist of the traditional western—"a heroic man, poised and ultimately isolated on the frontier between 'civilization' and 'savagery'"—reminds us that isolation is the condition of possibility for the hero of the western (875). In each volume of the Trilogy, McCarthy leaves the hero's quests either unresolved or settled in failure. Good and evil may be clearly distinct in the Trilogy, but good does not clearly triumph. Although John Grady is not wholly at odds with his world, it is fair to say that he has not found his place in it, nor can he, for his fate in the Trilogy is indissolubly tied to the old order of the range that is inexorably passing away.

John Grady seeks expiation from the judge, in part, because he had been forced to kill the "cuchillero" in the scene that marks McCarthy's return to symbolic violence in the Trilogy. The duel with the cuchillero in the prison mess marks the turning point in the novel and a shift in the hero's condition, from victim of the hacendado's revenge and Mexican injustice to avenging angel and redresser of wrongs. Though nearly killed in the knife-fight—a foreshadowing of his eventual demise in *Cities of the Plain*—Cole recovers and becomes the embodiment of retributive justice, recapturing his own horses, delivering the captain to the summary justice of the vigilantes, and bringing Blevins's horse back across the border. Present in the fight with the cuchillero are the novel's primary conflicts, and the action of the novel since John Grady's arrest on the hacienda Nuestra Senora de la Purisma Concepcion culminates in this moment. Cole and Rawlins encounter Blevins before they cross the border into Mexico, and from that moment the chain of events in the novel leads step by step to the scene of violence in the prison. By killing the cuchillero, John Grady initiates the reversal whereby Blevins's murder is avenged. Cole's opponent is a paid assassin, a coolly impersonal signifier of the forces he is pitted against—the hacendado's influence and the sweaty caricature of Mexican injustice. In their other fights in the prison, Cole and Rawlins had fought back-to-back, reminiscent of heroic stands in narratives of the "buddy" genre. But in this symbolic contest Rawlins has been removed, too badly wounded to figure in the hero's defining moment, and the mess hall clears out to reveal a stark tableau of violence, a narrow gate through which the narrative must pass. The opponents are equal in age and arms, their fight to the death a contest between both John Grady's values and his ignorance on the one hand, and a tattooed killer who represents the world's implacable and remorseless unconcern for the values John Grady represents. Cast in these terms, Cole's triumph over his ordeal is at best a temporary victory, for in the context of McCarthy's trademark pessimism (call it realism), the individual cannot truly win against the world. Nevertheless, in the context of the plot of *All the Pretty Horses*, the death of the cuchillero begins the hero's ascent out of darkness, out of prison, out of the tentacles of injustice, and toward a resolution of the novel that completes the quest structure, though that completion provides little solace for the hero.

McCarthy fittingly organizes the second volume of the Trilogy, *The Crossing*, around three border crossings into Mexico, by Billy Parham alone with the wolf, by Billy and his brother Boyd to recover horses stolen by their parents' murderers, and by Billy alone again to search for his brother. Having exhumed his brother's body from a Mexican cemetery for reburial at home, Billy laconically notes in the manner of the heroes of the Trilogy: "This is my third trip. It's the only time I was ever down here that I got what I come after. But it sure as hell wasnt what I wanted." (416). What Billy wanted was to find his brother alive and well, similar to the popular rescue fantasies of the 1980s where American POWs from Vietnam are snatched from work camps by selfless and patriotic (but antiestablishment) commandos. Instead, Parham is forced to settle for the repatriation of his brother's bones, and in the process his fraternal quest intersects with his brother's reinvention as the "hombre de la gente" in the mythology of the Mexican folk (317). All of the novels of the Trilogy feature sage figures that provide a meta-commentary on the narrative itself, or on other narratives told within the frame story. There are several in *The Crossing*—Senor Gillian, the ex-priest, the blinded revolutionary, the gypsy, the gerente Quijada—and it is Quijada who explains the significance of Boyd's fate for his brother, once again telling the McCarthean story of storytelling itself:

> What does the corrido say?
> Quijada shook his head. The corrido tells all and it tells nothing. I heard the tale of the guerito years ago. Before your brother was even born.
> You dont think it tells about him?
> Yes, it tells about him. It tells what it wishes to tell. It tells what makes the story run. The corrido is the poor man's history. It does not owe its allegiance to the truths of history but to the truths of men. It tells the tale of that solitary man who is all men. (387)

What Billy knows with certainty is that his brother was seriously wounded by the henchmen of La Babicora and later disappeared with "the girl." Whatever his actual fate, the circumstances of Boyd's life and death are absorbed and transformed into the "corrido," the ballad of the countryside that mythologizes the deep economic divide and political struggle between rich and poor in Mexico. The workers who save Boyd's life immediately christen him the "guerito," though they know nothing about who shot him or why. Boyd's wounds and his youth are all that is required to transform him into the guerito of their song, and the myth-making apparatus of the Mexican folk absorbs whatever material it finds into the story that sustains their struggle.

Billy Parham's quest to find his brother and bring him home is thus linked with the larger narrative of class struggle and national identity in Mexico. Film and media discourse in the 1980s frequently foregrounded the issue of surviving MIAs in Vietnam. The repatriation of remains of soldiers killed in action and the issue of surviving MIAs became an important political and cultural subject for nearly a decade. Hollywood cinema did its share in fueling speculation that American servicemen had been betrayed, mostly by weak and cowardly civilians and generals. The effect of "rescue discourse" on American public consciousness was to partially merge the narrative of repatriation with the politically conservative narrative of American renewal. Bringing the POWs home became a part of a new national narrative, culturally significant if election results are an indicator, whereby rescuing brave Americans from the netherworld of POW camps marked a symbolic movement analogous to rescuing national identity from the miasma of defeat in Southeast Asia and self-division at home. The narrative of the guerito and the narrative of American MIAs are similar in their role in the continuous reproduction of national identity, and both incorporate "real" events into a self-serving myth necessary for their respective communities.

Each of the Parham crossings into Mexico has at least one corresponding scene of symbolic violence: Billy and the young don face off in the fighting pit over wolf; Billy and Boyd contend with the agents of La Babicora; and last, Billy experiences a kind of "Mexican stand-off" in the bar with the drunken veteran of the revolution. In this last scene, bloodshed is averted only when Billy, himself intoxicated, backs down from a barroom dispute that seems to originate in simple ill temper. The confrontation is a scene rich in irony, however, for both men have reached a boiling point of frustration directly the result of their struggles against the same ruling powers in Mexico. The former soldier of the revolution refuses the American whiskey Billy proffers, signifying as it does to him the collusion of the American government with the despotic Mexican regime. Parham responds to the insult with belligerence of his own, fueled by the two adventures in Mexico that have proven so devastating for him personally. The violence in the moment remains latent, unrealized, and Billy achieves a moment of drunken clarity in "the sallow light of the cantina," one in which he recognizes that two narratives of futile struggle against the McCarthean "world" of indifferent force, so well represented by the rich and powerful in Mexico, have spiraled into violent contact with one another. When the veteran displays his bullet wounds from the revolution, Billy reflects "that the only manifest artifact of the history of this negligible republic where he now seemed about to die that had the least authority or meaning or claim to substance was seated before him" (363). This epiphany holds true to the McCarthean vision presented in the Trilogy: the uncertain validity of all that Billy has been a part of in Mexico haunts his consciousness and calls to mind the suspect quality of all narrative, while on the other hand the veteran's scars seem to tell an authentic story that ironically threatens the end of the road and his death.

Another rescue plot appears as the main action of *Cities of the Plain*, and the novel's resolution hinges on the rescue of John Grady's beloved from a Juarez whorehouse. While the closing of the range provides *Cities of the Plain* with a historical backdrop, the primary ground of the novel is ontological rather than social or political. The book's theme might be deciphered from an aphorism delivered by the nameless philosopher-transient to the aged Billy Parham: "You call forth the world that God has formed and that world only. Nor is this life of yours by which you set such store your doing, however you may choose to tell it" (285). There is certainly an air of authorial sanction to the words of the various sage figures in the Trilogy, and the mysterious tramp's observation concedes that while we do create reality in the act of perception, nevertheless because we are a part of that world we cannot falsify it, we cannot call it forth other than it is. This is McCarthy's trump, an acceptance of the postmodern condition while refusing the nihilism inherent in such a position. So it must be with the life and death of John Grady Cole, a character in a work of art that has the same status as the figure in the dream told by the philosopher-transient. Cole's entire romantic quest, beginning in All the Pretty Horses and concluding disastrously in his love for Magdalena, stands in the same relationship to the reader as the dream-figure for the philosopher-transient. McCarthy thus implies that John Grady's life in a work of art (or Billy's, or Boyd's) and the life of the man in the dream have the same ontological standing, as the philosopher-transient explains:

> My belief is this, and I say it again: His history [the man in the dream] is the same as yours or mine. That is the stuff he is made of. What stuff other? Had I created him as God makes men how then would I not know what he would say before he ever spoke? Or how he'd move before he did so? In a dream we dont know what's coming. We are surprised.
> All right.
> So where is it coming from?
> I dont know.
> Two worlds touch here. You think men have power to call forth what they will? (285)

The point is, clearly, that we do not. Like *Absalom, Absalom!*, the volumes of the Trilogy ultimately provide their own theory, and *Cities of the Plain* can hardly be equaled for artistic bravado in that it contains the formal justification of its own narrative as truth.

As the final installment of McCarthy's turn from serial to symbolic violence, the contest between Cole and Eduardo marks the culmination of the primary action that begins the moment John Grady sees Magdalena at La Venada. Having premised the novel on the redemption of a teenaged, epileptic prostitute sold into sexual slavery as a child, it is difficult to imagine, even given McCarthy's transformation as a storyteller, how such a tale could end happily and remain McCarthean. *Cities of the Plain* is a novel rich in narrative irony, and Cole's fatal duel with the pimp and the failure of his quest are predicated from the very beginning—in retrospect, no other outcome seems possible. The entirety of the novel is present in the single moment that a teenaged cowboy and a child prostitute recognize their destiny in a Mexican bar, their love sufficiently improbable within the vision embraced by McCarthy's work that we may without hazard foresee the outcome.

The knife fight between Cole and Eduardo serves as a contest of violence in which self-preservation is put aside for principle and the resuturing of the fabric of self-respect calls for blood. There is an unspoken agreement between the two men that their quarrel involve no other, not Tiburcio or Billy Parham, and that it be fought with weapons, knives, not only equal on both sides but also fiercely expressive of the desire for the retribution that each man in his own way seeks. During their deadly struggle over a prostitute, Eduardo supplements the practiced play of his switchblade with a running commentary on an old story in which John Grady is a player: "They [Americans] drift down out of your leprous paradise seeking a thing now extinct among them. A thing for which perhaps they no longer even have a name. Being farmboys of course the first place they think to look is in a whorehouse" (249). What Eduardo means by the nameless "thing" is of course the McCarthean mystery of existence, and the search for an answer to this mystery forms a thread that runs throughout his entire work. At an earlier stage in McCarthy's career, Judge Holden offers one answer: "Your heart's desire is to be told some mystery," he observes to the assembled band of scalphunters, and in *Blood Meridian* the answer seems to be that "The mystery is that there is no mystery" (252).

The novels of the Trilogy propose an alternative to the Judge's nihilism. When John Grady descends on Eduardo at the White Lake—"to kill you or be killed"—he embodies the bitter failure of his romantic quest, the aborted Pygmalion south of the border (248). At the moment of truth, Cole kills Eduardo by jamming his knife through his jaws and into his skull, thus symbolically shutting the pimp's mouth, but not before the pimp has made a home thrust, not only with his blade, but with an ontological sally: "They cannot seem to see that the most elementary fact concerning whores . . . is that they are whores" (249). On a symbolic level, John Grady's success in silencing the pimp would seem to indicate that Eduardo is, as Cole claims, "a liar," that Magdalena is no whore "to the bone," but rather an unfortunate victim of horrific circumstances. The elementary fact that escapes Cole, however, as it escapes all romantics, is that the reality of the world seldom if ever coincides with the reality of our desires, that Magdalena is indeed a whore, if not morally, then by a more insidious and unalterable definition: she is a whore because she is a whore, and for that reason the world opposes their love with a finality explained by the blind man: "Let me tell you only this. Your love has no friends. You think that it does but it does not. None. Perhaps not even God" (199). Their worlds cannot touch; their quest for a life together has no future.

Through the return to symbolic violence in the Trilogy, McCarthy reestablishes the connections to his predecessors Faulkner and, to a lesser degree, Warren that he had seemingly severed in his radical devotion to serial violence in the early work. McCarthy turns to the genre of the western for a mythic landscape suitable to conflicts stark and simple, and on that spare terrain the true subject of the novels becomes not so much the story he is telling but storytelling itself. That he does so without resorting to the elaborate narrative hijinks of his peers among postmodern novelists we may attribute to what is pre-modern in his artistic sensibility, viz., that storytelling is a historically transcendent means of knowing—stories reveal being because they are a part of being itself. McCarthy's novels of the Border Trilogy share equally with Faulkner and Warren a concern for the consequences of the crossing of the ways, of the passing away of one world and the emergence of another. Since this transcendent conflict oversees much of the work of these three writers, it is understandable that they find useful the organizing principle of symbolic violence as a means by which two antagonists can embody the contending forces within the narrative. Whatever McCarthy's other artistic motives for taking up the genre of the western, the centrality of symbolic violence in the Trilogy testifies to his meditation on the continuous quest for identity in the space created by violence.

Works Cited

Arnold, Edwin T. "The Last of the Trilogy: First Thoughts on Cities of the Plain." *Perspectives on Cormac McCarthy*. Eds. Edwin T. Arnold and Dianne C. Luce. Jackson: UP of Mississippi, 1999. 221–247.

Arnold, Edwin T. and Dianne C. Luce. "Introduction." *Perspectives on Cormac McCarthy*. Eds. Edwin T. Arnold and Dianne C. Luce. Jackson: UP of Mississippi, 1999. 1–16.

Bakhtin, Mikhail. *Rabelais and His World*. Trans. Helene Iswolsky. Cambridge: Massachusetts Institute of Technology Press, 1968.

Bataille, Georges. *Erotism: Death and Sensuality*. Trans. Mary Dalwood. San Francisco: City Lights, 1986.

Bell, Vereen M. *The Achievement of Cormac McCarthy*. Baton Rouge: Louisiana State UP, 1988.

———. "The Ambiguous Nihilism of Cormac McCarthy." *Southern Literary Journal* 15.2 (1983): 31–41.

Bold, Christine. "The Popular West." *Updating the Literary West*. Ed. Thomas Lyon. Fort Worth: Texas Christian UP, 1997. 874–881.

Herr, Michael. *Dispatches*. New York: Vintage, 1991.

Luce, Dianne C. "The Road and the Matrix: The World as Tale in The Crossing." *Perspectives on Cormac McCarthy*. Eds. Edwin T. Arnold and Dianne C. Luce. Jackson: UP of Mississippi, 1999. 195-219.

McCarthy, Cormac. *All the Pretty Horses*. New York: Vintage, 1992.

———. *Blood Meridian*. New York: Vintage, 1992.

———. *Child of God*. New York: Vintage, 1993.

———. *Cities of the Plain*. New York: Vintage, 1998.

———. *The Crossing*. New York: Vintage, 1994.

————. *The Orchard Keeper*. New York: Vintage, 1993.

————. *Suttree*. New York: Vintage, 1992.

Morrison, Gail Moore. "All the Pretty Horses: John Grady Cole's Expulsion from Paradise." *Perspectives on Cormac McCarthy*. Eds. Edwin T. Arnold and Dianne C. Luce. Jackson: UP of Mississippi, 1999. 175–194.

Nelson, Andrew. "Metaphysic or Metafiction: The Western Novels of Cormac McCarthy." *The Image of the American West in Literature, the Media, and Society; Selected Papers from the 1996 Conference of the Society for the Interdisciplinary Study of Social Imagery.* 263–266.

Sepich, John Emil. "What kind of indians was them?: Some Historical Sources in Cormac McCarthy's Blood Meridian." *Perspectives on Cormac McCarthy*. Eds. Edwin T. Arnold and Dianne C. Luce. Jackson: UP of Mississippi, 1999. 123–143.

Shaviro, Steven. "'The Very Life of Darkness': A Reading of Blood Meridian." *Perspectives on Cormac McCarthy*. Eds. Edwin T. Arnold and Dianne C. Luce. Jackson: UP of Mississippi, 1999. 145–158.

Slotkin, Richard. "The Movie Western." *Updating the Literary West*. Ed. Christina Bold. Fort Worth: Texas Christian UP, 1997. 874–881.

Stone, Robert. *Dog Soldiers*. Boston: Houghton, Mifflin, 1997.

SARA L. SPURGEON

Foundation of Empire: *The Sacred Hunter and the Eucharist of the Wilderness in Cormac McCarthy's* Blood Meridian

The Foundation of Empire is Art and Science. Remove them or Degrade them and the Empire is No more. Empire follows Art and not vice verse.

—William Blake

Cormac McCarthy's Southwestern works, and *Blood Meridian* in particular, have been seen as both archetypal Westerns and as anti-Westerns, as myth and counter-myth, as glorifications of American imperialism and as damning indictments of it. I will argue here that McCarthy does indeed evoke archetypal myths and mythic heroes that have traditionally been used to serve the cause of American westward expansion and imperialism. That is, in part, the function of myth—to legitimate current social structures through a stylized vision of the past, to offer blueprints for behaviors and attitudes, and to justify future actions. I will also argue, however, that by uncovering the most ancient bones underlying these myths and using them to construct a new mythic vision of history, McCarthy is deliberately deconstructing the imperialist aims and justifications of the old myths while disrupting assumptions about the ideas and identities they were intended to uphold. The result is indeed an indictment, bloody and accusatory, of an American national(ist) identity based on the violent conquest of both racialized Others and feminized nature. The new mythic vision presented in *Blood Meridian*

From *Exploding the Western: Myths of Empire on the Postmodern Frontier*, pp. 19–40. © 2005 by Sara L. Spurgeon.

offers a postmodern challenge to notions of essentialized ethnic and national identities and borders.

One of the many complex relationships McCarthy explores in *Blood Meridian, or, The Evening Redness in the West* is between humans, especially Anglo Americans, and the natural world. He does so in part through the manipulation of several archetypal myths closely identified with the European experience in the New World, tracing their collapse and rebirth in the border regions of the American Southwest. McCarthy moves *Blood Meridian* through the dark and disordered spaces of what Lauren Berlant terms the National Symbolic, but unlike the familiar icons of mythic frontier tales, McCarthy's characters seek no closure, nor do they render order out of the chaos of history. Rather, they reveal the chaos at the heart of history and the myths we make from it. The novel functions on the level of myth-making and National Fantasy as an American origin story, a reimaging, upon the palimpsest of the Western frontier the birth of one of our most pervasive National Fantasies—the winning of the West and the building of the American character through frontier experiences.[1]

Both of these related themes demand a wilderness to be conquered, either literally via ax and plow or metaphorically by defeating the Indians rhetorically tied to the wild landscape. Annette Kolodny has defined the American obsession with land, especially land-as-woman, as an American Pastoral, drawing some images from the European version, yet unique from it. The literary hero within this landscape, she says, is "the lone male in the wilderness" (*The Lay of the Land*, 147) struggling to define a relationship with the female landscape in its troubling metaphorical appearance as both fruitful mother and untouched virgin, one image offering nurturing fertility while the other demands penetration and conquest.

Blood Meridian chronicles the origin of this figure, sometimes called the American Adam, though not the benignly patriarchal John Wayne version. McCarthy's project is not simply to retell the familiar myths or dress up the icons of cowboys and Indians in modern, politically correct costumes. Rather he is using the trope of the historic frontier and the landscape of the Southwest within the genre of the Western to interrogate the consequences of our acceptance of archetypal Western hero myths. *Blood Meridian* rewrites and reorders those myths in such a way as to bridge the discontinuity Patricia Limerick identifies as being perceived by the public to exist between the mythic past of the American West and its modern realities.[2] This gap, marked by the feeling of discontinuity and limned by continued popular obsession with traditional Western and frontier icons that have thus far failed to cover it, is filled in *Blood Meridian* with a newly structured version of National Fantasy, though not one that imposes any kind of hoped-for order or control.

Instead McCarthy presents a counter-memory, a sort of anti-myth of the West, illuminating especially the roots of the modern American relationships between Anglos and non-Anglos and between humans and the natural world. In many ways McCarthy has produced a counter-history, in contradiction to the meaning generated from most official histories of the period. It is within the accuracy of the historical detail of *Blood Meridian* that McCarthy finds his mythic history, lurking within the liminal spaces of the familiar rhetoric of Manifest Destiny, the taming of the wilderness, John Wayne's famous swagger, and other pillars of the National Symbolic.

Kolodny argues that the American Pastoral was structured around the yeoman farmer responding to the female landscape and discusses this figure as he appears in Jefferson, Crevecoeur, Freneau, and others. However, as Henry Nash Smith notes, the image of the yeoman farmer was simply not romantic enough to sustain popular interest for long. What emerged instead was an American version of a far older figure—the hunter—that existed in both European and Native American myths.

The myth of the sacred hunter, as Richard Slotkin explains it, is one of regeneration through violence enacted upon the body of the earth. The hunter must leave the safety of his community, track his game (usually a representation of the spirit of the wilderness or an avatar of a nature deity), and slay it. In many versions, both Native American and European, the prey allows itself to be hunted and killed, willingly sacrificing its life to sustain the life of the hunter and his community, who must in turn give honor and thanks to the prey and to whichever nature spirit it represents. Following the hunt, he and/or his community either literally or symbolically consume the prey in a eucharist of the wilderness, thus renewing the hunter and providing life for those he serves. The eucharist, Slotkin says, is itself a sublimation of the myth of the sacred marriage that enacts a sexual union between the hunter and the body of nature. The game the hunter tracks in many versions of this myth is revealed at the end of the chase to be some female representative of the wilderness whom the hunter marries, instead of slaying, in a parallel renewal of self and community through sexual union with nature.[3]

Slotkin writes that, in the Anglo American version, "The hunter myth provided a fictive justification for the process by which the wilderness was to be expropriated and exploited" (554). It did so by seeing that process in terms of heroic male adventure commodified by visual and symbolic proofs of the hunter's heroic stature and, therefore, his rightful and proper triumph over his prey. The famous image of Davy Crockett standing proudly next to his stack of 150 bearskins, the legend of Paul Bunyon clearing miles of virgin forest with a single stroke of his ax, and the often-photographed mountains of buffalo skulls towering over the Great Plains embody this version of the myth.

The vision of a feminine landscape within the patriarchal bounds of Anglo American culture and the long-standing tradition of associating Native Americans with what appeared to early Anglo colonists as a "howling wilderness" both encouraged and justified this exploitation. In *Blood Meridian* these images are echoed in the scalphunters' collections of scalps, ears, teeth, and various other trophies, as well as described in detail on the plain of the bone pickers. What is echoed and amplified as well is the subtle shift evident in the modern Anglo version of the myth, from the imaging of the prey as symbol of divine nature sacrificed so that man may live, to simply that which deserves to fall before him.

The gigantic figure of Judge Holden, who is both a fictional version of an historical personage and an amalgamation of numerous archetypes from the mythic West, acts throughout the book as the author of the new version of the hunter myth. McCarthy consistently presents the judge as a priest, a mediator between man and nature, shepherding, or more accurately manipulating, the scalphunters' souls even as Glanton guides their physical bodies. The image of the judge as priest is consistent with the dominant mood and tone of *Blood Meridian* as origin myth—a sacred tale recounting how the world came to be. Bernard Schopen calls the entire novel "profoundly religious" and claims it takes place "in a physical and thematic landscape charged with religious nuance, allusion, and language" (191). That is not to say that *Blood Meridian* is a Christian book or particularly interested in presenting any kind of Christian worldview. At its deepest structural and rhetorical levels, *Blood Meridian* utilizes mythic and religious imagery both Christian and non-Christian in order to strip away the layers of blind belief myths compel.

The judge, a mythic figure in his own right, is the terrifying guide to the disintegration of the last vestiges of the old sacred hunter myth and its rebirth as the modern myth of the American frontier. The first time we see the judge is at the revival meeting tent where the primary charge he levels against the apparently innocent Reverend Green foreshadows the betrayal and perversion he will commit as the novel progresses. The minister, the judge claims, is wanted "On a variety of charges the most recent of which involved a girl of eleven years—I said eleven—who had come to him in trust and whom he was surprised in the act of violating while actually clothed in the livery of his God" (7). This violation of a child and the profaning of a sacred office by the figure entrusted with upholding and protecting it will be enacted again and again throughout the novel with the judge playing the leading role.

The judge deliberately cultivates a feel for myth, ritual, and religion and directs it toward his own ends. His goal is to harness the unconscious response to mythic heroes, invoke it with the rituals of the sacred hunter and the eucharist of the wilderness, and reorder, or perhaps disorder, it on a deep and essential level. The result is a new myth that restructures American attitudes and beliefs about what it means to be an American and how Americans must relate to the landscape they inhabit.

Throughout *Blood Meridian* the judge both exalts the natural world and strives to contain and destroy it, to usurp its power for his own ends. He is priest here, not only of men's souls, but of their minds as well, and he often appears as the spokesman of what is presented as a sort of new religion—science. As the novel progresses the figure of the judge becomes more and more godlike, while that of nature is debased. The judge manipulates the power and mystery of the natural world and its association with the sacred through his scientific knowledge, which gives him the ability to penetrate that mystery and therefore disrupt the assumptions of the other characters about the place of humans within the world. As the scalphunters are camped at an abandoned mine, the judge collects ore samples

> in whose organic lobations he purported to read news of the earth's origins. . . . A few would quote him scripture to confound his ordering up of eons out of the ancient chaos and other apostate supposings. The judge smiled.
> Books lie, he said.
> God dont lie.
> No, said the judge. He does not. And these are his words.
> He held up a chunk of rock.
> He speaks in stones and trees, the bones of things.
> The squatters in their rags nodded among themselves and were soon reckoning him correct . . . and this the judge encouraged until they were right proselytes of the new order whereupon he laughed at them for fools. (116)

The acceptance of traditional Christian dogma regarding the world and the place of man in the natural order of existence is deconstructed by the judge, built anew through the acceptance and belief of his listeners, then destroyed again. His audience now doubts their own understanding of nature as well as Christian doctrine, but the one figure whose personal power has increased in the eyes of his followers is Judge Holden. The judge is laying groundwork, gathering "proselytes," participants in the ritualistic myth he is enacting.

That nature plays the part of the sacred does not imply the sort of patriarchal relationship imagined by Christianity in which a merciful, all-powerful God cares for and watches over his children. As many have noted, in McCarthy's work nature is often brutal and almost always without mercy for humans, and yet the shadow of the sacred and the profane permeates

Blood Meridian and is constantly evoked by the judge through man's relationship to the natural world. That this destructive version of the myth he is bringing to fruition demands material evidence of its fulfillment does not lessen its ritualistic power. The judge, having symbolically dethroned the priest of the Christian rituals and myths at the revival tent, will make proselytes of the scalphunters and lead them in a cannibalistic perversion of the old myth made new in this place where "not again in all the world's turning will there be terrains so wild and barbarous to try whether the stuff of creation maybe shaped to man's will or whether his own heart is not another kind of clay" (5).

Whether the stuff of creation may be shaped to man's will, I would argue, is one of the central questions of the novel, implicating American attitudes regarding man's conquest of nature, the relationship of Anglo America to any non-Anglo peoples, and America's imperial mission especially as it was imagined in relation to the West. Dana Phillips claims that what McCarthy is questioning is "whether human beings have any privileged position in relation to the rest of the world" (443). His answer is that, according to McCarthy, they do not. Humans and nature are simply part of the same continuum, mutually ignoring each other throughout the novel. At first glance it would seem that indeed creation *cannot* be shaped to man's will, or, as Phillips says, "at least not for very long. Man's will does not seem a very relevant or potent force in this novel" (439). However, a closer examination suggests that in fact man's will is the most potent of forces as well as the central concern in the terrifying relationship between Holden and the kid. It is man's will that ultimately shapes myth, and, McCarthy implies, it is our myths that also ultimately shape the world. The agent of this shaping is not nature but Judge Holden who, as the only character who truly understands the immense power of will, acts almost as collective human will made flesh in order to shape the stuff of creation through the shaping of the myth that constructs it.

Phillips would likely disagree with this interpretation. He argues that there is no inherent meaning in the actions of the characters or of the natural world in *Blood Meridian*, that darkness is just darkness, death just death. McCarthy has even "dispensed with the concept of character" (441) in the traditional sense, Phillips says, in order to erase any hint of possible moral redemption for his band of scalphunters and their victims. I would argue, however, that the lack of traditional character development by McCarthy is more than a response to the "furious troping" (441) of Melville's Ishmael or an avoidance of Flannery O'Connor-style moralizing. McCarthy is interested in myths, not morals. It is true, as Phillips notes, that there are no real surprises in the plot of *Blood Meridian*, that "all the novel's complexities are fully present from the first page. . . . The novel does not seek to resolve 'conflicts' which trouble its characters" (443). This is so, not because there is no meaning or symbolism in the world of *Blood Meridian*, but because, like any mythic story, we already know the outcome. The characters are not explored in the Lukacsian sense because, as actors in a myth, their individualities are less important than the roles they are playing. The face of the hero is infinitely changeable; therefore the kid does not need a proper name, Judge Holden can be endowed with faculties that border on the superhuman, and Tobin can be referred to as simply "ex-priest" as often as he is called by name. Meaning resides solely in the actions the characters take and the power of their story to shape the world of those who hear it.

It is true that the Christian god and the moral structures he represents are absent in the natural world of *Blood Meridian*, at least as a cipherable entity to the travelers. The judge alone among the scalphunters claims the power to solve the mysteries of the natural world, and he does so through science and a skewed rationality cloaked with the rhetoric of religion. The myth of science, with the judge as its sacred high priest, is opposed to the earlier myth of nature served by the sacred hunter. Within the space of the National Symbolic and in the tradition of the earliest Puritan writings about the New World, the judge's figuring of wilderness as that which must be conquered by man lest it conquer him is a familiar trope, common to virtually every Western written after the mid-nineteenth century.

Kolodny argues this is part of the defining structure of the American Pastoral, born in conjunction with the first stirrings of the Industrial Revolution, that "implicit in the metaphor of the land-as-woman was both the regressive pull of maternal containment *and* the seductive invitation to sexual assertion" (67). Henry Nash Smith notes that by the late 1850s, as the myth of the garden and the land as fruitful mother began to fray, the archetypal frontier hero in the American wilderness had lost Leatherstocking's "power to commune with nature. . . . He no longer looks to God through nature, for nature is no longer benign: its symbols are the wolves and the prairie fire. . . . The landscape within which the Western hero operates has become . . . 'a dreary waste' . . . He is . . . alone in a hostile, or at best a neutral, universe" (89). And yet the relationship McCarthy explores is considerably more complex than the simple nihilism of "Nature does not care for man."

Dana Phillips refutes Vereen Bell's claim that human beings and nature compete in the novel by arguing that "this competition has been decided in favor of . . . the natural world even before *Blood Meridian* begins" (446). Humans and the natural world are not antagonists, Phillips claims, but are instead "parts of the same continuum" (446). That is indeed the case at the outset of the novel, and the balance of power between the various parts of the continuum appears fairly equal, but it is the fundamental change in this relationship, enacted on the level of the mythic and sacred, that McCarthy is interested in uncovering. That the nature of that relationship exists on a level significantly deeper than mutual indifference or antagonism is clear. Again and again, McCarthy invokes archetypal myths and references to the sacred when portraying humans in the natural world. Travelers of all sorts in the wilderness are commonly referred to as "pilgrims" and "proselytes." As the scalphunters cross a dry lakebed, the narrator claims that the earth itself notes their passing, "As if the very sediment of things contained yet some residue of sentience. As if in the transit of those riders were a thing so profoundly terrible as to register even to the uttermost granulation of reality" (247). The narrator continues with the often-quoted passage regarding the quality of light in the desert that "bequeathed a strange equality and no one thing nor spider nor stone nor blade of grass could put forth claim to precedence . . . and in the optical democracy of such landscapes all preference is made whimsical and a man and a rock become endowed with unguessed kinships" (247). These passages have often been interpreted as "a critique of our culture's anthropocentrism,"[4] and, as Phillips notes, "the human does not stand out among the other beings and objects that make up the world" (443). However, that relationship of indifferent equanimity is neither stable nor unchanging. It is the laying bare of the cataclysmic evolution taking place in the mythic formations that have created this structure that McCarthy seeks to document through the actions of his characters and their mythic roles.

If we view the relationship between man and nature in *Blood Meridian* in terms of the sacred hunter myth, a clear set of images appears. This myth implies the necessity of a certain kind of relationship between man and nature—a bloody and violent one to be sure and one that does not necessarily hold any moral overtones in the Christian sense of right or wrong or good or evil, but simply a set of rules governing what is, how reality and the natural world work, and a sense of order and balance in the roles of each. That, of course, is the most basic function of myth, to organize and impose order upon man and his world, though in *Blood Meridian* the revelation of the profound disorder at the heart of our myths seems to be the ultimate goal.

The scalphunters as a group can be read as playing the part of the sacred hunter, dark versions of classic Western heroes from the Deerslayer and Daniel Boone to Buffalo Bill, leaving their communities to enter the wilderness for renewal and regeneration through the act of hunting and killing. Although the scalphunters seek a human prey, it is a prey nonetheless rhetorically tied to the wilderness, and the goal of its killing is ostensibly the protection and renewal of the scalphunters' foster community—the Mexicans living in Sonora. And yet the fact that their prey is human begins the degeneration of the myth, tilts it off its axis. Of course the epigraph from the *Yuma Daily Sun* that opens the novel (detailing a 300,000-year-old skull found in the Afar region of Ethiopia that showed evidence of having been scalped) implies that such a perversion is equally as old as the myth itself. This idea is furthered by the name of the judge's gun, "Et in Arcadia Ego" (Even in Arcadia am I [Death]) implying as Leo Daugherty notes that "the point of the gun's name is not that because of its appearance in the landscape, or by synecdoche the judge's appearance, death has been introduced into an idyllic Arcadia: the entire novel makes clear (primarily through the judge, who continuously emphasizes the point in his preachments) that the human world is, and has always been, a world of killing" (126–27).

The figure of the judge within this space is a Conradian expression of white American civilization, or perhaps the brutal force of its will. Like Kurtz, the judge engages in a savage war that is both sanctioned and denied by various authorities; like Kurtz he carries his war forward from both sides, existing at once as the ultimate expression of Euro-American manhood (poet/scholar/warrior) and as the primitive savage he seeks to destroy and emulate, donning native clothing and defeating native peoples on their own ground. And more importantly, like Kurtz, the judge is the agent of the revelation of the savagery at the heart of the myth and the civilization that produces it. Once the prey of the sacred hunter becomes human, imperialism itself becomes a sacred act, mythically justified by the very narrative on which it depends.

Through the course of the novel, the judge will turn the old myth on its head, pervert it and cannibalize it. He leads the scalphunters in acts that violate the relationship contained within the sacred hunter myth while still seeming to follow its internal rules, in the same way the Black Mass was seen as an inversion of a sacred ritual and indeed depended on the sacred nature of the original for its own symbolic power. This degeneration of the myth from within sounds a striking note of prophecy, for it marks a change not only in the outer form of the hero and his universe (to be expected as cultures change with the passage of time), but also in the most basic narrative structure of the myth. A change on this level, Slotkin claims, "reflect(s) a fundamental alteration of the culture's conception of the relationship of man to the universe, a revolution in world view, cosmology, historical and moral theory, and self-concept. Hence such changes may be seen as marking the point at which a new epoch of cultural history or perhaps even a new culture can be said to begin" (*Regeneration through Violence*, 9). The neobiblical rhetoric of the novel and its blood-washed, apocalyptic images support this vision of revolution, of violent death and rebirth, of some enormous and profound change in the fabric of things imagined by McCarthy through the perversion of the sacred hunter and his position in the natural world.

In fact the first description in the novel of Glanton and his gang mark them equally as actors within the myth and as deviants from it, as both hunters and cannibals:

> a pack of viciouslooking humans mounted on unshod indian
> ponies . . . bearded, barbarous, clad in the skins of animals stitched
> up with thews and armed with weapons of every description . . .
> the trappings of their horses fashioned out of human skin and
> their bridles woven up from human hair and decorated with
> human teeth and the riders wearing scapulars or necklaces of
> dried and blackened human ears . . . the horses rawlooking and
> wild in the eye and their teeth bared like feral dogs . . . the whole
> like a visitation from some heathen land where they and others
> like them fed on human flesh. Foremost among them . . . rode
> the judge. (78)

The natural order of the original myth governing the relationship between
humans and nature has been upset so profoundly that even the horses are
seen as feral, feeding on flesh instead of grass, and the hunters themselves a
visitation of the profane rather than the sacred. Although Glanton is their
nominal leader, it is the judge who is "foremost among them." Their sacred
nature as hunter heroes is evidenced by the "scapulars" they wear and yet their
pollution is obvious as well. The scapulars are formed of scores of human ears
collected as trophies in the same skewed capitalistic spirit as Davy Crockett's
bearskins or Paul Bunyan's logs, and indeed the native people to whom
those ears belonged are viewed by the scalphunters more as natural resources
than human beings, just another part of an infinitely exploitable landscape.
Inevitably, however, the cannibalization at the heart of the new myth will
become reified.

The first instance of the judge's symbolic cannibalization of those
whom he is engaged to serve occurs when the scalphunters spend the night
with the doomed miners at the ruined mines. As the gang prepares to
retire for the night, "Someone had reported the judge naked atop the walls,
immense and pale in the revelations of lightning, striding the perimeter up
there and declaiming in the old epic mode" (118). The next morning the
body of the boy is discovered, lying naked and face down, while the judge
is seen "standing in the gently steaming quiet picking his teeth with a thorn
as if he had just eaten" (118). The sacred marriage and the sacred eucharist
in this scene are at once conflated and perverted, the whole echoing and
reimagining the sacred hunter myth as well as the Christian crucifixion
and eucharist.[5] The naked body of the innocent child "whose head hung
straight down" (119) when the miners grabbed his arms and lifted him,
mimics the image of the body of the innocent and sinless Christ on the
cross, drooping head ringed by a crown of thorns. As the judge watches
these procedures, he employs a thorn with which to pick his teeth clean of
the cannibalized flesh of the child.

The connotations of rape in the explicit nakedness of the judge and the murdered boy mock the fertility rite of the sacred marriage with a union that produces only violence and death in much the same way as the cannibalism implied by the judge picking his teeth "as if he had just eaten" mocks the intention of renewal and life in the ritual of the eucharist. The judge both literally and symbolically consumes that which is forbidden, the child as a living representation of the community the sacred hunter is bound to serve and protect. The boy is neither proper prey for the hunter nor a proper bride, and yet as the myth is inverted and turned in upon itself he becomes both. His childlike state—weak, helpless, and lost in the wilderness—at once feminizes him and marks him as prey for the foremost hunter in the gang. In the proper fulfillment of this emerging version of the myth, the judge rapes and cannibalizes him, absorbs his essence and emerges renewed. Indeed the entire gang appears rejuvenated, associated here with the symbols of life and rebirth as the narrator tells us: upon discovery of the boy's body they "mounted up and turned their horses to the gates that now stood open to the east to welcome in the light and to invite their journey" (119).

This sequence of actions, enacting the ritual of the hunt culminating in a perversion of the sacred marriage and sacred eucharist and the regeneration of the hunters ends chapter 9. The next major action within the narrative begins in chapter 10 with the ex-priest Tobin relating to the kid the story of how he first met Judge Holden, a story that again involves the judge as priest leading a group of men in the perversion of the ritual of the sacred marriage.

This narrative establishes the ritualistic heart of the judge's new myth, for Tobin's story shows the gang's initiation into their roles as sacred, or perhaps profane, hunters. It is important, therefore, that McCarthy have this tale originate from one labeled "ex-priest," fallen from the symbolic orders, both Christian and non-Christian, of the past, and ripe therefore to be baptized into the order (or disorder) to come.

Tobin relates the much-talked-about scene in which the judge appears, alone in the middle of the desert, acting as savior for Glanton and his riders who are without gunpowder and in a desperate flight from nearly a hundred Apaches. The judge uses an uncanny knowledge of the natural landscape to lead them on a new course to a distant mountain range that holds both a bat cave full of nitre and a sulfur-ringed volcano. Tobin recalls that the judge, before commencing his bloody ritual, tells the men "that our mother the earth . . . was round like an egg and contained all good things within her. Then he turned and led the horse he had been riding across that terrain . . . and us behind him like the disciples of a new faith" (130).

And like all converts, the men are required to unite in a group ritual pledging themselves to this "new faith," legitimizing the degeneration of the myth they have been enacting all along. The judge combines charcoal, the nitre from the bat cave, and sulphur scraped from the mouth of the volcano as Tobin continues, "I didn't know but what we'd be required to bleed into it" (131). The scalphunters do pour forth their own bodies, in the form of urine instead of blood, into the hole in the earth the judge has made for the preparation of his eucharist.

> He worked it up dry with his hands and all the while the savages down there on the plain drawin nigh to us and when I turned back the judge was standin, the great hairless oaf, and he'd took out his pizzle and he was pissin into the mixture, pissin with a great vengeance and one hand aloft and he cried out for us to do likewise. . . . We hauled forth our members and at it we went and the judge on his knees kneadin the mass with his naked arms and the piss was splashin about and he was cryin out to us to piss, man, piss for your very souls for cant you see the redskins yonder, and laughin the while and workin up this great mass in a foul black dough, a devil's batter by the stink of it and him not a bloody dark pastryman himself. (132)

Here again the sacred marriage and the eucharist of the wilderness contained within both the hunter myth and Christianity are conflated and perverted. Rather than the flesh of a deer or the sacred host, the judge kneads "a foul black mass, a devil's batter" made of elements of the natural world turned black and stinking by symbolic and ritualistic violence, with the men gang-raping the great vaginal hole in "our mother the earth," spewing piss instead of semen. The ritual reaches its violent climax with Glanton firing his rifle, primed with the foul mixture, straight down the open mouth of the volcano. The flesh of men and the flesh of nature are united here by science to birth gunpowder used to slaughter every last Apache, with the judge as a midwife and anti-priest. As the final ceremonial step cementing the men to the judge as their spiritual leader within this version of the myth, the judge "called us all about to fill our horns and flasks, and we did, one by one, circlin past him like communicants" (134). And indeed communicants are precisely what the scalphunters are, participants in a ritual of renewal dependent upon acts of violence and the perversion of the very myth (and mother) that gave them birth.

This scene, with its savage rape of the earth and resultant "butchery" (134) of the Indians, is a brilliant condensation of McCarthy's violent counter-memory of the winning of the West, his anti-myth of the frontier, deconstructing the forms of National Fantasy so often and so fondly used in building the space of the National Symbolic and shaping the attitudes that would come to justify American devastation of the natural world, genocide of native peoples, and imperial adventures from South America to Southeast Asia. Here we see that indeed "the stuff of creation may be shaped to man's will" (5). The results of the shaping, of the wholesale acceptance of this version of the sacred hunter as the governing myth of the new nation, are played out through the last half of the novel.

Immediately following this narrative, in revenge or perhaps fulfillment of the perversion of the sacred marriage/eucharist, a bear, a powerful symbol of the natural world for McCarthy, steals a Delaware. Like many chapters, this one begins with a detailed description of the natural world through which the scalphunters ride, this time the aspen and pine forests of a high mountain. The bear rises up unexpectedly beside the trail and is shot by Glanton. "The ball struck the bear in the chest and the bear leaned with a strange moan and seized the Delaware and lifted him from the horse . . . the man dangling from the bear's jaws looked down at them cheek and jowl with the brute and one arm about its neck like some crazed defector in a gesture of defiant camaraderie" (137). Acting as an avatar of the natural world, perhaps as nature's own sacred hunter, the bear escapes with his "hostage" (137). The relationship between them is something more than simply an unlucky rider falling prey to a random wild beast or indifferent nature. The Delaware has been consumed by the myth, as the narrator states, "The bear had carried off their kinsman like some fabled storybook beast and the land had swallowed them up beyond all ransom or reprieve" (138).

By this time all the scalphunters have been swallowed up beyond ransom or reprieve by the anti-myth they are enacting, their disconnection from the wilderness through which they ride so complete that even their shadows on the stones appear "like shapes capable of violating their covenant with the flesh that authored them and continuing autonomous across the naked rock without reference to sun or man or god" (139). The balance of power, which may be perceived as resting on the side of nature at the start of the novel, has by the final scenes shifted to the side of man. The original covenant has been violated, the sacred myths structuring the relationship of man to the natural world now perverted to an extent that McCarthy suggests cannot be redeemed, reprieved, or corrected.

The first powerful vision we receive of the results of this reordered myth is on the plain of the bone pickers, fifteen years after the main action of the novel. The kid, now a man, camps on the prairie where he meets an old hunter who tells him of the slaughter of the buffalo herds in which he had participated, an event Tom Pilkington calls "an ecological calamity so stunning as to be almost inconceivable" (317). Initially the old hunter paints pictures that, while bloody and full of gore, reflect the sheer abundance of life that once existed on the now empty and silent plains:

"animals by the thousands and tens of thousands and the hides pegged out over actual square miles of ground . . . and the meat rotting on the ground and the air whining with flies and the buzzards and ravens and the night a horror of snarling and feeding with the wolves half crazed and wallowing in the carrion. . . . On this ground alone there was eight million carcasses" (317). In contrast to this, the hunter then recalls the "last hunt" in which he and the other hunters searched the empty plains for six weeks for a sign of buffalo. "Finally found a herd of eight animals and we killed them and come in. They're gone. Ever one of them that God ever made is gone as if they'd never been at all" (317).

Here is the new covenant, this hunter and those like him proselytes of the new order the judge has helped bring into being in which man's relationship to the wilderness is one of butchery on a scale scarcely imaginable. The outcome is not regeneration, since no animals remain alive to carry on the relationship. This new version of the ancient hunter myth represents degeneration signified by the images of the enormous mountains of bones, miles long, stretching across the prairies in which the mythic figure of the sacred hunter has been reduced to that of the bone pickers, ragged children gathering dead evidence of the now-vanished herds. It is the logical culmination of the task the judge has set for himself early on, when Toadvine questions his taxidermy of one of every species of bird they have encountered. The judge replies, "Only nature can enslave man and only when the existence of each last entity is routed out and made to stand naked before him will he be properly suzerain of the earth. . . . The freedom of birds is an insult to me. I'd have them all in zoos" (198).

While the judge may be clothing it in the sacred rhetoric of the religion of science, we see that the will of man, far from being insignificant, is the most powerful force in the novel. If only nature can enslave man, conversely only man can enslave nature, even if by doing so he leaves a sky as empty of birds as the plains now are of buffalo. Through his will man can make himself suzerain of the earth, though in so doing he must destroy that which he would rule. Kolodny has identified this as "the pastoral paradox" and argues it is at the heart of the modern American relationship to the natural world. Within this paradox, she writes, "man might, indeed, win mastery over the landscape, but only at the cost of emotional and psychological separation from it" (*The Lady of the Land*, 28). And driven by the inexorable force of myth, man is incapable of stopping, his actions governed, directed, and justified by the myth his own deeds have reified.

This situation has been foreshadowed by the judge through the allegory he relates at the Anasazi ruins: "The father dead has euchred the son out of his patrimony" (145). In destroying the sacred power of nature and the myth that tied man to it, the father has robbed those sons to come of their right to take part in that myth and of the regeneration and rebirth to be had from it. Instead, ironically, by making himself suzerain, the hunter-father engenders his own demise, and thus has ensured that for the son, "The world which he inherits bears him false witness. He is broken before a frozen god and he will never find his way" (145). Like the son in the story, these sons will grow to be "killers of men" (145) rather than sacred hunters, resulting in generations of those "not yet born who shall have cause to curse the Dauphin's soul" (327).

And in fulfillment of the judge's desired containment of birds, the great patrimony of nature has been reduced to the level of a zoo or circus by the final chapter of the novel. The gigantic figure of the bear, formerly the magnificent and terrible avatar of the wilderness able to pluck a Delaware from the midst of the scalphunters, is now dressed in a tutu and dances on a saloon stage to the music of a little girl's crank organ. As the kid watches, a drunk from the judge's table shoots the bear, but there is nothing sacred or holy in this hunt. The prey is killed without even the intention of power or ritual and its death is a meaningless spectacle: "The bear had been shot through the midsection. He let out a low moan and he began to dance faster, dancing in silence save for the slap of his great footpads on the planks. . . . The man with the pistol fired again . . . and the bear groaned and began to reel drunkenly. He was holding his chest . . . and he began to totter and to cry like a child and he took a few last steps, dancing, and crashed to the boards" (326). This scene is the antithesis of the one that occurred in the mountains. The bear, like the last few buffalo and the defeated remnants of the native tribes, is now the hostage. In the place of the Delaware with his arm around the neck of the mighty beast who will carry him off crouches the sobbing child with her arms around the neck of the dead bear that "in its crinoline lay like some monster slain in the commission of unnatural acts" (327). This scene is capped with perhaps the most unnatural act of all: the judge's subsequent murder of the little girl, who, like most of the other children in the novel, is betrayed by the sacred hunter who should be her protector and is taken by him as prey.

The destruction and reordering of the original myth is now complete. This point for McCarthy is a meridian and a nadir, the final mastery of man over the wilderness and the prophetic embarkation of his descent. The judge tells the scalphunters, "in the affairs of man there is no waning and the noon of his expression signals the onset of night. His spirit is exhausted at the peak of his achievement. His meridian is at once his darkening and the evening of his day" (147). There is the implication here of something inevitable and preordained, more than the random tragedy of history. As the quote regarding the 300,000-year-old skull from Africa suggests, neither scalping nor any other vicious perversion is new or unique. The scalphunters and the Indians, the dancers in the saloon, the lone buffalo hunter on the empty prairie, and the long-dead scalper of the unfortunate Ethiopian whose skull now speaks to modern anthropologists are all tabernacled in the others' books (141), "each pass[ing] back the way the other had come, pursuing as all travelers must inversions without end upon other men's journeys" (121) in an "endless complexity of being and witness" (141).

The suggestion is that the myth has always contained within itself the anti-myth, the dark shadow double awaiting a Kurtz or a Holden to strip bare the original and turn it inside out. McCarthy's earth in *Blood Meridian* and many other works is hollow, full of empty caves and echoing caverns, at once womb and tomb, signifying the hollowness at the heart of all myths. There is no center to the sacred hunter myth, any more than there is to its antithesis. And yet the power of myth to move and shape us remains, and through *Blood Meridian*, McCarthy has done more than simply invert the sacred hunter and the eucharist of the wilderness; he has altered their form in several significant ways.

The most basic relationship enshrined in that myth, between man and nature, is ultimately replaced with a new ordering based upon the relationship between man and man in the form of sacred war. The death of a bear or deer, the sacrificial shedding of the blood of some symbol of divine nature, once an essential part of the ritual upon which the sacred hunter myth rested, is no longer sufficient for regeneration. Regeneration depends upon ritual, but as the judge explains, "A ritual includes the letting of blood. Rituals which fail in this requirement are but mock rituals" (329). The myth of science, therefore, is not enough. It must be enacted through the more ancient ritual of war. Because all generations following this one have been euchred of the patrimony of nature, invalidating the blood of bears or deer as sources of regeneration, the prey must now become humanity itself. The new version of the myth demands human blood, for now no other will suffice, and, therefore, as the judge suggests, the holiest of all acts is war.

And again the suggestion is that of inevitable procession toward this end. "War was always here," the judge says. "Before man was, war waited for him. The ultimate trade awaiting its ultimate practitioner" (248). War, in fact, is god, according to the judge, because, as myth or game enhanced "to its ultimate state" (249), it is the perfect embodiment of human will, the force of will made divine, driven to test itself against the very stuff of creation, "a forcing of the unity of existence" (249), beyond what the judge considers the petty concerns of moral judgments. In engaging in the act of war, in forcing the hand of existence to choose who shall live and who shall die, the sacred hunter becomes one with the prey, and man assumes the cloak of divine power himself. Moral law, good and evil, are simply trivialities enshrined by one church or another. Questions of right and wrong are subsumed by the force of human will made manifest in this mythic vision of war. To prove this notion the judge challenges Tobin, the de facto representative of religion and moral order:

> The judge searched out the circle for disputants. But what says the priest? he said.
> Tobin looked up. The priest does not say.
> The priest does not say, said the judge.... But the priest has said. For the priest has put by the robes of his craft and taken up the tools of that higher calling which all men honor. The priest also would be no godserver but a god himself....
> I'll not secondsay you in your notions, said Tobin. Dont ask it.
> Ah Priest, said the judge. What could I ask of you that you've not already given? (250–51)

The judge's new myth has long ago swallowed up Tobin and the religion and morality he symbolizes, the impotent state of those institutions marked by Tobin's status as "ex" priest. The churches are empty shells, like the Anasazi village, crumbling ruins of an order dead and vanished, now "wondered at by tribes of savages" doomed to erect new churches, new edifices of stone in their attempts to "alter the structure of the universe" (146). But all such attempts, the judge insinuates, will ultimately fail. "This you see here, these ruins . . . do you not think that this will be again? Aye. And again. With other people, with other sons" (147). The judge has proven that the only thing that can truly alter creation is the brute force of human will, sharpened and focused through the lens of a mythic structure unconcerned with morality and bent to the task of godlike war. The eucharist of the wilderness has now become a eucharist of humanity.

Everyone now is a participant in the dance of war, either as hunter or as prey. All in the gang have been baptized into the new myth, have partaken in its ceremonies of cannibalism and rape. Only the kid finally attempts to renounce the dance and to assert a will independent of the judge and his anti-myth. By giving up his position as a hunter of men within this new myth, he makes himself prey. At the ruins, the judge supplied the blueprint for raising hunters, explaining that at a young age children should be put into pits with wild dogs, forced to fight lions and run naked through the desert. Only those with the most perfect and powerful wills would survive such tests (mercy, we are to assume, would produce weakness instead of strength), and, ironically of course, only those adults with the most potent of wills could administer the trials without succumbing to the urge to help the children.

The kid faces several such trials throughout the narrative and fails them. He alone of the gang answers David Brown's call for aid in removing an arrow from his leg (162). By the rules of the anti-myth, Brown should have been left on his own, like the child in the pit of wild dogs, to triumph by the force of his will alone or to fail and die in the desert. Tobin warns the kid of the danger of his actions: "Fool, he said. God will not love ye forever. . . . Dont you know he'd of took you with him? He'd of took you boy. Like a bride to the altar" (162–63).

The "he" here refers to the judge, who has earlier refused to help Brown and who tests the kid later by calling for help himself in the killing of a horse (219). None of the other members of the gang answers him, and Tobin again warns the kid not to respond. In doing so, the kid violates the internal order of the myth, though the prospect of being taken "like a bride to the altar" by the judge is perhaps not such an appealing one. While the phrase echoes the rhetoric of the sacred marriage common to both Christianity and the sacred hunter myth and perverted by the act of rape in this new order, in this instance we can understand Tobin to intend a positive meaning. While the relationship between the judge and the kid might be more properly characterized as that between father and son rather than husband and bride, the implication at least is of renewal and rebirth, the promise of regeneration that the kid betrays.

As Tobin and the kid crouch in the desert after the slaughter at the ferry crossing, the kid receives his final chance to seize his place as hunter within the new myth and fails once again when he refuses to shoot the unarmed judge. To do so would only have been right and proper within the relationship of hunter and prey, human will against human will in sacred war, as well as within the relationship of father and son, since as the judge has said at the Anasazi ruins, it is the death of the father to which the son is entitled. When the kid will neither shoot him nor join him, the judge charges, "There's a flawed place in the fabric of your heart. . . . You alone were mutinous. You alone reserved in your soul some corner of clemency" (299).

The kid ignores the judge's warning and over the final section of the book covering the last decades of his life, attempts to return to the previous mythic order, to reestablish the relationship of the sacred hunter as guardian and protector of his community. He becomes a guide for other travelers passing through the wilderness, protecting them from the forces of nature, from Indians, and from those like his old companions who have become hunters of men. Most significantly, he begins to carry a Bible, a book already made defunct by the judge as a false book and symbol of the empty moral laws thrown down before the force of human wills in war. Like the church it represents, the Bible is a kind of ruin here, silent and without reference in the world shaped by the new myth. Especially for the illiterate kid, the Bible is a mute emblem of a fallen system, "no word of which he could read" (312).

Its futility as a symbol within the world shaped by the new order is reified by the kid's encounter with the penitents he finds butchered in a canyon and his attempts to speak with one of them:

> The kid rose and looked about at this desolate scene and then he saw alone and upright in a small niche in the rocks an old woman kneeling in a faded rebozo with her eyes cast down.
>
> He made his way among the corpses and stood before her. . . . She did not look up. . . . He spoke to her in a low voice. He told her that he was an American and that he was a long way from the country of his birth and that he had no family and that he had traveled much and seen many things and had been at war and endured hardships. He told her that he would convey her to a safe place, some party of her country-people who would welcome her and that she should join them for he could not leave her in this place or she would surely die.
>
> He knelt on one knee, resting the rifle before him like a staff. Abuelita, he said. No puedes escucharme?
>
> He reached into the alcove and touched her arm. . . . She weighed nothing. She was just a dried shell and she had been dead in that place for years. (315)

The kid attempts here to perform the act of confession, a ritual based upon the acknowledgement of a moral order the speaker has in some way violated, but the kid has himself been a participant, as his confession makes clear, in the destruction of that moral order that has rendered this ceremony empty and meaningless, the authority of the church now "just a dried shell." The kid has turned his back on the new myth he helped bring into being, but it is too late to revive the old ones. He prostrates himself before a dead body that cannot hear his confession and can therefore offer no absolution or forgiveness, cannot even move to accept his proffered aide, and is as mute as the Bible he carries but cannot read. He even clasps his rifle, not like a weapon of divine war, worthy of the name the judge has bestowed on his gun, the tool of death in the garden, but like a staff, symbol of the doomed priest, administrator of an empty office, and a figure the kid is said to have come to resemble.

The kid has in fact betrayed the sacred office he once occupied as a hunter of men in this new myth, and it is this betrayal for which the judge castigates him in the prison. "You came forward, he said, to take part in a work. But you were a witness against yourself. You sat in judgment on your own deeds. You put your own allowances before the judgments of history and you broke with the body of which you were pledged a part" (307). And it is for this betrayal that the judge, described as immense and bearlike (having subsumed the figures of the old myths within himself), finally kills the kid in a horrible embrace, a corrupted hug, a perversion of the act of reproduction performed in the midst of human excrement (333), and yet despite all this, an act that is holy and proper within the structure of the new myth, for after the killing the judge emerges renewed and rejuvenated to join the dance in the saloon.

If we accept Slotkin's claim that any fundamental alteration of the narrative structure of the myth signals some profound shift in the culture that produces it, then the sense of momentous change is inescapable. Here is the bloody tie binding America's mythic past to its troubled present, here in this mythic dance is the violent birth of a National Symbolic that has made heroes out of scalphunters and Indian killers and constructed the near-extinction of the buffalo and massive deforestation as symbols of triumph and mastery, the proud heritage of the modern American citizen. This is one possible interpretation of the novel's rather obscure epilogue. The man progressing over the silent plain digging postholes is striking out of the rock with his steel, the fire, and symbolically the life, "which God has put there" (337), the first step before stringing barbed wire along that "track of holes that runs to the rim of the visible ground" (337).

The barbed wire fence is a potent and deeply paradoxical symbol in the American West. On one hand, it is the triumphant emblem of Anglo America's conquest of the land once referred to as the Great American Desert, of the sheer force of human will necessary to empty it of those animals like the buffalo that do not serve Anglo America's needs and to fill it instead with cattle—nature tamed and controlled by the sharp-edged product of Eastern factories. It is also, for many Westerners, the sign of some final closure, usually expressed nostalgically as the loss of the wandering horseman's right to travel freely and without restriction across the landscape. That wandering horseman, the lone cowboy with his bedroll and his rifle, is the most commonly recognized modern American expression of the sacred hunter, the lone male in the wilderness, here digging the postholes that mark his own demise and performing the final fencing-in of the natural world.

The plain in the epilogue is empty of life, no buffalo, no bears, wolves, or antelope, the patrimony of nature gone, only "bones and the gatherers of bones" (337), following behind the diminished hunter striking out hole after hole. The act of the posthole digger "seems less the pursuit of some continuance than the verification of a principle, a validation of sequence and causality" (337), the consequence of our national acceptance of the judge's perverted anti-myth, of the disruption of the continuum identified by Dana Phillips in which some balance or relationship between man and nature has been destroyed and replaced with a mythic structure few besides McCarthy have dared to gaze at unflinchingly. American identity, as constructed through the national(ist) narrative of frontier myth, cannot be seen as innocent, either of intent or deed. Nor can national identity as the product of myth be viewed as essential in any way. Rather, identity must be seen as fragile, tenuous, and unfixed, as McCarthy suggests all empires of man are. In the first of his Western works, McCarthy has recast the lens of myth through which American history and identity is viewed, thus challenging the mythic language by which the American nation understands itself, its beliefs, and its role in the world.

NOTES

1. I use the term "palimpsest" here as Daniel Cooper Alarcón has employed it in *The Aztec Palimpsest*: "a site where texts have been superimposed onto others in an attempt to displace earlier or competing histories. Significantly, such displacement is never total; the suppressed material often remains legible, however faintly, challenging the dominant text with an alternate version of events" (xiv).

2. In *The Legacy of Conquest*, Limerick argues that the association of the Western landscape with "a potent and persistent variety of nationalistic myth" (30) coupled with the government's official declaration of the end of the frontier in 1891 resulted in a public perception of "a great discontinuity between the frontier past and the Western present" (31). The perception has persisted, she claims, in part because of the romanticization of the frontier experience and in part because such a discontinuity allows the grim realities of conquest and colonization to be viewed from a safe remove, as associated with the distant past and unrelated to the present day.

3. Slotkin argues, for example, that the common and extremely popular folktale regarding Daniel Boone's first meeting with his future wife Rebecca Boone is a version of this myth. The story claims Boone was hunting deer by torchlight one night when he saw two eyes shining among the trees. He raised his rifle to shoot but at the last moment stayed his hand. What he had believed to be a deer was actually Rebecca, walking at night through the woods. This portion of the story, though widely repeated, may or may not be true. Neither Boone nor Rebecca denied it, though their children, feeling it to be primitive and pagan and thus reflecting badly on their father, who was already well on the way to achieving mythic status, did so vehemently. We do know that Boone married Rebecca soon after their first meeting. Within the bounds of the myth working at the level of popular culture, this act would have been the proper fulfillment of the rules of the sacred marriage, which culminated the hunt and which decreed that woman or deer, married or slain, the hunter must love and honor that which he hunts for its sacred nature in order to receive union, and communion, with it. For a further discussion of the Boone myth as the first truly American (i.e., combination of European and Indian) version of the sacred hunter story, see Slotkin's *Regeneration through Violence*, pp. 152–56.

4. Bell, p.124.

5. The connection of the symbolic cannibalism of the Christian eucharist and the figure of Christ with both Old and New world versions of the sacred hunter myth in which the hunter himself must die in a symbolic mirroring of the hunter as stag and prey has been noted by many; see Slotkin's *Regeneration through Violence*, especially chapter 2, "Cannibals and Christians."

JAMES R. GILES

Discovering Fourthspace in Appalachia: Cormac McCarthy's Outer Dark *and* Child of God

Few American novelists have so thoroughly explored the various and complex ramifications of violence as Cormac McCarthy. Sustained critical attention was late in coming to McCarthy, and, especially in recent years, it has focused on his western novels: the anti-Western *Blood Meridian; or, The Evening Redness in the West* (1985) and the Border trilogy, *All the Pretty Horses* (1992), *The Crossing* (1994), and *Cities of the Plain* (1998). Certainly this attention is deserved. No text so thoroughly deconstructs the myth of a heroic American West as *Blood Meridian*, with its constantly accelerating body count; it demonstrates that Anglo domination of the North American continent was made possible by illiterate and violent men acting outside any established legal system. Thus the subtitle with its implication of a frontier that, even while vanishing, leaves behind its blood-soaked legacy. The Border trilogy—especially the first two volumes, *All the Pretty Horses* and *The Crossing*—represents a much more lyrical and forgiving modernist evocation of the frontier myth. *All the Pretty Horses* first brought McCarthy significant popular recognition and thereby inspired the re-publication of his neglected earlier novels.

In these texts, all set in Tennessee or in some less identifiable realm of Appalachia, McCarthy had been exploring the phenomenon of violence for two decades. The ambitious *Suttree* (1979) is set in a relatively contemporary

From *The Spaces of Violence*, pp. 16–41. © 2006 by the University of Alabama Press.

Knoxville and is largely realistic in narrative approach. In contrast, *Outer Dark* (1968), while unmistakably set in rural Appalachia, seems to transcend precise definitions of space or time. While the setting of *Child of God* (1973) is identified as Sevier County, Tennessee, sometime around the mid-twentieth century, the text evokes a comparable sense of unreality. What Vereen M. Bell says about *Outer Dark* is, to some degree, true of both novels: "The topography is vague, dreamlike, and surreal in a way that imposes an unwholesome, deranged aspect upon the entire scene" (33). In both texts, physical and social space are, at times, obliterated. While both short novels explore a desperation born of degrading poverty and stultifying ignorance, and can thus be seen as exposés of the disabling effects of systemic oppression, this is nevertheless only one of the levels on which the two texts are intended to function.

The elusive nature of space in the two texts is witnessed in three perceptive but contrasting critical discussions. In *Cormac McCarthy*, Robert L. Jarrett discusses the problems in attempting to approach the fictional landscape in McCarthy's Appalachian novels from familiar historical and literary sources. He notes that, in sharp contrast to the fiction of William Faulkner, a writer with whom McCarthy is often compared, McCarthy's novels, and especially *Outer Dark*, seem almost untouched by nineteenth-century southern history, specifically by "the antebellum South, the Confederacy, and Reconstruction." If there were a single identifiable county in McCarthy's Appalachia, it would defy the talents of any mapmaker. While McCarthy does not completely ignore race, it is far from being the overwhelming issue that it is in Faulkner's Yoknapatawpha County (Jarrett 24–25). In part, Jarrett attributes the seeming absence of history in McCarthy's fictional landscape to Appalachia's geographical and cultural isolation from the rest of the South; because slavery was never profitable in eastern Tennessee, he points out, the plantation system never flourished there. In addition, Appalachia has historically existed in political isolation from the rest of the South (24–27).

Brian Evenson and Gary M. Ciuba approach McCarthy's world from considerably more abstract critical perspectives. Evenson discusses the central characters in both the Appalachian and the western novels in a post-structuralist context defined by Gilles Deleuze and Felix Guattari in their analysis of "nomadology in *A Thousand Plateaus*" (Evenson 42). Dividing McCarthy's protagonists into two categories, "wanderers" and "nomads," Evenson places the three dark, murderous outlaws from *Outer Dark* and Lester Ballard from *Child of God* in the second category. Citing Deleuze and Guattari, Evenson writes that the defining characteristic of the nomad is a search for "smooth spaces," that is, open spaces free from limiting, regulating forces: "Such a topography can be actual or it can be the metaphorical equivalent: a moral or ethical open ground. The nomad's existence is a series of movements which explore the limitless, open possibilities of the smooth space" (42). McCarthy's complex aesthetic in *Outer Dark* and *Child of God* projects landscapes or spaces that fuse the "actual," the "metaphorical," *and* the "psychological" to create something that is simultaneously all of these and none of them.

This imagined landscape can perhaps be described as a kind of fourthspace, existing in a dimension somewhat similar to, but ultimately extremely unlike, Edward W. Soja's thirdspace. The fourthspace that distinguishes the world of *Outer Dark* and *Child of God* merges the material, the metaphoric or linguistic, and the psychological or subconscious, and only the darkest forms of freedom, the most horrific possibilities, result from the merger. Ultimately, nothing is transcended in McCarthy; no one is given the opportunity to explore spiritually affirming "borders" of existence.

The three grim outlaws of *Outer Dark* and the necrophilic murderer Lester Ballard act in a perverted realm of "smooth space." They perform acts of evil characterized by sheer excess, and McCarthy's two novels are, in part, explorations of such excess. On this level, they can usefully be read in the context of comments by Georges Bataille on work, reason, excess, and violence. Bataille posits an inherent duality in human beings that he defines through the binaries of work, a realm dominated by reason and secured through taboos, and excess, a realm of violent transgression of taboo: "One cannot fail to observe mankind's double nature throughout its career. There are two extremes. At one end, existence is basically orderly and decent. Work, concern for the children, kindness and honesty rule men's [the gender-specific language is in this case appropriate] dealings with their fellows. At the other, violence rages pitilessly. In certain circumstances the same men practise pillage and arson, murder, violence and torture. Excess contrasts with reason" (186).

McCarthy's fiction has always been focused on the second half of this duality; the excessive violence that dominates his fiction is thus an essential element in his aesthetic. The characters who inhabit the worlds of *Outer Dark* and *Child of God* are either exiles from the realm of work and reason or nomadic wanderers who have never even known it. The kind of "smooth space" they explore exists on several levels, all distinguished by the kind of extreme freedom that Bataille associates with excess; the violence in McCarthy's fiction must be senseless, is often unmotivated, and above all is supremely irrational.

McCarthy's art is thus intended to disturb by revealing a world from which the protective taboos that characterize what Bataille identifies as the realm of work have been torn away. For Bataille, this kind of intentionally disturbing art is essential for revealing the full dimension of human beings, for probing into a level of the natural so extreme that it may become unnatural:

"Man has built up the rational world by his own efforts, but there remains within him an undercurrent of violence. Nature herself is violent, and however reasonable we may grow we may be mastered anew by a violence no longer that of nature but of a rational being who tries to obey but who succumbs to stirrings within himself that he cannot bring to heel" (40).

In this context excess is an essential human characteristic, and one with which artists have long been fascinated. At times McCarthy's nomads seem almost bloodless embodiments of such excess, and as Evenson points out, they are inevitably at war with "civilized" human spaces. When they encounter a settled space, violence inevitably results; the nomad's quest for smooth space can only be pursued outside the boundaries of settlements. Evenson argues that McCarthy's ability to dramatize the violent confrontations of nomads with settled spaces is "precisely the appeal of McCarthy's greatest fictions" (43).

In an essay that should be read in conjunction with Evenson's (both are included in a collection of McCarthy criticism entitled *Sacred Violence*), Ciuba interprets *Child of God* through René Girard's theories concerning violence and sacrifice. In this context, he provides an interpretation of the relationship between the title of the novel and its protagonist, the murderous Lester Ballard:

> Lester Ballard is the child of an ancient tradition of sacred violence. René Girard contends that the sacred of primitive religion rose out of the salutary transcendence of violence by violence. At the founding moment of culture, humankind overcame internecine strife by focusing its mutual hostilities on slaying one of its own. The violence that once threatened to destroy the community became the violence that graciously delivered it.... Since the sacrifice transformed an accursed outcast into the redeemer of a fractious community, the godhead assumed both the maleficent and beneficent aspects of violence. The transgressor became the savior; the most heinous was also the *Child of God*. (77–78)

Thus, Lester Ballard becomes both sacrifice and sacrificer in an Appalachian community historically defined by violent injustice and oppression. It is as if a plague has been let loose upon the land, and Lester redeems it through the excess of his own transgressions. "Like some violent voluptuary in the religion of Georges Bataille," writes Ciuba, "he makes transgression the very sign of its transcendence" (78). Girard offers a further gloss on this paradoxical concept: "From the purely religious point of view, the surrogate victim . . . inevitably appears as a being who submits to violence without provoking a reprisal; a supernatural being who sows violence to reap peace; a mysterious savior who visits affliction on mankind in order subsequently to restore it to good health" (86).

Lester does not perfectly fit Girard's description. He submits to his initial displacement from the community only after he is knocked unconscious and forcibly removed from what was first his father's and then his own farm while it and the things on it are being auctioned off. Thus Lester's victimization is, to some degree, systemic; he is the product of decades of poverty and ignorance. Moreover, he exists in a world in which religious faith, to the degree that it exists at all, has been debased to a malevolent doctrine offering no genuine redemptive promise. While his crimes are certainly excessive in nature and execution, no one in the communal world of the novel would view him as a supernatural being. The sheer savagery of his acts serves to reinforce his undeniable humanness. He embodies the violent side of Bataille's concept of human duality; certainly work is as foreign to his being as excess is natural to it.

After he is forced off his farm, Lester gradually evolves into a representative of Evenson's nomad, living on the edge of cultivated space. In the course of the novel he is transformed from a communal outcast to a mysterious nomadic presence that periodically assaults the settlement. In an early scene, he is falsely accused of rape and, while being interrogated in the sheriff's office, pronounces what amounts to his judgment on the community: "you sons of bitches. . . . Goddamn all of ye" (52). Periodically the novel shifts into a communal narrative voice, which at one point summarizes the disgraceful history of the Ballard family, concluding on a note of perverse pride: "I'll say one thing about Lester though. You can trace em back to Adam if you want and goddamn if he don't outstrip em all" (81). It is significant that this judgment ties Lester's origins firmly to the first *human* sinner rather than seeking a supernatural explanation for his actions. In distinct contrast, the "grim triune" from *Outer Dark*, while always appearing in human form, seems something other than human. Even more than *Child of God*—in fact, more than any other McCarthy novels—*Outer Dark* seems to take place in some ambiguous physical-social space devoid of history.[1] In part, this almost surreal setting can be understood as exemplifying Jarrett's description of Appalachia as a space on the periphery of the South and its history and traditions. In the opening of the novel, its two central characters, Culla and Rinthy Holme, brother and sister, are so isolated as to barely know that any larger community exists. This isolation is, moreover, not strictly spatial; Culla and Rinthy are victimized by a profound ignorance that is not simply a matter of literacy. It is as if they have somehow been untouched by any sustaining cultural values or accepted social customs. At one point Rinthy says, "They ain't a soul in this world but what is a stranger to me" (29). The brother and sister appear parentless and, except for each other, cut off from any family; the only reference to their background comes when Rinthy tells a family that takes her in and feeds her, "I bet I ain't eat two pones of lightbread in my life. I was raised hard" (60). Certainly, she seems never to have known anything approximating kindness or gentleness.

On one metaphoric level, Culla and Rinthy are re-creations of Adam and Eve, doomed to commit anew the unpardonable sin that threatens to exile them from human or divine mercy, to make them wanderers through a grotesquely fallen world. Thus their last name is cruelly ironic—they have never really known anything approximating "home" or even a safe space. Isolated from virtually everyone else, they almost doom each other. Before the novel opens, they have committed incest; the reader is introduced to them as the baby is about to be born. Culla delivers the baby himself after refusing to go in search of a midwife, since he wants to keep their sin secret. After delivering the child, he makes an ominous prophecy: "I don't look for it to live" (15).

Culla does not kill the child, though. Instead, he takes the infant and leaves it to die in some neighboring woods. McCarthy's description of Culla's misfortunes while carrying out his secret and desperate mission is, one assumes, deliberately excessive. After Culla stumbles and falls to the ground, he "lay there with his cheek to the earth. And as he lay there a far crack of lightning went bluely down the sky and bequeathed him an embryonic bird's first fissured vision of the world and transpiring instant and outrageous from dark to dark a final view of the grotto and the shapeless white plasm struggling upon the rich and incunabular moss like a lank swamp hare" (17).

While this kind of McCarthy prose has been condemned as excessive and imitative of Faulkner, in this case it serves a legitimate purpose. The quick shift to the "fissured vision" of the "embryonic bird" evokes a timeless, primal space underlying the mimetic Appalachian setting. Incest (however it is defined) is, of course, one of the oldest of human taboos, Girard believes, because, like murder, it assaults communal order in the most profound of ways. By destroying culturally accepted distinctions, it bequeaths chaos: "Incestuous propagation leads to formless duplications, sinister repetitions, a dark mixture of unnamable things" (Girard 75). Carrying his child, the result of "incestuous propagation," Culla has ventured into this "dark mixture of unnamable things" as much as, if not more than, he has entered forested material space. McCarthy seems to have emphasized Culla and Rinthy's cultural and social isolation partly in order to emphasize the extreme and primal nature of their resultant guilt.

Culla compounds his guilt by telling Rinthy that the baby is dead. When she demands to see where it is buried, he takes her into the woods where he has left the infant. Once there, they discover that the infant has been taken, either alive or dead, by a tinker who had intruded upon their isolation and tried to sell Culla a book of amateurish pornographic drawings. One remembers folkloric associations of tinkers with Satan, and this tinker seems to possess supernatural insight into the lives of the isolated brother and sister. The tinker is, in fact, the first of several prophet figures, usually demented to some degree, in the novel. The tinker's theft of the child forces Culla and Rinthy out of their isolated worlds as they separately seek to find the lost child, and McCarthy's linguistic excess merges with the psychological guilt of Culla and the maternal need of Rinthy to produce the debased fourthspace in which the novel takes place.

In their quests, both discover grotesquely fallen worlds, haunted by poverty, ignorance, and sheer malice. Bell describes *Outer Dark* as being "as brutally nihilistic as any serious novel written in this century in this nihilistic country" (34). Refuting Bell, Edwin T. Arnold asserts that a redemptive moral center underlies *Outer Dark* and all of McCarthy's fiction, including *Blood Meridian*, with its unrelenting evocations of social, rather than strictly individual, acts of violence: "While I recognize and appreciate the postmodern celebration of McCarthy's exuberant violence, his astonishing approximation of chaos, his grand evocation of the mystery of the world, there is also evident in his work a profound belief in the need for moral order, a conviction that is essentially religious. There is, in addition, always the possibility of grace and redemption even in the darkest of his tales, although that redemption may require more of his characters than they are ultimately willing to give" (46).

Nihilism and something like religious affirmation are at war throughout McCarthy's novel. In this context, it is significant that the space through which Rinthy travels is more conventionally mimetic and more accepting than the dark and deadly landscape Culla encounters. Arnold perceptively analyzes Culla's descent into something that seems a great deal like both Christian and Sartrean imaginings of hell as resulting from a failure of courage, an attempt to flee from sin. That Culla's journey is at least as much a psychological and a spiritual experience as an actual exploration of mimetic space is foreshadowed by a horrific nightmare that opens the novel and haunts him for the remainder of the text:

> There was a prophet standing in the square with arms upheld in exhortation to the beggared multitude gathered there. A delegation of human ruin who attended him with blind eyes upturned and puckered stumps and leprous sores. . . . It grew cold and more black and silent and some began to cry out and some despaired but the sun did not return. Now the dreamer grew fearful. Voices were being raised against him. He was caught up

in the crowd and the stink of their rags filled his nostrils. They
grew seething and more mutinous and he tried to hide among
them but they knew him even in that pit of hopeless dark and
fell upon him with howls of outrage. (6)

Now Culla has been transformed into something closer to a Cain than an
Adam figure. He has been banished and set apart from the rest of humanity.
This introductory nightmare functions as a metaphoric introduction of the
remainder of the novel. The pornography-selling tinker was merely the
first of the ominous prophets Culla will encounter as he travels among "the
beggared multitude." To some degree, the emphasis on the stinking "rags"
of "the human ruin" evokes the more real or mimetic landscape of soul-
killing poverty through which he will travel. It also alludes to the sinfulness
and viciousness in which Culla finds human beings clothed and to his own
sin, already that of incest and soon to be of child abandonment as well. Like
Hawthorne's Young Goodman Brown, Culla undertakes a journey in which
physical space, psychological guilt, and spiritual despair merge so completely
as to become indistinguishable.

Shortly after the scenes of birth and abandonment, the novel depicts
an incident that reoccurs in different forms throughout McCarthy's fiction.
On a Sunday, Culla goes to the nearest store to buy some food for the
weakened Rinthy. Inevitably he finds the store closed and hears a voice
calling down at him "from an upper window": "We still christians here"
(26). As indicated by the deliberate withholding of the uppercase C from
"christians," the scene constitutes, on one level, condemnation of a southern
Christian fundamentalism that denies support to those who exist outside it.
Such "faith," McCarthy seems to imply, is divorced from any meaningful
association with Christ; it merely looks down on and condemns those in
physical or spiritual need. In this and comparable McCarthy scenes, God
seems not so much absent as harsh and vindictive, as if looking down from
an elevated space upon a desperately flawed humanity. Still, the most severe
judgment on Culla comes from within; he believes that he has so violated
established rules of human behavior as to stand in judgment outside the
possibility of forgiveness. Most of all, it is Culla who withholds forgiveness
from Culla.[2]

Once Culla undertakes his search for the stolen child, comparable
judgments meet him at every turn.[3] Sometimes they seem innocent enough
on the surface, as when a "squire" for whom he briefly works lectures him
that "I hope you've not got a family. It's a sacred thing, a family. A sacred
obligation" (47). Inevitably, Culla hears this pronouncement in the context
of his sins of incest and child abandonment and cannot deny that he has, in
fact, violated "a sacred obligation." Here as elsewhere in the text, outsiders—

some of whom, like the squire, look down upon him from perspectives of social class or legal power—are, in some mysterious way, aware of his transgressions. Such judges exist on two levels, that of mimesis and psychological projection. The squire is a representative of class and economic superiority, of what Henri Lefebvre describes as the "power" of vertical space and the "submission" of horizontal space, as is made manifest in the squire's initial meeting with Culla in which the squire looks at the desperate young man "as he would anything for sale" (42). The squire's dominant position in the socioeconomic hierarchy is based on the power to objectify others, to treat them as commodities that can be used and then discarded. His power is transitory, however, as he ultimately runs into the three nomadic killers who coldly and senselessly murder him. But he is also an emblematic figure who embodies Culla's self-condemnation.

After the doomed squire, the next "judge" Culla encounters is an old man from whom he begs a drink of water. Twice, the old man tells Culla that he "wouldn't turn Satan away for a drink" (117). Like the squire, the old man appears to possess some mysterious knowledge of the primal nature of Culla's sins. Moreover, he turns out to be a snake hunter given to telling grotesque stories about victims of snakebite, and inside his cabin he has the skin of a monstrous rattlesnake tacked above his fireplace: "He was eight foot seven inches and had seventeen rattles. Big in the middle to where ye couldn't get your hands around him" (122). The scene recalls traditional associations of serpents with death and evil ranging from Genesis to Satan's magical staff in "Young Goodman Brown"; on a Freudian level, the phallic overtones of the monstrous snake recall Culla's intercourse with Rinthy. Later a man who has lost his entire family to cholera charges Culla with being a plague carrier, to which Culla responds not at all honestly, "Ain't nobody plagued" (138). Like that of Oedipus, Culla's incest seems to have let loose a plague on the countryside. One also recalls Camus's division in *The Plague* of human beings into the categories of plague carriers and plague fighters.

Near the end of the novel, Culla comes close to being executed in a black comic "(mis)reading" of an incident recounted in the New Testament book of Mark. He abruptly finds himself in the midst of a herd of hogs driven by men "gaunt and fever-eyed with incredible rag costumes and wild hair" (213). After some wildly absurd discussion between Culla and one of the drovers about "unclean" hogs, split hooves, and Jews ("What's a jew? That's one of them old-timey people from in the bible"), the drover concludes: "A hog is a hog. Pure and simple. And that's about all ye can say about him. And smart, don't think they ain't. Smart as the devil. And don't be fooled by one that ain't got nairy clove foot cause he's devilish too." Culla can only concur with such immaculate logic: "I guess hogs is hogs" (216). This exchange is a reminder of what the bleak central vision of *Outer Dark* can lead the reader to forget—there is wonderful black comedy in the novel, most of which has roots in southern and old southwestern folklore.

The mood of the scene quickly takes a more serious turn when the hogs inexplicably begin stampeding off the edge of a cliff into a river and the desperate drovers are transformed into beings barely recognizable as human: "[The swineherds] had begun to assume satanic looks with their staves and wild eyes as if they were . . . disciples of darkness got among these charges to herd them to their doom" (218). In the stampede, the younger brother of the drover with whom Culla had been talking is driven over the cliff to his death in the river below. Nevertheless, the scene undergoes another daring mood shift when Culla resumes conversation with the surviving drovers:

> [One of the drovers]: That beats everything I ever seen.
> [Culla]: That's pitiful about your brother.
> [The drover]: I don't know what all I'm goin to tell mama.
>   Herded off a bluff with a parcel of hogs. I don't know how
>   I'm going to tell her that.
> [Culla]: You could tell her he was drunk.
> [The drover]: Tell her he got shot or somethin.
> [Culla]: You wouldn't need to tell her he went to his reward with
>   a herd of hogs. (219)

Given the brutish behavior of most of the characters in the landscape through which Culla travels, McCarthy seems to be saying that, should anyone somehow manage to receive "his reward," he will do so in the company of a herd of hoggish human beings. It is not insignificant that Culla and the drovers both assume that their mother would find lies about the deceased man dying drunk or as a result of human violence more acceptable than the truth.

In the biblical text that McCarthy is intentionally "(mis)reading" (Mark 5:1–17), a man with an "unclean spirit" whose "name is Legion; for we are many" asks Christ to save him. In response, Christ sends the legion of "demons" out of the man and into a herd of two thousand swine, who then rush off "a steep place into the sea" and drown. Frightened by such power, those who have witnessed the miracle promptly beg Christ to leave the region. The savior is immediately rejected and symbolically banished. In this context, it is not surprising that, with no evidence whatsoever, the surviving drovers decide that Culla mysteriously caused the hogs to stampede, and another of Culla's "judges," fittingly in this context the most deranged of all, abruptly enters the text: "A parson or what looked like one was laboring over the crest of the hill and coming toward them with one hand raised in blessing, greeting, fending flies. He was dressed in a dusty frockcoat and carried a walking stick and he wore a pair of octagonal glasses on the one pane of which the late sun shone while a watery eye peered from the naked wire aperture of the other" (221). McCarthy's absurdist humor continues to be in evidence as the "parson" almost condemns Culla first to being lynched and then to being thrown off the cliff into the river with the hogs by asserting that such acts of retribution would be wrong: "Boys I believe he's plumb eat up with the devil in him. But don't hang him. . . . Don't flang him off the bluff, boys, the preacher said. I believe ye'd be better to hang him as that" (223).

After some deliberation, the drovers decide that hanging Culla would be the best course, and the preacher offers to baptize him first. When the outraged Culla refuses such a mode of salvation, the minister comments: "I guess a feller mires up so deep in sin after a while he don't want to hear nothin about grace and salvation. Not even a feller about to be hanged." To this speculation, one of the drovers adds this gloss: "It ain't no use, Reverend. He's too mean to be saved" (225). Of course, in this particular instance Culla is innocent, and not surprisingly, the reverend is later revealed to be a charlatan. Like the early scene at the store, this episode parodies a judgmental religious fundamentalism. Culla is, however, still in flight from the sins that drove him out into the world, and until he acknowledges them he is unworthy of salvation, not because he is "too mean" but because, as Arnold points out, he is too cowardly.

Yet such judges as these, as potentially deadly as they are, pale in comparison with the grim triune whom Culla encounters twice in the novel. The first occasion occurs after Culla has almost been drowned on a ferryboat; in this scene, the rampaging river that swallows up everyone on the ferry but Culla is no bad substitute for the river Styx. It is not then surprising that Culla, after crossing the river of death, encounters the three outlaws. It is in McCarthy's evocation of these three nightmarish figures, who exist on both mimetic and metaphoric levels, that the text's fourthspace is most overtly dramatized. At one point they are described as emerging upon the landscape out of nowhere, "*armed with crude agrarian weapons*, spade and brush-hook . . . parodic figures transposed live and intact and violent out of a proletarian mural *and set mobile upon the empty fields, advancing against the twilight*" (35). They are grotesque parodies of the naturalistic figures created by Thomas Hart Benton in his American murals. Now as re-created by McCarthy, they threaten violent assault on an agrarian economic system that exploits and objectifies the small farmers of Appalachia, and thus their cold murder of the squire constitutes, on one level, retaliation against an exploitative social order. Described as coming across a field "attended by a constant circus of grasshoppers" (51) in the scene in which they murder the squire, they seem personifications of some delayed and apocalyptic judgment, this time recalling the plagues unleashed on Egypt in the Old Testament story of the clash between Moses and the pharaoh.

On another level, they can also be understood as "psychic avengers," projections of Culla's guilt over his sins of incest and child abandonment.[4] In this context, they demonstrate the degree to which the fourthspace of *Outer Dark*, in contrast to Soja's concept of a liberating thirdspace resulting from a merger of material space and cerebral recognition of the material, is frightening and restrictive. When Culla stumbles upon their camp, they, like several of the other "judges" in the text, appear to know about his past and recent experiences. Their unnamed leader, for instance, insists three times that Culla is the now drowned ferryman, thereby forcing the young man to deny three times that he is metaphorically the ferryman to hell.[5] While Culla may not correspond to Charon, he did set the progress of his secular damnation in motion through his sinful actions involving the lost child and thus transports himself into an earthly hell. Culla, feeling that he is in the presence of some not-quite-human force, tries to look into the eyes of the leader with unsettling results: "In the upslant of light [the leader's] beard shone and his mouth was red, and his eyes were shadowed lunettes with nothing there at all" (171).

In a preview of the novel's denouement, the satanic presence then insists that Culla partake of some almost inedible and never identified meat that the trio is cooking. Subsequently an ominous discussion of names ensues. Indicating one of the other two men, the leader and spokesman of the deadly trio says: "That'n ain't got a name. . . . He wanted me to give him one but I wouldn't do it. He don't need nary. You ever seen a man with no name afore?" (174).[6] The leader is identifying himself as the namegiver who possesses the power to withhold or bestow identity upon others and has thus assumed Culla's role as an Adam figure. He then proceeds to tease Culla with the mystery of his own name: "I expect they's lots would like to know that" (173–74). In part, the leader is playing a role derived from such popular-culture genres as the Western of the unnamed and thus doubly terrifying villain. More significantly, he is identifying himself with some force too powerful to be named, an Old Testament god of vengeance.[7]

With Culla and his transgressions clearly in mind, the leader next observes that "some things is best not named." Because it so threatens the social order, incest has traditionally been a sin too fundamentally unsettling to be acknowledged. The reference to things best left unnamed seems intended as a reminder to Culla of the infant he has abandoned and thereby caused to be abducted by the peddler. In this context, he later mocks Culla in a speech that appears to refer to his nameless companion but actually seems intended to evoke the child: "I wouldn't name him because if you cain't name somethin you cain't claim it. You cain't talk about it even. You cain't say what it is" (177). The words are apparently a reminder to Culla that he has forfeited any right to the child, and they also reveal an awareness that the young man's concern for the lost infant is pretended. Certainly in contrast to Rinthy's, Culla's search is, at best, halfhearted. Reinforcing his satanic role, the leader comments, "I like to keep the fire up. . . . They might be somebody coming" (175). He is thus identifying himself as the guardian of the fires of hell, as the enforcer of eternal punishment, perpetually on the lookout for sinners like Culla.

The multileveled nature of the trio's identity becomes manifest in this scene. On a strictly mimetic level, they are a savage gang of roving outlaws who assault the community out of sheer malevolence. But the several metaphoric levels on which they exist are more important. They are simultaneously "proletarian" warriors and agents of a vengeful god. In this context, it is significant that they execute the peddler after taking the infant from him. Their chosen mode of execution is lynching, an act that evokes the history of southern violence and injustice as well as the fate that Culla almost experiences at the hands of the charlatan minister and the simple-minded drovers. Moreover, they are projections of Culla's subconscious guilt, representatives of his sin and self-condemnation, a self-judgment that, as Arnold observes, he is too cowardly to acknowledge publicly. But they also embody a capacity for excessive evil that places them outside human comprehension. It is as if they are committed to violating all behavioral taboos, as if they are engaged in a prolonged assault on the order that is essential to preserving human community. Besides the several horrendous murders of which they are guilty, they unearth the dead, stealing the clothes of corpses and leaving them in positions that mock homosexual embrace. Girard points out that social taboos emerge out of a need to maintain order and that the ultimate threat to such order is death. Through their grave-robbing, the grim triune make this threat overt. It is hardly irrelevant that Culla is accused of the violation of the corpses, since in the course of the novel he is accused of virtually everything else. He has, in fact, violated those taboos that the three outlaws, existing outside any communal structure that includes women, have no opportunity to violate.

The full metaphoric role of the trio is not revealed until their last, climactic encounter with Culla. When he comes upon them this time, the child, now hideously disfigured, is with them: "It had a healed burn all down one side of it and the skin was papery and wrinkled like an old man's. It was naked and half coated with dust so that it seemed lightly furred and when it turned to look up at him [Culla] . . . saw one eyeless and angry red socket like a stokehole to a brain in flames" (231).

Perhaps not fully human themselves, the three have dehumanized the child, transforming it into something monstrous. Moreover, the leader continues the harsh questioning of Culla that he began in the earlier scene, again seeming possessed of some kind of supernatural insight. He knows, for instance, that the tinker stole a child from Culla and asserts that the child was Culla's as the result of an incestuous act. Twice, in what Arnold sees as the young man's culminating moment of cowardice, Culla denies the accusation and any responsibility for the child: "He ain't nothin to me" (235).

Subsequently, in an action that echoes Girard's description of the ritual sacrifice of the scapegoat in *Violence and the Sacred*, the leader holds the mutilated child over a burning fire and slits its throat with a knife. In committing incest, Culla violated one of the most basic of cultural taboos and thus instigated a sacrificial crisis that profoundly threatens the social order. As Girard explains, the sacrifice of an innocent is necessary to restore the order that Culla's acts of incest and child abandonment have endangered. Girard further specifies that, in order to prevent a destructive cycle of retributive violence, the victim should be powerless, with no ties to the individual whose violations of taboo have brought on the crisis. Above all, such cyclical violence is to be avoided:

> Vengeance professes to be an act of reprisal, and every reprisal calls for another reprisal. The crime to which the vengeance addresses itself is never an unprecedented offense; in almost every case it has been committed in revenge for some prior crime. Vengeance, then, is an interminable, infinitely repetitive process. Every time it turns up in some part of the community, it threatens to involve the whole social body. There is the risk that the act of vengeance will initiate a chain reaction whose consequences will quickly prove fatal to any society of modest size. The multiplication of reprisals instantaneously puts the very existence of society in jeopardy, and that is why it is universally proscribed. (14–15)

The leader's sacrifice of the unnamed child both clarifies and complicates the role of the grim triune as agents of retribution. Obviously, the infant, the very product of Culla's sin, is not an arbitrarily chosen victim with no connection to the original violation of taboo. It could, though, hardly be more powerless, since it has been abandoned and remains nameless. The leader slits its throat only after Culla again denies responsibility for it. In the several brutal murders they commit, the triune seem to be agents of retributive vengeance, punishers of unnamed crimes, devoted above all to putting the communal order at risk. An example of McCarthy's calculated narrative excess is evident in the remainder of this grim scene: "The child made no sound. It hung there with its one eye glazing over like a wet stone and the black blood pumping down its naked belly. The mute one knelt forward. He was drooling and making little whimpering noises in his throat. He knelt with his hands outstretched and his nostrils rimpled delicately. [The leader] handed him the child and he seized it up, looked once at Holme with witness eyes, and buried his moaning face in its throat" (236).

The mute one is the one from whom the leader has withheld a name, just as Culla has left his own child nameless. Now as punishment he is forced to witness its bloody sacrifice. The child, however monstrous it has become in the hands of the three, remains an innocent, and the mute's act of drinking its blood is a parody of Christian communion. Any doubt the reader might have that the strange meat which Culla was forced to eat in his earlier encounter with the trio was human flesh is now removed. Unwilling to confront his guilt, he has nevertheless been forced to partake of "the body" and, fully unrepentant, he can hardly chew it. All of this is not, of course, an endorsement of cannibalism. It represents McCarthy's vision that human beings are god, and god is human beings. The excess in this scene seems intended as testimony that any human action one can imagine, however diabolical, has almost certainly been already committed. In this context, it is perhaps worthwhile to see McCarthy as a post-Holocaust writer, since the Nazis exceeded any previously known boundaries of evil and thus threatened to make the word itself meaningless. Nevertheless, as the largely benevolent experiences of Rinthy, who is searching for her lost child and trying to negate Culla's sin, indicate, god's grace has not vanished from the world.

In one scene, the denuded and grotesquely arranged corpses that the triune has unearthed are brought into a town on the back of a wagon. Seeing them, an unidentified man says to Culla: "I hate known they is such people, don't you?" (88). One assumes that he does not mean the grotesquely displayed corpses but rather people who could do such things to the dead. One aspect of McCarthy's aesthetic is a determination to force upon the reader the awareness that, in fact, such people exist in the world. But in the context of the novel's fourthspace, actions like the triune's murders take on added dimensions. In part, they personify Culla's willingness to commit incest, abandon his child, and then repeatedly deny that the child is his, as well as embodying Culla's self-condemnation for such actions. Excess in style and details of plot are essential parts of the linguistic dimension of the text's fourthspace. They contribute to its merger of a grotesquely detailed mimesis, its metaphoric and sociological implications, and its surrealistic feeling as a projection of Culla's subconscious. The space Culla enters is more complex and thus ultimately more inescapable than the forest into which Goodman Brown ventures. Because they exist completely outside the community (unless they are in fact projections of communal sin and guilt), the grim triune is only privileged to move freely in an extended smooth space.

Child of God is a more clearly mimetic novel. Its geographical setting is identified as mid-twentieth-century Sevier County, Tennessee, and its fourthspace is thus less complex and—somewhat paradoxically, given the content of the novel—less intimidating. Culla and the grim triune of *Outer Dark* coalesce in the figure of Lester Ballard, who, hideous though his actions are, remains recognizably human throughout the novel. Thus one dimension of the fourthspace of *Outer Dark* is inevitably absent: Lester as recognizable human being cannot be a projection of Lester's own subconscious guilt. Psychology, especially abnormal psychology, is a concern of *Child of God*, though in a subtle manner. As several critics point out, the narration rarely intrudes on Lester's consciousness; he is seen almost exclusively from a narrative distance, from outside. It is then difficult to know what, if any, degree of guilt Lester feels as a result of his horrific actions. A severely curtailed psychological dimension is part of the fourthspace of the novel. Mimetic and metaphoric dimensions are extensively developed in the novel.

Evenson sees Lester Ballard as being "a nearly unadulterated nomad" (43). This definition is appropriate, but it is important not to overlook the factors that underlie the qualification. Evenson correctly observes that throughout most of the novel, "Ballard lives absolutely on the fringe, his dependence on society reduced to a minimum. Like the movie *Badlands*, *Child of God* portrays directionless violence, an amorality which refuses to apologize for itself, which denies judgment" (44). Lester is forced onto "the fringe" by the suicide of his father and the resulting auction of his home and the false charge of rape; he makes attempts, however halfhearted and doomed they may be, to rejoin the community before his final descent into mad and senseless violence; and at the end he voluntarily submits himself to society's judgment. Edwin Arnold points out that "what Lester wants is permanence, even (or especially) the permanence of death, but what he experiences in his life is change in the form of desertion and denial and loss. He expects to be abandoned" (56).

Lester is forced to retreat to society's fringe after the auction because he has literally nowhere else to go; after existing in virtual isolation since his father's suicide, he no longer knows, if he ever did, how to function in human society. He is then almost fated to occupy the kind of smooth space Evenson describes. Imprisoned because of the false charge of rape, Lester meets a black prisoner whose past and future foreshadow Lester's own. The African American's crime, in its sheer excess of brutality, previews the extremes of perversion that Lester will soon explore: he has beheaded a man with a pocketknife. Moreover, he feels no remorse for what he did ("all the trouble I ever was in was caused by gettin caught" [53]), and his self-definition is appropriate for Lester as well: "I'm a fugitive from the ways of the world. I'd be a fugitive from my mind if I had me some snow" (53). Still a kind of innocent at this point, Lester doesn't know anything about "snow" or any other narcotics. But he will soon become a fugitive from his own mind; he will evolve into the very prototype of excess that constitutes the binary opposite of reason in Bataille's paradigm. McCarthy sometimes employs a kind of after-the-fact communal narration to describe Lester, and one early such passage describes a propensity for sudden and frightening acts of violence.

Still, before committing acts that make his exile from the human community complete and irrevocable, Lester makes failed attempts to rejoin at least its outer limits. In fact, he once makes an overture for something approaching mainstream acceptance by abruptly entering a country church, but his presence merely serves to shock the preacher and the congregation, which he inadvertently further outrages: "Ballard had a cold and snuffled loudly through the service but nobody expected he would stop if God himself looked askance so no one looked" (32). Lester is condemned partly because of his family's history of poverty and lawlessness, and in this context he ironically attains a kind of stature in the community by entering its folklore. He is defined as being the most sinful member of two sinful families, the Ballards and the human race; the communal voice concludes a summary of the Ballard family with this: "I'll say one thing about Lester though. You can trace em back to Adam if you want and goddamn if he didn't outstrip them all" (81). This pronouncement is crucial to the judgment the text is making concerning the human capacity for evil—as shocked and disgusted as they are by his actions, the community feels a degree of genuine pride in having produced the sinner of sinners. In Hawthorne's dark forest, Satan tells Young Goodman Brown that "evil is the nature of mankind" and then welcomes the once innocent Puritan to the witches' sabbath, the "communion of your race." The community's pride in Lester's violent assault on the communal order indicates at least that evil is a strong part of human nature.

Not surprisingly, Lester is rejected by women throughout the novel. He attempts a grotesque courtship with a young woman who has a mentally retarded child. Having captured a live robin, he brings it to the child as a present, telling the woman that he has something for her, to which she replies: "You ain't got nothin I want" (77). When the child chews the legs off the living bird, Lester offers an explanation for the disgusting act: "He wanted it to where it couldn't run off" (79). McCarthy may well be venturing too obviously into the territory of William Faulkner and Flannery O'Connor in this scene, yet the episode of the young woman, the ghoulish child, and the robin is relevant to the rest of the text. Beginning with his father's suicide, people have been running away from Lester for some time. Moreover, the rejection by the young woman, as understandable as it is, effectively summarizes the communal response to Lester, who truly has nothing that anyone wants.

Comparable in its evocation of the deliberately repulsive is McCarthy's description of a deranged "dumpkeeper" and his family of nine daughters, each of which is "named out of an old medical dictionary gleaned from the rubbish he picked": "These gangling progeny with black hair hanging from their armpits now sat idle and wide-eyed day after day in chairs and crates about the little yard cleared out of the tips while their harried dam called them one by one to help with chores and one by one they shrugged or blinked with sluggard lids. Urethra, Cerebella, Hernia Sue" (26). Almost inevitably, the dumpkeeper discovers one of the daughters having sex in the woods and, after chasing the unknown young man away, tries to force himself on her. While such Erskine Caldwell-like misogyny and stereotyping of "poor white trash" is objectionable, the scene is thematically relevant to McCarthy's narrative strategy. *Child of God* is devoted to exploring the boundary between the human and the animal, the spiritual and the material, the rational and the excessive. McCarthy is deliberately assaulting the reader; his aesthetic is inherently transgressive in nature. Moreover, the "community" of the dumpkeeper's family, which exists outside any moral or ethical values, is the only one in which Lester is truly welcome; the family represents a transitional stage in Lester's descent into a horrific and multileveled smooth space.

The misogynistic overtones of the textual moments involving the woman, her monstrous child, and the robin and the dumpkeeper and his daughters pale in comparison to what is still to come. From an exile with some yearning still to be a part of the social order, Lester degenerates into a ghoulish figure so consumed by madness as to be scarcely recognizable as human. He becomes a murderer of women who collects the corpses of his victims in order to have sex with them. Moreover, he begins to dress in the clothing of the dead women and wears a literal fright wig "fashioned whole" from the scalp of one of his victims.

Nevertheless, as Edwin Arnold, John Lang, and Dianne C. Luce have argued, McCarthy goes to considerable lengths to prevent readers from misunderstanding Lester as an inhuman monster. Arnold points out that the first third of McCarthy's text is devoted to the stages of Lester's exile from society, and Lang analyzes the ways in which the condemning communal voice ironically creates compassion for Lester. Lang further comments that "ultimately, *Child of God* testifies not to the anomalous outrages committed by Lester Ballard but to the potential of violence inherent in all human beings. Lester's actions are often shocking, but they are not, unfortunately, unique" (94). In describing Lester before he begins his murderous rampage, Luce offers the most perceptive analysis of the role of sexuality in the novel: "Ballard's predicament is dramatized in terms of his human needs not only for a home and shelter but also for sexual contact. Considered peculiar, he finds it nearly impossible to approach the women he knows. They rebuff him not because they are chaste, nor because they are less crude than he, but because he is in some way marked as a pariah. As his parents and the law have dispossessed him of what he considers his by right, so the women he approaches deny him both sexual outlet and intimacy" (125). Of course, dead women cannot reject Lester; nor can they resist whatever he does to them. As Evenson points out, Lester "does not ask, as most of us would, what is the proper thing that should be done with a dead body, but rather what can be done with a dead body. For Ballard, a woman's dead body is a smooth space, open to myriad possibilities" (44).

None of this, of course, really resolves the issue of the novel's misogyny. In *Child of God*, McCarthy is intent upon exploring the extremes to which male appropriation and objectification of the female can be taken. If there is a more profound way to objectify a woman (or, for that matter, anyone) than killing her, it would be by sexually desecrating her corpse. It is important to remember that *Child of God* is an exercise in excess, in the outer limits of violation of the body and the spirit, and that it is set in a rural southern culture in which women have traditionally been objectified. Evenson is correct in seeing the dead bodies of women as representing a cumulative smooth space for Lester, but they are only one such space for McCarthy's "part-time ghoul" (174). The ultimate smooth space for Lester is madness, an insane discarding of any restrictions on or limitations to his murderous needs. Perhaps the defining aspect of his kind of madness is its seeming unawareness of all boundaries, not only those separating him from other people and even from nature itself but also those that separate the living from the dead. In his madness, McCarthy's protagonist is free to explore fully Bataille's dimension of excess, of the total renunciation of reason and order. His dressing in the clothes of his female victims and even constructing a wig out of the scalp of one of them can be understood in the context of a smooth space originating in his insane need to appropriate the bodies of his victims even more completely than by sexually violating them. Lester, in fact, wants to merge his body with theirs until what is left is a pure physicality from which all boundaries have been removed.

It is in this context that McCarthy's title is intended to be provocative, potentially even offensive, but ultimately inclusive of all forms of human behavior. In *Madness and Civilization: A History of Insanity in the Age of Reason*, Michel Foucault valorizes the madness that underlies some of the most memorable products of Western art:

For Sade as for Goya, unreason continues to watch by night; but
in this vigil it joins with fresh powers. The non-being it once was
now becomes the power to annihilate. Through Sade and Goya,
the Western world received the possibility of transcending its
reason in violence, and of recovering tragic experience beyond
the promises of dialectic. After Sade and Goya, and since them,
unreason has belonged to whatever is decisive, for the modern
world, in any work of art; that is, whatever any work of art
contains that is both murderous and constraining. (136)

Foucault believes that an essential element of the aesthetic power of the art
of unreason comes from the fact that society attempts to deny and repress
the vision that sustains it. McCarthy can certainly be placed in this tradition;
his work is rooted in a dimension of murderous unreason that is nevertheless
undeniably human. In the fourthspace of *Child of God*, this dimension
becomes increasingly dominant as the text progresses, often submerging the
mimetic to such an extent that Appalachia as a place is almost forgotten.
Truly, Lester and all he represents might emerge anywhere. Lester exists
initially on the boundary between reason and unreason, but for a time he
finds his own kind of liberation in crossing over into madness.

Lang writes that "Lester's crimes would not place him beyond a human
continuum on which we find John Wayne Gacy, Ted Bundy, and Jeffrey
Dahmer" (93), and indeed an underlying concern of McCarthy's aesthetic
is to show that human beings are capable of any act that one can imagine,
however violent it may be. Thus McCarthy is careful not to make Lester seem
as abstract and metaphoric as he does the grim triune of *Outer Dark*, even
though Lester's crimes differ from theirs only in being more clearly rooted in
sexuality. Bell emphasizes the complex implications inherent in McCarthy's
insistence that such crimes do not place Lester beyond the possibility of
grace and redemption: "This is at once strange and not strange, for if Lester
is in a state of grace—if such grace were in fact possible—this seems to be
precisely and incomprehensibly what true grace would be like" (68).

In part, grace is possible for Lester because, despite the horrific nature
of his crimes, he exists as a naturalistic victim and a sacrificial scapegoat.
From the beginning of the novel, when his life is auctioned away and he
is knocked unconscious, Lester is depicted as being controlled by external
forces, some of them systemic and others fundamental and permanent. As
one of Evenson's nomads, however reluctantly he joins their ranks, Lester
necessarily exists outside the protection of the social order. In this context,
it is not surprising that the loyal sheriff, significantly named Fate, declares
himself Lester's merciless judge early in the novel. It is as if Fate knows
that his antagonist will inevitably assault the social order he is charged

with protecting, prophesying early in the novel that Lester will become a murderer. Moreover, like Culla and Rinthy Holme, Lester is also the victim of long-standing economic oppression and profound cultural ignorance.

At one point, McCarthy even goes to elaborate lengths during which he initially appears to shift the narrative perspective away from Lester to establish a historical context for his protagonist. A flood threatens to submerge the town and in fact most of Sevier County, after which Sheriff Fate joins some communal volunteers in rescue boats.[8] They begin to reminisce about local history and especially rival vigilante groups known as the White Caps and the Bluebills, both prototypes of the Ku Klux Klan. About the White Caps, one old man says: "They was a bunch of lowlife thieves and cowards and murderers. The only thing they ever done was to whip women and rob old people. And murder people in their beds at night" (165).[9] This discussion soon evokes memories of a legendary sheriff named Tom Davis who managed to subdue the White Caps. Paradoxically, but in the world of Cormac McCarthy inevitably, Davis eradicated violence only to celebrate it. The old man remembers a communal lynching of two White Caps that took on all the aspects of a carnival: "People had started in to town the evenin before. Slept in their wagons, a lot of em. Rolled out blankets on the courthouse lawn. . . . Women sellin sandwiches in the street. . . . [Davis] brung em from the jail, had two preachers with em and had their wives on their arms and all. Just like they was goin to church. All of em got up there on the scaffold and they sung and everybody fell in singin with em" (167). One remembers that the auction of Lester's farm also turned into a carnival. In Sevier County, violence has always been as close as the courthouse lawn, and the boundary between reason and the excess of unreason has always been an illusion. Thus Lester is merely the historic culmination of the communal legacy of violence. He is the naturalistic victim of historic, as well as economic, forces.

But Lester's victimization goes even deeper. Nature itself seems to have willed his destruction, a fact that Lester vaguely comprehends. Early in the novel he sees a pack of hunting dogs catch and destroy a wild boar and is fascinated by the bloody, choreographed violence unfolding before him: "Ballard watched this ballet tilt and swirl and churn mud up through the snow and watched the lovely blood welter there in its holograph of battle, spray burst from a ruptured lung, the dark heart's blood, pinwheel and pirouette, until shots rang and all was done" (69). Lester will become both boar and hound, the hunted and the merciless hunter fascinated with "the dark heart's blood" of his female victims. What is most significant here is that the hunters (the godlike producers of the ballet) remain out of sight, as such controlling powers must in literary naturalism.

The text directly challenges the reader on the second page, describing Lester as "a child of God much like yourself perhaps" (4). McCarthy's narrative strategy here is clear: the reader, at this point not really knowing Lester and certainly not having encountered him as murderer and necrophiliac, is not likely to resist such identification. *Child of God* demands that McCarthy's implied reader, at the novel's end, still accepts Lester as a human being different from other human beings only in the extremity of an isolation brought on by his descent into the realm of madness, by his insistence upon the discovery of the ultimate smooth space, by his assault on the boundaries between his own need for gratification and the bodies of others.

The early reference to Lester as "a child of god much like yourself perhaps" is superseded in the novel by a later and more confrontational passage, which is interestingly one of the few places in *Child of God* where McCarthy indulges in the kind of stylistic excess that characterizes *Outer Dark*. In it, Lester attempts to cross a flooded river by riding a crate filled with an "odd miscellany" consisting of "men's and ladies' clothes, [and] the three enormous stuffed toys" (155). When the crate is swept out from under him, he is near drowning until he is able to grab a log that has come close to smashing into him. The external narrative perspective then isolates him in the midst of the raging river: "Ballard was lost in a pandemonium of noises, the rifle aloft in one arm now like some demented hero or bedraggled parody of a patriotic poster come aswamp" (156).[10] Having isolated Lester in a cinematic manner,[11] the text now adopts a dialogical mode from which to issue its strongest challenge for the reader to view Lester as a "child of god": "He could not swim, but how would you drown him? His wrath seemed to buoy him up. Some halt in the way of things seems to work here. See him. You could say that he's sustained by his fellow men like you. Has peopled the shore with them calling to him. A race that gives suck to the maimed and the crazed, that wants their wrong blood in its history and will have it. . . . How is he then borne up? Or rather, why will not these waters take him?" (156). "Fellow men like you" belong to a human race that gives birth "to the maimed and the crazed"; the legacy of such beings is both monstrous and definitively human. Through this dialogical approach, McCarthy is insisting that the reader acknowledge a shared humanness with "the maimed and the crazed."

Whether or not the reader is willing to drown Lester, the human community of the text understandably demands that his prolonged assault of taboos central to the social order must be stopped. It also needs to sacrifice him as an embodiment of sacred violence gone mad; in the words of Ciuba: "Ballard eliminates the difference between the pious regard for sacred violence and the desire to arrogate such heavenly fury for his own power. . . . Like some violent voluptuary in the religion of Georges Bataille, he makes transgression the very sign of his transcendence. . . . The savage Lester is godlike precisely because he seems most ungodly" (78). Lester's rampage is the result of the sacrificial crisis evoked by the legacy of the White Caps and other such agents of Appalachian violence, and he must be stopped in order to avoid another cycle of reciprocal violence.

Having abandoned himself completely to smooth space, Lester has issued the most fundamental of challenges to the striated space of the community. His madness, which removes all boundaries from his insatiable demands, simultaneously liberates him and sets in motion his inevitable destruction. Lester becomes so much a part of the open space outside the community that he can almost merge himself with the landscape at will. Still, his narrow escape brings home to him the communal hatred, and this epiphany dismays him. He has a chance unspoken encounter with a young boy on a school bus that evokes a recognition in Lester of the sheer madness of his actions and of a time when he was not the communal outcast that he has become. It is as if he confronts suddenly the image of his own human innocence, of the same need for belonging that inspired his visit to the carnival. Now his smooth space has been compromised, and his insane assault on taboos and boundaries must end.

He thus presents himself at the county hospital, telling a startled night nurse that he belongs there. Ironically, he is never indicted for his crimes but is sent instead to the state hospital at Knoxville, where he is "placed in a cage next door but one to a demented gentleman who used to open folk's skulls and eat the brains inside with a spoon" (193).[12] It is as if the community's frenzied need for a scapegoat has simply played itself out, as if the moment for retributive sacrifice has passed. Finally, in 1965, Lester dies of pneumonia, after which his body is shipped to the medical school at Memphis, where an autopsy inevitably yields no insights into his behavior.

Child of God is a less complex novel than *Outer Dark*, eschewing the stylistic excess that characterizes the earlier novel, substituting for it excess of violent incidents. By denying himself narrative access to Lester's consciousness, McCarthy forces the reader to impose his or her own understanding of abnormal psychology on the text. Unlike the grim triune of *Outer Dark*, Lester Ballard cannot be understood on a purely mythic level. During the rescue trip in the boat, a sheriff's deputy asks the old man, who assumes something close to an authorial voice in the scene, if people were "meaner" during the days of the White Caps than they are at present. The old man's answer is crucial to an understanding of *Child of God* as well as *Outer Dark*: "No. . . . I don't. I think people are the same from the day God first made one" (168). Incest, child abandonment, murder, and necrophilia have been human actions since the beginning. Thus, society is always faced with the potential of a sacramental crisis. Still, in McCarthy's world, human beings are children of god and thus never completely beyond the possibility of salvation unless, like Culla Holme, they flee from it through cowardice or, like Lester Ballard, descend so deeply into madness that they exile themselves from redemption. And even then, Lester can experience a sudden awareness of his humanness that will bring him back into the arms of the community. Only the grim triune of *Outer Dark*, who exist in a largely metaphorical dimension and are thus not truly human at all, are beyond redemption.

NOTES

1. For a good summary of the biblical sources of McCarthy's title see Arnold 46.

2. One especially memorable such scene occurs when the "innocent" Gene Harrogate, violator of melons and planner of inept criminal schemes, passes beneath the window of a "viperous" evangelist who calls down a curse upon him (*Suttree* 106).

3. Arnold relates the circular structure of *Outer Dark* to Culla's doomed flight from judgment: "His sin still unspoken, his guilt yet unnamed . . . Culla, wandering in his state of nothingness, seems fated to return again and again to the site of his sin" (54).

4. I am borrowing this term from Richard Wertime's discussion of the symbolic significance of the street gang that serves as the central unifying structure in Hubert Selby Jr.'s *Last Exit to Brooklyn*.

5. The most important application of the number three is obviously to the three outlaws, the "grim triune," and they are indeed a dark parody of the Trinity, bringing violence and death instead of hope and salvation. Culla's thrice-repeated denial that he is Charon may well be intended to echo Peter's denial of Christ.

6. Especially in view of McCarthy's later revisionist novels about the American West, it is possible that "the man with no name" is a veiled reference to the protagonist played by Clint Eastwood in the 1964 Sergio Leone "spaghetti Western," *A Fistful of Dollars*. The Eastwood character also appears out of nowhere with a mission to punish evil. Since Eastwood, though of unknown origins, is a heroic figure in the film, such an allusion would be in keeping with the parodic subtext of McCarthy's novel.

7. William C. Spencer applies an allegorical reading to the three outlaws. Picking up on the Old Testament feel of the novel, he argues that "the three marauders of *Outer Dark* comprise a triple allegory of evil, with the bearded leader symbolizing lawless authority and destruction, Harmon [the only one of the three named in the novel] representing violence, and the idiot corresponding to ignorance" (76). He adds that "like the God of the Old Testament, the bearded one of the three is an authoritarian. He gives all the orders; he clearly is in charge at all times. Furthermore, like the Father of the Holy Trinity, he acts as judge and as a dispenser of 'justice'" (74).

8. The text makes overt the biblical overtones of this scene through dialogue that recalls early floods and fires that have threatened the community.

9. By the exclusion of African Americans from this list of victims, one is again reminded of Jarrett's discussion of the strong differences between McCarthy's Appalachia and the race-dominated and history-plagued South of Faulkner and other writers.

10. The scene inevitably recalls the aborted river crossing in Faulkner's *As I Lay Dying*. Again, Bloom's ideas about the ephebe's need to "appropriate the precursor's landscape for himself [sic]" (105) through creative "(mis)reading" are relevant to any discussion of the relationship between the fiction of Faulkner and McCarthy.

11. In a perceptive discussion of the shifting levels of narrative perspective in *Child of God*, Bartlett discusses the cinematic aspects of the text, pointing out that Lester is sometimes viewed as in a cinematic "freeze frame."

12. The kind of difficulty that confronts a writer like McCarthy, for whom shock effect is a central element in his chosen aesthetic, can be seen in the fact that a realistically staged act comparable to those performed by the "demented gentleman" can be seen in the most recent Hannibal Lecter film, *Hannibal*. Even though the movie was made almost three decades after McCarthy wrote his novel, one could argue that his appropriation of cinematic narrative techniques constitutes McCarthy's recognition of film's advantage over fiction in evoking purely visceral reactions. It has, after all, been a long time since Buñuel imaged the slicing open of an eyeball.

JAY ELLIS

Fetish and Collapse in
No Country for Old Men

The fathers shall not be put to death for the children, neither shall the children be put to death for the fathers: every man shall be put to death for his own sin.

(Deuteronomy 24:16)

The other thing is that I have not said much about my father and I know I have not done him justice.

(Sheriff Bell; *NCFOM* 308)

COLLAPSE

We may see many more novels yet from Cormac McCarthy. But on first reading *No Country for Old Men*, it is hard to believe so. Everything in this novel seems to have collapsed, or seems headed that way. The book's structure seems to collapse, starting with a bang into what seems to be one genre that only slides down into another. The villain, an avatar of Judge Holden, even kills people by collapsing their frontal lobe with a cattle gun, which at first seems simply to dispatch them through the same damage as a bullet, except that the closeness of the killer—"He placed his hand on the man's head like a faith healer" (*NCFOM* 7)—might make us look for more than madness in this method.

From *No Place for Home: Spatial Constraint and Character Flight in the Novels of Cormac McCarthy*, pp. 225–261. © 2006 by Taylor & Francis Group.

The apparent protagonist is killed three quarters of the way through the novel. The true protagonist grumbles along in monologues that begin each chapter. For all his West Texas stoicism, these soliloquies begin to run on, well beyond the framing device we thought they were, into an increasingly tangled mix of memories and stoic Western conservative positions on past and present. Sheriff Bell, this true protagonist, is trapped in time. So haunted by the past that he can only see the present as a dark and confusing mourning over the dead, Bell follows his grumbles about how much worse things are with fearful prognostications about how worse will be what days may come. Structurally, his italicized monologues begin to rush in sooner after each dwindling parcel of the apparent story (which hardly resolves). Bell's confessions take longer—and again longer—until the book collapses into one of his dreams.

Given this book's screenplay antecedent, one wonders at the possibilities of shifting light: the bright sunlit desert over Moss, the antelope, and the drug deal gone bad might imperceptibly fade into the darkness of that dream. Thus *No Country for Old Men* gradually reveals itself to have begun as one book, under one reading of its title in a bright light, only to slip away into another book, eventually fulfilling the depth and darkness of the title's reference to a poem by Yeats. It begins as a (relatively) young man's book, and ends in the voice of a middle-aged man who nonetheless seems to be quite old—as old as "Sailing to Byzantium" demands.

I must confess that in one reading, this novel simply seemed a failure, a tossed-off screenplay barely redacted into a novel in a genre that does not hold much interest for me. It seemed even to fail at that, as if the author's heart was not secure in the pot he might have meant to boil. *No Country for Old Men* starts hot, but then cools, and finally mists over. I ought to know better, and yet the novel's apparent conservatism seemed so insistent that against all better judgment I began to suspect (as many reviewers have) that this indeed indicated the frightened political views of an author now twenty years older than Bell and yet speaking through him. The structure collapsed so obviously as to raise the question of waning aesthetic powers; why not (the critic in hubris wonders) a waning political sensibility as well? (As if to disagree with a few readers is to have lost marbles.)

But then I reread it.

In short, everything about this book seems one way, but then does not—thus my repetition of "seems" fits a first impression. On subsequent readings, it becomes clearer that all these apparent collapses derive from the reality that this story is told with an awareness that many things have already collapsed in the previous novels. The title works in its reference to a retreat: after we are meant to begin in one country, with one book, we are meant to end in another space and another book, the true *No Country for Old Men*.

And whatever the author's politics, Bell eventually voices the fearful feelings and positions of many Americans.[1]

For this chapter, I will refer to those aspects that stand out most in the book's beginning, that do not immediately (in a first reading) likely reveal themselves as parodic, and that create those aspects of genre fiction that have led to the labels applied to it as a "crime novel," etc., as the Young Man book. This is Moss's book. The Old Man book, however, is that simultaneous novel, buried early on (at least before rereading) and apparently set up as a generically typical narrative foil for the Young Man book. This is Bell's book, initially only italicized, and it is the book that ultimately sounds deeper resonances with the title, *No Country for Old Men*.

This novel simply does not work as a direct delivery of the Young Man book, nor should it. This is one of those works whose apparent failures create unexpected difficulties which can only resolve in rereading, where the novel then resonates in quiet success. I will attempt to offer a reading that, rather than pretending to have interpreted the book in that second way (the way I read it now), will instead parallel what the novel itself accomplishes: the appearance of one book with merely two voices, until those two views compete, and finally one overtakes the other. This is the only way I can answer several questions that first struck me about *No Country for Old Men*. Why would McCarthy deliver a taut, if thin, crime novel that only collapses into jeremiad? Who, really, is the main character of this novel? And why does this novel's structure so obviously collapse?

Among the reviews of the book so far, those reviewers obviously predisposed toward the strengths of this author (such as Joyce Carol Oates) find in *No Country for Old Men* a winnowed-down version of what they liked, but also what they did not like, in previous McCarthy books. Others simply praise whatever seems likely to satisfy, and disparage what surprises, a reader acquainted only with *The Border Trilogy*. Still others give the book its due but only (as I was tempted to do) by praising the power of its initial genre, writing off apparent weaknesses either as aspects of the genre or failures to fit that genre of fiction in which McCarthy seemed suddenly to be indulging. The quickest description of that genre well fits the limited space of the synopsis for the book among the *New York Times Book Review*'s "100 Notable Books of the Year" for 2005: "Women grieve, men fight in this hard-boiled Texas noir crime novel" (33).

This genre label underestimates *No Country for Old Men* because it proves accurate only for the reader's first acquaintance with the book. The ease, however, with which we might agree with that label reminds me of Glanton underestimating Caballo en Pello. Whether the book proves to be that powerful or not will depend on whether continued rereading rewards the reader. This is not *Blood Meridian* in its initial effects. But it is not supposed to be. Neither is it ultimately a "hard-boiled Texas noir crime novel" at all. It merely starts out that way.

It ends up as a coda to *All the Pretty Horses*. And in that way, *No Country for Old Men* not only extends but also begins to resolve the son and father anxiety found in McCarthy, even if doing so means a step backward into a nostalgic evocation of mythic archetype. The image closing the book can only be arrived at, without thoroughgoing sentimentality all along the way, by opening the book in a different genre—a different country, as it were. This movement creates the structural shift I referred to already as a collapse. While *No Country for Old Men* reinforces the loss of space to place that we have already explored, it does so by answering many remaining questions about the father and son tension developed through the previous eight novels.

Granted, McCarthy is known to hold onto manuscripts (as most writers do). *No Country for Old Men* began as a screenplay and may have sat around in a drawer for some time before McCarthy turned it into a novel. But the book's ending can hardly be imagined on film, or at least cannot be imagined in anything approaching the "hard-boiled Texas noir crime" film that McCarthy may have originally envisioned. As it refuses those genre labels, the book collapses under the weight of the son and father anxiety that is only forestalled by the fetishism and violence preoccupying its opening.

Fetish

What makes readers call *No Country for Old Men* a crime novel is not the commitment of any number of crimes, nor the violence in its depiction of those crimes. Nor has this label stuck to the book because of its comparatively terse style, or rather, not for that reason alone. After all, *Blood Meridian* certainly details more crimes. And a terse prose style characterizes much work that we would never think to call "noir" or "hard-boiled" for that reason alone. The salient characteristics of the cheaper forms of the genre fiction with which McCarthy seems to be working have more to do with technological fetish.

This begins with Anton Chigurh's cattle gun. At first, the cattle gun seems merely a small hook for the screenplay that preceded this material's present form as a novel. "The pneumatic hiss and click of the plunger sounded like a door closing" (*NCFOM* 7). This attention to sound, and the fact that Chigurh wears this apparatus in a nearly cyborg fashion, recalls Frank Booth in *Blue Velvet*. It feels like a gimmick. Although the cattle gun might provide a manner of killing someone with less noise than a conventional gun, so would a knife. Given the difficulty that law enforcement has in getting across the wide spaces between this book's crime scenes, and given Chigurh's ready use of guns for close-range as well as long-range killing, its purpose is not practical.

Thus, the detail becomes truly important. By killing people with a cattle gun, Chigurh is turning them into livestock, denying their humanity. Moreover, by shooting them in the forehead with it, Chigurh simultaneously deprives them of their living sight while imprinting in them a symbolic third eye—a visual representation of the enlightenment on matters of chance and destiny that he sometimes provides in a brief pre-murder Socratic dialogue. But we must also note that Chigurh's requirement of this tool to accomplish what Holden does with his hands (*BM* 179), points to his mortality (as do his wounds from combat and the car crash).

Chigurh can extend his thin line of philosophical argument regarding free will so as to extend Holden's (and McCarthy's) larger arguments on this. On first reading, these feel like comparatively weaker forms of philosophical additions to a narrative that would otherwise rest more perilously on the voice of Bell. And ultimately, Chigurh's dependence on technology (not only weaponry, but on medicines, for instance, or on a telephone bill to track his victims) increases the distance between him and Holden. Chigurh needs gadgets, technology, to get around; he could never carry his own rock to sit on in the open desert. What seemed a weakness in the novel here, however, proves necessary to the way it works. Chigurh cannot be Holden because we no longer see devils or angels in our time, and Anton Chigurh is a villain of our time, and of the places created by the *Blood Meridian* Epilogue I discussed in Chapter Five. Although he kills everyone he sets out to kill, we last see him limping away, looking relatively mortal: "They watched him set off up the sidewalk, holding the twist of the bandanna against his head, limping slightly" (*NCFOM* 262). He has even had to buy this bandage from one of the boys who caused the wreck. Why doesn't he just shoot these boys and take it?

So they can see him. After all, apart from his secondary function in providing the novel with some philosophical content alternative to Bell's jeremiads and confessions and dream vision, Anton Chigurh's visual possibilities as a striking movie villain fit perfectly his primary role in this novel's opening. He is himself a fetish of a villain, boiled down to a few villainish characteristics. Moss notices only these: "Blue eyes. Serene. Dark hair. Something about him faintly exotic" (*NCFOM* 112). Beyond this politically safe "faintly exotic" and the mix of dark hair but blue eyes, Chigurh lacks any striking physical characteristics for us to remember him by (again, unlike Holden), except for the contrast between relatively sensitive features (blue eyes, a serene countenance) and his lethality. His name even serves first to suggest the geographically indeterminate origins favorable for a post–cold war movie villain, and then second to point us on to his philosophy. In this way, Chigurh is the villain whose character resides only in what he does and says. This, too, is not only characteristic of many film villains, but also of the crime novel genre. By "crime novel" I do not mean to refer to Chandler or Himes or other deft authors, but rather to the interchangeable serial novels that rely on formula and fetish in order to satisfy the desires of young male readers.

Weaponry fetish nearly overcomes the novel's first chapters. Even before the cattle gun, Chigurh satisfies that fetishistic need of crime novels not only to describe killing, but also to describe killing and other crucial activities of the hero and villains through the use of some surprising stratagem or technological apparatus. The characters must do things that the reader might not think of, such as blow the cylinder out of a lock "with the cobalt steel plunger of the cattlegun" (*NCFOM* 80). Note the specificity of the metal: "cobalt." To pre-adolescent (and increasingly, adolescent and older) male readers still uncertain about their vulnerability and power in the world, their sexuality and its possibilities, and (compared with women at the same age, on average) their intelligence, the minutiae surrounding objects that seem to afford their user power in that world become all-important. The phallic thrust of the cattle gun is so obvious as to deserve no further comment.

Anything that can be added on to an already desirable object that will afford greater lethality, greater speed, greater vision, or more information, fills in for what young men fear they lack. True intimacy with a young woman, friendship with someone they can completely trust and confide in fully, respect (or even time—let alone emotional intimacy) with a parent, acknowledgement from teachers—whatever is possible at any age among most of these things cannot be secured until after adolescence. But within the pages of a science fiction novel, or a crime novel, or as members of a car club, etc., young men can find ready substitutes for feelings of innate power, and honest emotional connection.

The details provided in descriptions of the fetish objects in *No Country for Old Men* call on the very generic terminology that the novel ultimately shrugs off. The string of qualifiers in the phrase, "hard-boiled Texas noir crime novel" narrows and specifies whatever aesthetic space might still be granted any "novel." The definitions of "hard-boiled" as a trope are "2. Callous; unfeeling" and "3. Unsentimental and practical; tough." The stereotypes regarding the location, "Texas," are too numerous to go into, but suffice to say this aspect of *No Country for Old Men* will seem to continue in the line of stoic cowboy existentialism that made *All the Pretty Horses* so popular, but which it, and particularly *Cities of the Plain*, also called into question, even to the point of parody.[2] But it will nonetheless allow Moss to go shopping for more fetish items.

Lest we assume that this "crime novel" might work in an optimistic mode where justice prevails and the hero lives, the word "noir" signals the disappointed male idealism that would complete the shield against vulnerability that this genre requires. *No Country for Old Men* so thoroughly exploits the fetishes of its apparent genre that by the third chapter I kept expecting one of the characters to slap around an obviously effeminate gunsel. But this book would not even allow such a vulnerable man on the side of the villains. Any sign of weakness at the surface level of characters marks them for dead. Thus, Moss never even seems to consider the loss of his wife when dealing with Chigurh. And when he knows he must run from the drug dealers—on foot—"he realize[s] that he would never see his truck again. Well, he said. There's lots of things you aint goin to see again" (*NCFOM* 29). Such as his wife, which is not the first thing to occur to him as lost.

Moss's character is first seen burdened not only by gear and descriptions of gear, but by the stereotypical situation in which we find him and the body language he assumes there. To be fair, anyone hunting in that part of the country might want that gear, and sitting on volcanic rock requires—even of someone accustomed to the back country—a slightly careful pose; a volcanic ridge is not, after all, a desk chair and does not feel like one. But the attention paid to all these aspects of the scene keep the reader safely distant from any deep identification of Moss's character:

> Moss sat with the heels of his boots dug into the volcanic gravel of the ridge and glassed the desert below him with a pair of twelve power german binoculars. His hat pushed back on his head. Elbows propped on his knees. The rifle strapped over his shoulder with a harness-leather sling was a heavybarrelled .270 on a '98 Mauser action with a laminated stock of maple and walnut. It carried a Unertl telescopic sight of the same power as the binoculars. (*NCFOM* 8)

Even if we need to think about whether the .270 could hit the antelope at nearly a mile's distance (one supposes in order for readers up on their gun knowledge to infer something about Moss's willingness to take chances that could result in harm to other creatures), why do we care about the material of the stock?

That is not a complaint. Rather, this brief look at a passage that precedes many more fetish descriptions makes it clear to whom the book seems to be aimed: a Young Man enamored of these details.[3] We soon see "a Canjar trigger set to nine ounces" let loose a "150 grain bullet" fall short enough to ricochet "off the pan" to hit one of the antelope in the leg (*NCFOM* 9, 10). So much for all that gear and knowledge. Even the ground has been turned into something one might possess—a "pan"—in its flatness. Nonetheless, in this scene just before Moss's world collapses around him, turning him into the prey, he simply was too far away from these antelope for even the "twelve power german binoculars" and the "Unertl telescopic sight of the same power" to make it clear to him that he was too far away. And that his impressive gun could not shoot far enough.

Here is where, on rereading, the genre fetish gives itself away as self-conscious, and either parodic, or momentarily indulged in to set up the Old Man part of the novel. Having succeeded in seeing the antelope but failing to see the impossible distance between those desired objects and the power of his gear, Llewelyn will soon have to put his knowledge to use in recognizing the gear of others. Note that these items are recognized by Moss in detail, as the narrative remains close to him. (We do not get nearly so many of these details when the narrative follows Chigurh, let alone Bell.) Moss's knowledge of their particularity and appreciation of their value stands in for the dreams and details of deep character provided John Grady, for instance. Those levels of deep character—provided not only in dreams, but also in descriptions of setting and character movement involving John Grady, and even Lester Ballard—in *No Country for Old Men* have dried up into volcanic ridges and hardpan desert. By contrast, the vulnerability of John Grady and Ballard is revealed, while Moss's is concealed by fetish. I cannot find a dream, a gesture, or a pose in an environment from which to infer anything about Moss's character except that he is tough.

Moss's discovery of the rip-off focuses on the men only after, and even then among, their gear. He notices first that their "vehicles were four wheel drive trucks or Broncos with big all-terrain tires and winches and racks of rooflights" (*NCFOM* 11). When, on his return to the rip-off site, the truck pursues him, he hears its "slow lope of the cam. Big block engine" (*NCFOM* 28). Moss, a welder, might note that this truck—as indeed any truck that could clear rocks and other variations in the "pan" of a real desert without losing its oil pan or getting stuck would have to be—has been improved on. It can go farther, and (with that cam) faster from a dead stop, and this matters if it will be chasing you. Yet, it is highly doubtful that even Moss would be thinking about these things when he has every reason instead to be concentrating on, perhaps, the particular guns they might have and how they will use them on him. But realism is not the point here (if it ever is). The point is to add the next group of items to our list of Moss's knowledge of fetish presumably important to the Young Man reader.

The guns will soon regain their importance, of course. Moss has already found "a shortbarrelled H&K machinepistol with a black nylon shoulderstrap" lying in the lap of the dying drug dealer (*NCFOM* 12–13). As in a video game, where the player picks up one after another weapon, weighing the relative accuracy and lethality of each weapon for different situations, Moss's tour of the rip-off site leads him through a small arsenal, including a shotgun modified to delight David Brown, "fitted with a pistol stock and a twenty round drum magazine" (*NCFOM* 12). The "nickel-plated government .45 automatic lying cocked in the grass" that Moss finds "between [the] legs" of the man with the money—now dead—(*NCFOM* 17), reveals the obvious connection between guns as fetish objects and male sexual power. This "cocked" pistol (of a high caliber, we might note) has done the dead man no more good than did the .270 Moss used against the antelope. We might also note that this weapon is "government" issue, and therefore use our knowledge of that to suspect that some arm of law enforcement—whether acting undercover, or illegally—was involved in this drug deal gone wrong. But this proves to be a red herring, as nothing significant along those lines ever turns up in the plot.

Characters in this genre must also do things in a particular way, either in a manner that is immediately recognizable and manneristic, such as in the *Dragnet* dialogue to come, or through some surprising novelty of detail that fills in for the lack of more standard character development. Thus, instead of writing that Moss merely looked through his binoculars, the noun for the fetish object is turned into a powerful (and new) verb: "He glassed the terrain slowly" and finds the scene of the rip-off, and then later "glassed the country to the south" to find the man with the money (*NCFOM* 10–11, 15).[4] Any strong writer knows to find strong verbs. But this one highlights the object used to enhance Moss's vision more than it does what he is looking at. Scopophilic power depends on the differential of seeing and not being seen, as we are reminded when Moss is the one on the run, emasculated in the desert sand, worrying in a suddenly not-so-macho fashion about the very realistic dangers of spiders and snakes he might be inviting up the legs of his jeans (*NCFOM* 30). Furthermore, Moss "glass[ing]" the desert floor seems to possess enough heat along with light to melt the sand that comes into his view, to turn it into glass.

His trick of hiding the money in ventilation shafts similarly provides the particularity that promises to distinguish what would otherwise be a run-of-the-mill scene of, well, hiding the money. We need to believe that the man who seems to be our troubled hero is intelligent and powerful; even when he is outnumbered and outgunned, his sheer toughness (inexplicable as a distinction when guns are involved), his disciplined refusal to become attached to women, let alone anyone else, and his cleverness are all stand-ins for those qualities desired (and therefore felt lacking) by the insecure reader of genre fiction. But the neat verb given to Moss to use with his binoculars does not help him hit his target.

And hiding the money in the ventilation shaft only fools everyone but the one man he hopes to fool, Anton Chigurh. Compare the descriptions of the two men involving ventilation ducts serving Moss as a cache. Moss goes first, having cleverly bought a shotgun (and again, recalling David Brown's visit to the farrier), "a hacksaw and a millfile," tent poles, sidecutters, and that most useful of items for ingenious men: duct tape (*NCFOM* 87).

> He untied the little nylon bag and slid the poles out. They were lightweight aluminum tubes three feet long and he assembled three of them and taped the joints with duct tape so that they wouldnt pull apart. He went to the closet and came back with three wire hangers and sat on the bed and cut the hooks off with the sidecutters and wrapped them into one hook with the tape. Then he taped them to the end of the pole and stood up and slid the pole down the ductwork. (*NCFOM* 101)

All this careful detail only stiffens the symbolism. Moss goes to much trouble first to shove the money down one vent, only to pay for a second motel room that he luckily is correct in assuming contains a vent connecting to the same trunk line of a central air conditioning system.[5] Then he must construct this single "pole" from the tent poles to create yet another extension of himself so that he can reach the money. Not only is all this activity conspicuous, but it is also time-consuming and liable to failure—in a Hitchcockian moment the hook on his pole nearly fails him in reaching the goodies. But at least it can be said that Moss, no sentimental fellow, refuses to be loyal to one air duct.

Here is Chigurh retrieving the bag after Moss has been killed by one of the many gang members looking for him:

> He pulled the little bedside table over to the wall and stood and took a screwdriver from his rear pocket and began to back the screws out of the louvered steel cover of the airduct. He set it on the table and reached in and pulled out the bag and stepped down and walked over to the window and looked out at the parking lot. (*NCFOM* 243)

By comparison, Chigurh retrieves the bag without all the improvised phallic extensions and cleverness of Moss, who in any case seems to have become less consummate in his ductwork insertions by this point.

So, we note both that Moss's knowledge of and care with fetishistic objects always fails him. And we note that he is the only one so deeply caught up in all these details of the crime novel genre. Moss's character is indeed a parody of the hard-boiled hero for a Young Man genre novel. Moss reveals this to a comic degree in two of his later scenes.

In the first, he goes shopping again. Granted, Moss needs clothes, as he is in the quintessential tough-guy position of walking out of a hospital wearing nothing but the backwards gown. Earlier, he has bought clothes at a Wal-Mart, but in this shopping trip, he is preparing for imminent combat and must look the part. Moss has already noted the "expensive pair of Lucchese crocodile boots" worn by Wells (*NCFOM* 154). Now in a clothing store after hours, Moss receives the kind of service that might make Bell rethink his cynicism about the loss of manners. The details here prove that Moss is no dime store cowboy: he buys the least expensive boots and is only particular about his jeans. When the owner asks him if "white socks" suit him, he replies, "White socks is all I wear." In this shopping scene so typical of Hollywood films of the last twenty years, we are forced to wait until Moss gets everything he needs—and we even get his underwear size (*NCFOM* 190–191). The attention to details continues to boil down his character until he seems dangerously malleable in fitting the requirements of genre fetish.

In the second scene, Moss picks up a hitchhiker. The dialogue then finishes out the stereotypes, with lines like "I dont know where you're at because I dont know who you are" (*NCFOM* 225), and the hitchhiker's question, "So are you sorry you become a outlaw?" and Moss's answer: "Sorry I didnt start sooner" (*NCFOM* 228).

The easiest interpretation of all this is that McCarthy simply meant to boil the pot (or rather, in this case to boil his new novel in it to a hard-boiled consistency), and deftly managed these details to create the taught noir hard boiled crime novel that readers seem to be recognizing in *No Country for Old Men*. But if so, why do all these gadgets so miserably fail their users? Usually, when loving detail is lavished on something possessed by the hero of genre fiction, it will save his neck. Here, the details prove meaningless as Moss is failed by his binoculars, his scope, his rifle, his airduct stratagem, and essentially by his clothes and his dialogue. Why?

The first sentence of *No Country for Old Men* reads, "I sent one boy to the gas chamber at Huntsville" (*NCFOM* 3). Many readers noticed that Texas had never executed anyone in a gas chamber. Complaints from enough of those who somehow enjoy McCarthy's work and yet are sticklers for accuracy in the correspondence between novels and life, grew loud enough that McCarthy actually released a statement through his publisher: "I put it in there to see if readers were on their toes" (Garner).

Perhaps. But only if we do not make the foolish assumption that this author—who almost never comments directly on his work—means by "on their toes" that a reader should be attuned to meaningless correspondences between the details of fiction and the details of life. What difference is there, really, between a gas chamber and an electric chair, a needle and a firing squad, except in absurd quibbles over the process chosen by the state putting a man to death? These differences are either analogous to those between a "Canjar" trigger and some other type, or they are differences of symbolic import. By "on their toes," the author of *Blood Meridian* might more likely mean that a reader ought to be alert to the foolishness of falling for literal truths in a book, of falling for the fetish instead of reading for the symbol.

As an intentional "error," the gas chamber reference strengthens the first sentence for a novel that seems to be aimed at a Young Man readership, but that proves to be something else. As with the fetish details that also mislead a first reader, this first sentence makes it clear that in *No Country for Old Men* there can be no simple recognition of just what the book is about. Not with any particularity in one answer. In general, it is about movement, and thus, about space. First Moss, and then Bell, flee the spaces in which we first find them, even as the world-narrowing power of Anton Chigurh threatens to collapse that space into a coffin. When Moss is finally killed at that three-quarter mark, the collapse of the Young Man book forces readers to acknowledge the true protagonist, and to recognize an altogether different genre at work. As Bell's voice takes over, so does the new genre—even as the chapters begin to fall inward and dwindle down. In the meantime, the spaces of *No Country for Old Men* have become differently unstable for both Moss and Bell.

SMUGGLING SPACES

First, *No Country for Old Men* merely echoes the collapse of space already occurring in *Cities of the Plain* and begun with the Epilogue to *Blood Meridian*. Allowing for numerous exceptions, we can see that throughout the novels, the general run allowed characters in flight first extends, and then contracts. With John Wesley and then Cornelius Suttree both leaving the terrain of the Southern novels, we actually find the greatest latitude of movement when *Blood Meridian* takes us back a hundred years earlier. After its meridian, we have seen the journey narratives of *The Border Trilogy* were doomed to collapse into a smaller and smaller space, like a lasso tightening around the necks of those characters. In "The Last of the Trilogy: First Thoughts on *Cities of the Plain*," Edwin Arnold commented on what many readers saw with some surprise in that novel: "adjustment to a diminished existence, illustrated by the growing number of confined spaces found throughout this novel: barn stalls, hotel and bordello rooms, long dark corridors and back alleys, hospitals and morgue labs, all leading to the packing crate in which John Grady, the all-american man of the west, meets his death" (235).

Not only the Epilogue of *Blood Meridian*, but also the kid, meeting his death in the jakes, should have prepared us for this. As David Holloway and others have observed, McCarthy's understanding of the twentieth century includes the story of increasingly unavoidable commodification: not only every activity, and every place, but every person becomes subject to the strictures of economic activity. As I have put it, space becomes places. No, John Grady and Lacey, "they" do not "expect"—or really allow—"a man to ride a horse in this country" any more (*ATPH* 31). Not, at least, across the separately owned parcels of land demarcated by those barbed wire fences these boys have to cut and mend in order to make their way across West Texas.

Space, therefore, has collapsed into smaller places well before *No Country for Old Men* begins. That Llewelyn Moss takes an ill-advised shot at too great a distance and probably fatally wounds an antelope, and that it takes him so long to walk toward it (as if he would get close enough to shoot it again), fools even this native of the area into thinking that out there in the desert, he can pick up what does not belong to him and get away with it.[6] A visit to this area confirms the ease with which Moss might feel he has all the space in the world. Indeed, despite his modern equipment, Moss fails to get close enough to the antelope for a successful shot. But this does not erase the border observed at the Rio Grande River that Moss ends up splashing into and crossing back and forth. As soon as Moss picks up the wrong prize in this frontera space, he is in smuggling country. There, the movement of the man with the contraband, or the money, is constrained more than he might know, while the sense of place of those, such as Bell, who are not directly involved in smuggling feels suddenly unstable. Smuggling spaces confound the usual laws of physics regarding spaces collapsing into place. Moss's hope to disappear nonetheless proves foolish.

As it happens, another disappearing act in the book involves the drugs. We might reasonably expect that a plot retailing the found-drug-money conceit in any novel might have a bit more to do with the drugs. Money has not been a direct concern in McCarthy novels. But smuggling has, in a variety of ways. And given the noir aspect of the book, we might even expect someone to use drugs: at least a secondary picaró similar to a Blevins or Harrogate might get high. But the drugs here only briefly serve the direct purpose of providing evidence (among much other evidence cited by Bell) that civilization is falling apart. Beyond that, they prove merely to be the kind of contraband that we have seen before in McCarthy, even if the black tar heroin Moss finds in the back of the dying man's truck is, compared with previous contraband, an inherently dangerous substance of no legitimate value to Moss.

Nobody does the dope in *No Country for Old Men*, although we do get head-shaking *Dragnet* dialogue about frying brains without a cattle gun. "What am I supposed to do with this?" asks the sheriff of Eagle Pass, referring not to the drugs but to the nifty transponder. Bell's Joe Friday says log it for evidence and then begins the hard-boiled editorial duet taking us back to the drugs:

Dope.
They sell that shit to schoolkids, [the other sheriff] said.
It's worse than that.
How's that?
Schoolkids buy it. (*NCFOM* 194)

For Bell, drugs merely represent a larger post-sixties slide in American moral values. He won't disagree with Moss Senior, who won't blame Vietnam but says, "Vietnam was just the icin on the cake. We didn't have nothin to give to em to take over there." That last explanation recalls the regularity with which these novels surprisingly revolve around exchange goods.[7] The elder Moss goes on, "You cant go to war like that. You cant go to war without God" (*NCFOM* 294–295). Here "God" seems to have been the missing thing to "give em to take" to Vietnam. Drugs are the substitute for God, then, in the fallen world according to Bell. By contrast, the transponder receives more attention in this novel. It tells you the location of a man who thinks he can disappear. It collapses space into place with a beep.

Drugs turn out not to be the point. The heroin here is more symbolic than realistic. In *No Country for Old Men*, the reduction of space includes one constraint doomed to failure: the control of a border and the eradication of smuggling—truly an unfulfillable dream. In the most circumscribed space of Knoxville in *The Orchard Keeper* and *Suttree*—its government buildings and their controlling reach beyond their walls—what is regarded as contraband is that which otherwise might move around uncontrolled on its own, spreading disease or preying on livestock. The government there seeks regulation of movement; where it cannot hope for that, it demands the eradication of what moves.

The government therefore attempts to tax the movement of alcohol, and eradicate raptors and bats. But in the case of the bounties, this reversal of the usual transaction little matters. The results are the same as with all commodified goods, whether organic or synthetic, alive or dead: they transport more easily when reduced to their essence—or at least the essence visible in the market that, because of some disparity or surfeit, offers a bounty for them, dead or alive. This reduction of the commodity becomes easier, though, if what the economy desires is its erasure. To erase wolves or bison, a bounty on just their hides should suffice—though perhaps also their bones, as we see before the kid reaches Fort Griffin in *Blood Meridian*. Bats and birds are small enough to move whole. If it is the erasure of a people that is desired, then for the purposes of transportation those people can be reduced even further, given their size—to nothing but their scalps, as we see in *Blood Meridian*.

Holloway examines the many objects exchanged in McCarthy:

In a fictive realm where scalps, children, buffalo bones, ferry crossings, ornate weaponry, whisky, landscape, and life itself are all merely "things" to be bought and sold according to the laws of the marketplace, the heterogeneous diversity of the object world is reduced to a single identity, a homogenous mass of matter, a collection of things linked together by their common exchange-value, their shared status as commodities in a commodity world. (104–105)

I would argue only that *Blood Meridian* includes some uncommodified terrain, spaces not yet rendered into places. At least not until the book's Epilogue. But it, too, depends on a type of proto-smuggling.

The border fiction renders smuggling in more obvious terms. After the reinscription of any a border's power by *Blood Meridian*'s Epilogue, the illegal transport of commodified objects amounts to literal smuggling, if not to those doing the carrying. Billy Parham believes he is repatriating the she wolf. And John Grady is, in more than just the legal sense, recovering the horses in a reenactment of older border struggles. Mr. Johnson tells of a 1917 raid "to cross some stolen horses we'd recovered" (*COTP* 63). But the phrase "stolen horses" comes before "recovered" in such a way as to remind us that there can be disagreements about horse ownership. To "cross" your own horses amounts to "recover[y]," but to "cross" someone else's amounts to smuggling. In *No Country for Old Men*, we hardly see any border crossing at all. And yet, the fact of smuggling hovers over the destroyed men and trucks found by Moss.

Bell professes some knowledge of the bloody history of the area. "*That country had not had a time of peace much of any length at all that I knew of. I've read a little of the history of it since and I aint sure it ever had one*" (*NCFOM* 307). Nonetheless, that history seems lost on him. Or, as would be more typical not only of someone professing Bell's views, but also of most people professing political views that seem opposite them, he has likely read selectively; he has read only one side of a many-sided subject. In his arguments notably all of which are appeals to emotion written by an author who, in Holden's case, has proven himself quite capable of working the corners of ethos and logos as well—Bell refers only to the "settler" side of that history. When he argues that for "*the early settlers,*" watching their wives "*and children killed and scalped and gutted like fish has a tendency to make some people irritable*" (*NCFOM* 195, my emphasis), Bell reveals that he has forgotten about, or is ignorant of, the peoples already living in that area for centuries before those "*early settlers,*" receiving the same treatment from the very real Glanton gang and their ilk.

This seems so obvious to me, and that it ought to be obvious to anyone reading this book, that *No Country for Old Men* has begun to assume an important position for me in our time of divisive, even polarized lack of genuine civic rhetoric. Bell's use of the word "early" echoes the empty repetition of the word "aboriginal" or "native" on the other side of this history, reducing an understanding of our collective bloody past to a sibling argument over who had dibs on a territory, or on who started the violence over it. As if either putatively white "settlers" or idealized "native americans" knew of no violence until they encountered one another and began the scalping.

Bell's fearful and therefore selective history leaves him ironically more, not less, vulnerable to the realities of the continual and inevitable violence of smuggling spaces. The seemingly sudden killing in his county (with a law enforcement response that, ineffectual as it is, leads Bell to compare the rip-off to a historic flood twenty years earlier) feels like an invasion of lawlessness previously unknown to those parts. Even if we ignore the illegal crossing of humans and horses in Bell's younger years, his willful ignorance that things were not, indeed, better in the old days *in toto* weakens his legs for standing strong wherever he finds himself.[8] Bell's sense of place falls away from under his feet, like the desert and mountains in that area when, after an inland sea dried up, heaved itself into a landscape that is more often than not sideways or upside down. We see Bell driving, more and more, across larger swaths of West Texas—but always a bit slow (unhurried enough to stop for coffee and pie) so that once he arrives, the most recent history has not only missed hurting him, but has also rendered the horror at his destination—of a drug shoot-out, a burned car, a motel shooting, a grieving father—distant to him. When these places become a single frighteningly open space to Bell—a borderland where the border keeps nothing back—he retreats.

Smuggling spaces therefore reverse the otherwise inexorable human trend toward reinforcement of boundaries and commodification of goods under cross-boundary agreements, such as NAFTA. They resist the recognition of borders agreed on in treaties, of taxes levied by governments they hardly recognize, or refuse to recognize at all. Most of the traffic on the international highways in the epilogue of *Cities of the Plain* may be sanctioned by NAFTA, but a significant proportion of it is sanctioned by underground economies trafficking in illegal narcotics and illegal aliens, both supplied on the cheap to the U.S.

The world cannot be wide enough, however, to run from Anton Chigurh. Despite the reversal of place into frightening space for Bell, Moss's actions put him under the power of the same constraints as those limiting the movements of John Grady and Billy in *Cities of the Plain*. All are endangered by the determination of space by a more powerful other. This is another reason why McCarthy chose the gas chamber for the execution visit that opens the book: the gas chamber is the only modern means of executing a man or woman that already creates a controlled space around the condemned, separating him or her from the rest of the world before death makes that separation irrevocable. (In lethal-injection—the method used at Texas's Huntsville prison—the use of intravenous tubes, rather than syringes directly injected into the condemned, along with the removal of those administering lethal injection to a separate space from the room containing the man or woman strapped to the cross-like table, are all attempts to translate this spatial distinction into our drug-obsessed and medicalized culture.) The gas chamber recalls the "hiss and click of the plunger" from Chigurh's cattle gun, sounding as it does "like a door closing" (*NCFOM* 7). As such, the closing door of the gas chamber collapses space.

FLIGHT TO JERUSALEM

Although it begins in italicized remembrance, the subject matter of that opening (Bell's visit to an execution) seems on first reading to be of a piece with the action that follows it. With all the violence in the roman type, it seems that this typographical remove for a relatively contemplative voice will serve merely to offset the violence, even to comment on it in ironic detachment—as if Bell is standing outside action that is occurring within a space safely sealed off from him. These monologues raise at least three questions.

First, how do Bell's monologues compare with previous italicized prologues for McCarthy chapters? After all, McCarthy has often used this technique. Here, contemplation alternates with the action. But not on anything like the level of the fireside chats of Holden, where philosophy asserts itself over history, between each massacre in *Blood Meridian*. Neither does the typographic switching provide the social voice of an oral history outside the action of the main character, as in *Child of God*. Whatever distance there is between Sheriff Bell's regular italicized reflections (actual thinking, or so it seems) and the action on the ground—following Llewelyn Moss and Anton Chigurh and even Carson Wells—we realize that rather than functioning within the generic expectations of the crime novel genre, these monologues begin to overwhelm that action.

Second, then, how do Bell's monologues fit the genre shift in *No Country for Old Men*? Initially by presenting that spatial separation for comment on the Young Man book, but eventually, by accomplishing the genre shift begun by that book's structural collapse. Particularly when the Young Man book later refuses to provide standard (or even cleverly modified) plot points that would have satisfied a crime novel structure, something has to fill the void. Bell's voice is there to fill in the relatively lengthening silences between gunfire. Indeed, the structure of the Young Man's book within this novel runs backwards, in comparison with the usual escalation of violence to a climactic shoot-out. Here, mayhem explodes along the border one third of the way into the book, opposite the end of a second act in a conventional three-act screenplay. We never actually see Moss die but are rather told the story third-hand, from the point of view of a deputy who got his version from a witness. Moss and his hitchhiker have simply disappeared from us, like Ophelia, with only their bodies making a reappearance to occasion a few words from the true protagonist. Bell's monologues pick up the pieces after the characters starring in the Young Man book within *No Country for Old Men* have run out of luck, time, and space.

By providing us with a character that is not so hard-boiled as is Moss to comment on the action, the narrative includes a moral center that Bell, laconic in his speech during that action, could not otherwise provide outside the tight-fitting constraints of *Dragnet* quips. In a work of film noir such as *Double Indemnity*, Leonard Neff's voice-over narration accomplishes both an ongoing confession and an ironic distance from the action that will conclude with his death. In that film, the voice-over performs Neff's confession to Barton Keyes, the "bulldog" who remains forever watchful, and yet who proves to be one step behind helping Neff by catching him. By the end of *No Country for Old Men*, Bell has similarly failed to help Moss by catching *him*. But as here the genre shift moves the weight of the novel onto those monologues, we have our last question about them.

Third, what is the deeper nature of Bell's italicized monologues? Bell has begun a very different confession from that of the central figure in a noir narrative. The book ends with Bell so defeated that he can only retreat into an image of a past that never existed, into a mythology that seems more of a defense than a viable dream. Instead of a vision of how a man might live outside the space of his dreams, Bell's dream only throws into sharper relief the losses in his life. In this sense, Bell's monologues serve as evidence that his conscious control of life has become overwhelmed by unconscious fears more than those myriad worries he cites in his earlier grumbling over the state of society. The narrative including his combat confession points to guilt over his behavior during combat. But that, too, proves to be another red herring (the circumstances of his position with the machine gun prove that his guilt over leaving that post is notably inflated). Bell's real fears lie deeper, and thus his monologues employ the comparatively dreamlike quality of italicized type to take us into those fears, in the darker space of the unconscious.

As I had first read into the new country of the Old Man book, however, the force of the genre fiction that preceded it—despite its failures, ultimately, to conform to that genre—kept me from recognizing the new genre as a total replacement of the earlier book. The new genre turns out to be, on rereading, evenly and fully realized throughout most of Bell's monologues. Until this new genre itself collapses into the unconscious, it repeats the laments of Jeremiah in the Old Testament.

In the King James Version of that book, Jeremiah's first worry is that he is insufficient to his god's purpose. God has to inform him that he is his son in a special way, that he has already "ordained" him to be "a prophet unto the nations" before his birth (1:5). Jeremiah nonetheless exclaims, "Lord GOD! behold, I cannot speak: for I am a child" (1:6). God solves this problem of insecurity in two ways. First, he tells Jeremiah simply not to say that he is a child (in other words, to grow up by pretending to be grown up). Second, God assures him that he will put his words into Jeremiah's mouth. It is a father's reassurance to a son that the son will become a man, but nevertheless that the son will always keep within him the power and truth of the father's word—that he will always be a son.

The "evil" that God is worried about first comes from another space, "out of the north" (1:15). At first, God's purpose is to empower Jeremiah to guard against this by building "a defenced city, and an iron pillar, and brasen walls against the whole land" to protect what seems to be a remarkably small space within which God is not offended and his new prophet cannot be harmed. But immediately, the evil appears to be within that space, as well. This is the jealous and vindictive God displeased with the failures of his chosen people: "And I brought you into a plentiful country, to eat the fruit thereof and the goodness thereof, but when ye entered, ye defiled my land, and made mine heritage an abomination" (2:7). A bit more will suffice:

> Hath a nation changed their gods, which are yet no gods? but my people have changed their glory for that which doth not profit. Be astonished, O ye heavens, at this, and be horribly afraid, be ye very desolate, saith the LORD. For my people have committed two evils; they have forsaken me the fountain of living waters, and hewed them out cisterns, broken cisterns, that can hold no water. (2:11–13)

Bell's complaints recapitulate these concerns of his God. First, he sees the evil as having arrived from outside his place in the form of somehow invading Indians that "*scalped and gutted like fish*" the women and children of those "*early settlers*" (*NCFOM* 195). Here, Bell's patriarchal assumption that the actual "*early settlers*" were the men, and not so directly "*their*" women and children, fits perfectly the typology of the Old Testament, as well as the archetypal unconscious idealization of masculinity for which we are headed. Second, the evil arrives from the outside in the form of drugs, run and dealt by "Mexicans." As Bell seems to assume that all of these are Mexican nationals (indeed, it is unclear if Bell regards Mexican-Americans as part of his flock), these dealers are outsiders.

But here is where the problem collapses one spatial degree, from xenophobia to the mistrust of one's own tribe, matching perfectly the collapse of God's fears in the book of Jeremiah: the second threat is that the children inside the walls of the space protected by God's prophet have not heard God, or have forgotten him, and that they will therefore adopt foreign gods and customs. Bell's *Dragnet* dialogue now assumes a biblical tone, echoing God's shift from xenophobia to a frustrated wrath against the children who have forgotten him: "It's worse than that," he tells the Sheriff who has commented on the outside threat (the drug dealers who sell to "schoolkids"). "Schoolkids buy it" (*NCFOM* 194). In other words, no one makes them use drugs; they choose them. The most heart-felt expressions of jeremiad fears in Bell's monologues concern children, whether unborn, of school age, or grown up and gone to war. He worries about Moss, and the other inhabitants of his county, with a patriarchal feeling for them as his figurative children.

Bell is a model for the god in McCarthy's philosophy: a slightly doddering figure old before his time, worried first about the evil from without the space he keeps for his people, but then secondly worried about the evil taken into that space, and ultimately worried that, quite apart from whatever evil might exist outside that space, his people have lost their way—they have forgotten to listen to him. But it is also the case that he may have forgotten how to speak to them. Thus the third, inmost worry of God and Bell is that their children have given up their acknowledgement of what is good and righteous because of some failure on the part of God or Bell; the parent ultimately owns all failures of the child.

Asked about the (apparently sudden) high crime rate in his county, Bell looks within that place: "*It starts when you begin to overlook bad manners. Any time you quit hearin Sir and Mam the end is pretty much in sight*" (*NCFOM* 304). Here again Bell's worry is centered in the children (the ones buying the drugs, rather than the ones selling them), whom he sees as having lost their sense of place, in the sense that they no longer automatically show verbal respect for people who have gone before them. The first identification of the problem, however, points to parents. Bell doesn't point right back at himself, but at the reporter with that "you." By no longer exercising sufficient authoritative control, however, the patriarch is really the origin of the sin. The trope embedded in "overlook" suggests not only a hierarchical differential of power, but also distance.

McCarthy shows us this the first time we see Bell as a character in the narrative: "Bell climbed the rear steps of the courthouse and went down the hall to his office. He swiveled his chair around and sat and looked at the telephone. Go ahead, he said. I'm here." After this grumbling—like a father who knows he is about to be bothered again with something trivial to him and yet important to his child—Bell picks up the phone and we infer the other side of the conversation from his. "Mrs Downie I believe he'll come down directly. Why dont you call me back here in a little bit. Yes mam" (*NCFOM* 41).

This cornball moment almost dropped the book from my hands. Worse than a formulaic film, this seems closer to something from a long-running television series whose best writers have all wandered off to better gigs. It introduces Bell in the perfect manner, of course, for the Young Man's book as it so perfectly fits the cliché of the beleaguered and bored country lawman about to be overwhelmed by the excitement of the plot that will engulf him. And yet, it also introduces how Bell sees himself. Surprisingly, long after one endures this scene, it echoes through the collapse of Bell's jeremiad into his dream.

First in this telephone scene, note Bell's good manners: at age fifty-seven, he uses both the honorific "Mrs" and "mam" for a woman who is probably older. The cat stuck up a tree emergency is so clichéd as to bring on the severest pain in the reader: yes, our sheriff character's office is normally a slow place. My, how Anton Chigurh will, by comparison, shake things up. Bell first resents this call. "It's money, he said. You have enough money you dont have to talk to people about cats in trees." On second thought, however, he remembers his role as the protector of people whose concerns may seem trivial to them, but for whom those concerns are important. "Well." The period suggests another pause. "Maybe you do" (*NCFOM* 41).

Maybe. But we notice Bell's ambivalence here, his understandable feeling of being put out to little purpose, and even the uncertainty permeating his reminder to himself that indeed, as sheriff in a largely empty county with a few frightened people scattered across the desert, his job does include reassuring old women about their cats. His errands quickly involve chasing after Moss (or might have involved chasing after Chigurh, which he seems assiduously to avoid). Nevertheless, his stops at the house, the pace of his dialogue, his pauses for coffee and pie, reveal that his favorite part of the job really is not in having to listen to his children, but rather in an enjoyment of the places of his office. Moving between his desk, his car, a booth in a cafe, and across somewhat frightening wide open spaces to various towns in which he is always known and recognized, give him the feeling that his children recognize in him the patriarchal figure who deserves recognition, verbal respect, freedom of movement, and pie.

But this does not mean he has been speaking to his children with regularity, much less with success. And even if he has, on what authority can he speak? His ethos seems limited to that of a reluctant counselor for the tremulous owners of wayward cats. It might also be his job to actually protect them. But he knows he is ineffectual at this (as indeed was the God of Jeremiah worried about those people to the north): he is so outgunned and outnumbered as to make it ridiculous for him to take a stand against the drug dealers. And they know it. *"I think for me the worst of it is knowin that probably the only reason I'm even still alive is that they have no respect for me. And that's very painful"* (*NCFOM* 215). Bell's only hope, as God's in the book of Jeremiah, is that his children will again recognize righteousness, show respect for his authority, and refuse to take up the evil customs (drugs, another religion) from outside the place of safety within the larger wilderness.

Why would Bell's children listen to him? Bell, like many a real sheriff in West Texas counties, and like the god regularly discussed by many McCarthy characters, is powerless to do anything about evil. Or—and this provides evidence of a more troubled theology, and one that must retain some of the resentment of the distant father so hated by Cornelius Suttree—God is merely preoccupied. In *Suttree*, he busies himself with floods and dams and collapsing slate walls, oblivious to the carnage beneath his play. Like a giant child himself, he moves things around from time to time, sometimes curious about the progress of an individual ant—perhaps even an ant-on-sugar—but he does not preside over a simple top-down universe in which he regularly mediates the activity on lower levels of existence.[9]

This is why I argued at the end of Chapter Four that Holden's claims should not be too readily discounted as inaccurate. Morality may be something conjured up, like a trick, by human beings living in a nonmoral universe. Morality may be inevitably medial, with no connection up or down. Our feelings of connection below, to animals and the natural world, proves to be no more than our inability to evolve out of anthropocentric habits of epistemology. So, too, our feelings of connection above, to the larger universe: these may only be an unkillable figment of the empathic systems our brains have evolved for our life as social creatures. Just as we are good (and terrible) at imagining what someone else is thinking and feeling, we might simply have the habit of projecting a god onto a universe that has none.

Bell's final dream makes it difficult to tell whether Freud, or Jung, should be our guide on this last question. Freud, of course, derided "oceanic" feeling as a delusion resulting from the failure to recognize "the reality principle" (11–12). Jung, on the other hand, believed that such feelings evidenced the truth of a collective unconscious. This isn't the space to settle between these two, but I remain curious as to how McCarthy's visions, dreams, and descriptions of feelings of a deep connection with the universe ultimately come out: true, or delusional?

I cannot see this resolved within the books. But either way, we are headed down to myth and the unconscious with Bell, as his role speaking the worries of Jeremiah wears down under the terrible weight of God's absence, and as his role as a symbolic god proves that he, too, remains too far from people to really help them. The possibility that any god might intervene on the behalf of Bell and his people seems ruled out by Bell's uncle when he asks him,

> Do you think God knows what's happenin?
> I expect he does.
> You think he can stop it?
> No. I dont. (*NCFOM* 269)

Riding from Jerusalem

Thus, even the jeremiad, the genre that so takes over *No Country for Old Men*, itself wears out, collapsing into confession and dream. The key to Bell's inability to meaningfully intervene on the behalf of his citizens goes all the way back to his departure from an absurd situation where he most certainly would have been killed and probably would not have accomplished anything but killing a few more German soldiers. And yet, this memory seems to ruin his ability to think of himself as effective in any way. Bell's war experience seems to have damaged him irrevocably; he has already fought, even bravely, and yet the hopelessness of continuing that fight emasculates him. But this obsession with a particular guilt proves to be an unreliable inflation. As such, it leads inevitably to a projection of that inflated archetype that remains outside Bell's ability to integrate the god-like power of his position into a whole personality.

Bell's concluding dream, as well as his jeremiad worries, echoes another father in McCarthy. As with the god of The Old Testament, we have only a general name for him, his family name alone: "Cole." As with so many other names in McCarthy, this one resonates with meaning. One step down the alphabet from "Cold" (and thus more remote), the name sounds the same as "Coal," that last cinder that carries within its heart the fire that must not be allowed to burn out in movements through the endless space of darkness. Perhaps only now does the insistence of the narrator about John Grady's name ring true: "The boy's name was Cole. John Grady Cole" (*ATPH* 7). Even seeing his mother with another man does not flush him from the San Antonio hotel where he spies on her. He must be sure that she is sleeping with someone other than his father before he can leave San Angelo, or at least that she has indeed renounced his father's name. By checking to see if she has used that name to register for her own room, he finds out: "No," the clerk tells him. "No Cole" (*ATPH* 22).

Like Bell, John Grady's father first appears to us as an already defeated, emasculated, and sorrowful man. He tells John Grady that "[w]hat you won was gravy but what you lost was hard come by" (*COTP* 214). This pronouncement comes as a posthumous recollection two novels after the father's admission that in one poker game he "won twenty-six thousand dollars in twenty-two hours of play," including the hand for "four thousand dollars in the last pot," "with three natural queens" (*ATPH* 12). Judging by the reduced circumstances of his domestic space in the hotel, we know that Cole Sr. has lost more money than he has ever won. The one "queen" he had in life deserted him, long before the war took away his masculinity in some other way. He tells his son that "It aint her fault. I aint the same as I was" (*ATPH* 12), even though well before Cole Sr. left for World War II, John Grady's mother abandoned them both. "She left out of here. She was gone from the time you were six months old till you were about three" (*ATPH* 25). Like many of McCarthy's young male would-be fathers, this mother headed West, to California.

The failure of Cole Sr. as a father figure originates in this, and subsequent, emasculations. He is just as ruined as Bell, and even shares the idiosyncrasy of stirring his coffee out of nervous habit—with no sugar in it (*ATPH* 24, *NCFOM* 90). Like Bell, he cannot assimilate the news, where even the domestic conflicts of movie stars echo his own private sense of failure: "How can Shirley Temple be getting divorced?" he asks his son. Then he continues, "The Good Book says that the meek shall inherit the earth and I expect that's probably the truth. I aint no freethinker, but I'll tell you what. I'm a long way from bein convinced that it's all that good a thing" (*ATPH* 13). Cole's cynicism here may seem atheistic, but no more so than Bell's ultimate inability to believe in a God who can, or will, intervene on earth.

Nonetheless, Cole Sr. gives his son a saddle as an early Christmas present (*ATPH* 14), and it is the father, rather than the son, who at least verbally pushes for some time together—riding horses—telling John Grady, "You dont have to if you dont want to" (*ATPH* 9). This remains the only scene in all of McCarthy where a father makes any gesture toward emotional connection with a main character. What follows?

First, John Grady puts off this ride. But eventually, they go out together, and we seem to see the son from the eyes of a father who appreciates him:

> The boy who rode on slightly before him sat a horse not only as if he'd been born to it which he was but as if were he begot by malice or mischance into some queer land where horses never were he would have found them anyway. Would have known that there was something missing for the world to be right or he right in it and would have set forth to wander wherever it was needed for as long as it took until he came upon one and he would have known that that was what he sought and it would have been. (*ATPH* 23)

The highly biblical language here ("but as if were he begot" and the finality of "and it would have been") is actually King James diction. As such, it points us as readily to myth as to the religion that seems less powerful for John Grady, that seems unrecognized by his father, and that has failed Bell.

Spatially, this scene enacts a dream fulfilled as it could rarely be in that fenced country of 1949, and as it never occurs for McCarthy's other protagonists. These two, father and son, are moving through open spaces without the violence of the Glanton gang and yet among ruins that suggest the impermanence of some of the constraints on space that have appeared here since the kid rode through. "The wreckage of an old wooden windmill fallen among the rocks" and "[a]n ancient pickethouse" almost suggest the decay of a pastoral. They even pass "crippled fenceposts propped among the rocks that carried remnants of a wire not seen in that country for years." This could be the fencing from *Blood Meridian*'s Epilogue. Indeed, after that fallen windmill, we get the quintessential *Blood Meridian* sentence: "They rode on" (*ATPH* 23).

John Grady knows his father is dying, however, and that he is already powerless—was always powerless—to preserve the family's reserve of a land where horses can still be found. As I have argued in Chapter Six, he must ride on to replace everything he is losing outside San Angelo. But we have now seen that not only his grandfather, but also his father will be left behind—one buried, and the other heading for the grave.

Bell's father has also died, while Bell was still relatively young. Meanwhile, Bell's marriage has survived the loss of an only child. At his first mention of her, he immediately says he will not talk about her. Then, later, as the chapters collapse around his monologues, he confesses that he talks *to* her. "*She would be thirty now. That's all right. I dont care how that sounds. I like talkin to her. Call it superstition or whatever you want. I know that over the years I have give her the heart I always wanted for myself and that's all right. That's why I listen to her*" (*NCFOM* 285). This confession turns out to be only an admission that the father keeps a lost child alive through his own voice.

But either this remains too private for Bell to elaborate on, and end with, or it does not ring in his heart as does the loss of his father, or even his confessed feelings of guilt over combat and as a failed father-figure for his county. Because here we have an idea, a thought, more than an image. And thinking never matches the power of image. Bell's evocation of his daughter remains at the level of sound—possibly quite powerful to him, but we cannot know for sure. "*I listen to what she says and what she says makes good sense. I with she'd say more of it. I can use all the help I can get.*" It may be moving that here the father is listening to the child, and has indeed traded places with her, taking advice from her. But we know nothing about what it is that she tells him. Bell cuts off these thoughts and we never return to them: *"Well, that's enough of that"* (*NCFOM* 285).

This is thinking. And for the first time since *Suttree*, and fundamentally in a different way, McCarthy has characters thinking all over the place in *No Country for Old Men*. Bell sometimes uses the phrase to lead up to what he is actually thinking about. But more often, a phrase such as "he thought about that" refuses to tell us more than what we could already have inferred. McCarthy also uses such phrases to collapse the space between psychology and a social tension between characters in this novel. In a parody of this, Chigurh picks up a signal from the transponder and wonders who still has it. "He could think of no reason for the transponder unit to be in the hotel. He ruled out Moss because he thought Moss was almost certainly dead. That left the police. Or some agent of the Matacumbe Petroleum Group. Who must think that he thought that they thought that he thought they were very dumb. He thought about that" (*NCFOM* 171).

This "thinking" is nothing like *Suttree's* interior monologues, but is rather the often meaningless expository thinking on the part of characters in genre fiction—again, filling in the spaces of their absent characters with plot machinations of no import. The inclusion of the full name of the evil corporation involved in the drug smuggling even takes us back to fetish; here the specificity of the name stands in for the much deeper complexity of the relationships between real corporations and drug smuggling. But that would take time, and Chigurh is busy thinking.

My reference to this last evidence of the genre book we have already left behind is meant to point out how much Bell, too, has been "thinking." And it does him no good. Rather, his "thoughts" revolve much less around matters of immediate responsibility and possibilities of action than do Moss's and Chigurh's. Rather, Bell is continually trying to think himself free from feelings without denying their power. Rejecting the Western assumption that all psychological phenomena are the products of each individual mind that is experiencing them, Jung argued that the contrary is the case: "Psychic existence is the only category of existence of which we have *immediate* knowledge, since nothing can be known unless it first appears as a psychic image. Only psychic existence is immediately verifiable. To the extent that the world does not assume the form of a psychic image, it is virtually non-existent" (*Portable* 486, his emphasis).

It may be that the loss of his daughter remains an important component of Bell's character. And Bell's confession about his actions in combat may also inform his sense of guilt as a failed father. By telling his uncle that story, we approach an image that occasions Bell's thoughts about it. But the description of Bell's actual use of the machine gun nearly tilts back to the gun fetish of the earlier book.

> That thing was aircooled and it was belt fed out of a metal box and
> I figured if I let em run up a little more on me I could operate on
> em out there in the open and they wouldnt call in another round
> cause they'd be too close. I scratched around and I dug around
> some more and come up with the ammo box for it and I got set
> up behind the section of wall there and jacked back the slide and
> pushed off the safety and here we went. (*NCFOM* 275)[10]

This has its merits, but they are not strongly related to Bell's guilt. In fact,
this is not at all the language of a confession, but rather the deftly handled
transcription of a good storyteller not at all averse to having himself imagined
in a heroic act. Furthermore, there is no image here, but rather another of the
good storyteller's stock in trade: expert "doing."

In place of "thinking," we have the same kind of impressive "doing"
that I earlier characterized as another aspect of the crime novel genre: the
things handled, and the way they are handled here, is what is important.
And in another echo of Moss and his guns and truck fetishes, this is a scene
of modern warfare, centering on the specificity of technology involved. It
can of course be objected that any question of Bell staying in that position
is absurd, as eventually a half-competent officer among the Germans would
have them pull back as a shell blows this machine-gunner to pieces. Bell
earned his medal by picking up the machine gun at all. Beyond that, his guilt
is misplaced. Why?

Because the power of images around his father keeps that man at an
impossible remove from Bell. Even as Bell confesses that he knows he is, in
some ways, "*a better man*" than his father (*NCFOM* 308), it is hard to believe
that Bell truly feels this way.[11] The image we have of the father includes in
him an impossible power, one that Bell can never hope to assume. We might
imagine this broken-down sheriff waking from his dreams, pleading as did
Jeremiah, "Lord GOD! behold, I cannot speak: for I am a child" (1:6). Here
is the image of the father who was not even on the battlefield with Bell that
day, and yet is so assumed to possess a superior courage that this image will
surpass Bell's description of fumbling for an ammo box. In Bell's words, his
father would have "set there till hell froze over and then stayed a while on the
ice" (*NCFOM* 279).

BELL's DREAM

Bell's final dream includes an image familiar in Freud, but with a figure whose
archetypal power can best be understood through Jungian theory. First,
the fact that the father is carrying fire. In *Civilization and its Discontents*,

Freud discusses a primeval scene around a fire. In a now-famous footnote, Freud ponders what might have been a first realization of the human (and particularly, and as Freud would have it, only male) capacity for control of emotions in order to control nature. In this mythic scene, Freud imagines the first person to realize that fire might be preserved, and carried forward.

> Putting out fire by micturating—a theme to which modern giants, Gulliver in Lilliput and Rabelais' Gargantua, still hark back—was [...] a kind of sexual act with a male, an enjoyment of sexual potency in a homosexual competition. The first person to renounce this desire and spare the fire was able to carry it off with him and subdue it to his own use. By damping down the fire of his own sexual excitation, he had tamed the natural force of fire. (37)

This imaginative idea suggests the overemphasis on constraint and repression that refers most accurately here to Moss, and the Young Man book. But we can keep this in mind as something behind Bell's dream.[12]

Second, as I have argued in my interpretation of Bell's combat confession, his father looms too large in his imagination. And the tension between image and "thought" running through Bell's monologues further calls on Jung for another interpretation of the final dream. In Jungian terms, the image precedes all of Bell's ideas, and the grotesquely heavy mythological weight of the father in his dream explains Bell's inability to work out any coherent thoughts to explain an overwhelming feeling that, in comparison to his father, he must forever remain a child. Jung insists that before the idea comes the image, tracing "idea" back to the ideal forms in Plato and before that, to "the 'primal warmth' of the Stoics" and the "ever-living fire" of Heraclitus (*Archetypes* 33). Because Bell cannot see an image of himself realizing his father potential, that potential is only available projected outside him, in the form of the archetypal father figure we recognize in his final dream.

As Jung also saw that in the presence of the image, there is a release of emotion, we can also see why this dream closes *No Country for Old Men*: the archetype in this dream is so emotion-charged that it generates more emotion than any other for Bell. Archetypes also become strongest during abandonment, or after a loss. The murders in *No Country for Old Men*, particularly the death of Moss and the hitchhiker, remind Bell of the death of his daughter. He talks about his daughter in the second monologue after he views the bodies in the morgue (*NCFOM* 240–241, 285).

Another reason to continue with Jung, more than Freud, is that Jung's acceptance of a mythological explanation for "oceanic" feeling provides us with an explanation for Bell's thoughts and visions without merely pathologizing them, as would Freud. For Jung, the telos of humanity is the recognition of godhood, and the self is the recognition of the god-like in temporal life. Instead of projecting this out into religion, Bell's recursive and obsessional thinking about the problems besetting his sense of place and his relationship with both his lost father and his lost daughter eventually move him away from his role as Jeremiah. But he cannot manage to find the god in himself, particularly as he feels that he is a failure for the citizenry he will leave behind. He therefore falls back on an archetypal image that signals his past and current failures, even as it seems to point to nostalgia.

The move to archetype for Bell becomes clear in his comments about the water trough:

> You could see the chisel marks in the stone. It was hewed out of solid rock and it was about six foot long and maybe a foot and a half wide and about that deep. Just chiseled out of the rock. And I got to thinkin about the man that done that. That country had not had a time of peace much of any length at all that I knew of. I've read a little of the history of it since and I aint sure it ever had one. But this man had set down with a hammer and chisel and carved out a stone water trough to last ten thousand years. Why was that? What was it that he had faith in? It wasnt that nothin would change. He had to know bettern that. [...] And I have to say that the only thing I can think is that there was some sort of promise in his heart. And I dont have no intention of carvin a stone water trough. But I would like to be able to make that kind of promise. I think that's what I would like most of all. (*NCFOM* 307)

Thinking about this trough, Bell nearly advances farther than he does in his last dream toward Jungian individuation. Of course, the creator of this trough did have faith—in himself, but also in all those who would follow his passing in archetypal terms. The "promise in his heart" had to be that he would simply show up, and do this work for the sake of its own creative exercise, the skill it takes, and some sense that what he works at would indeed endure. That promise is the promise one makes in creating something in a bid for immortality. Three resonances we find in the trough advance all this in Jungian terms, but also in more particular terms for McCarthy.

First, in Jungian terms, the trough represents the mythical possibilities of taking over the power of God. One of the first complaints that God makes to Jeremiah involves the control of water: "For my people have committed two evils; they have forsaken me the fountain of living waters, and hewed them out cisterns, broken cisterns, that can hold no water" (2:13). By hewing their own troughs, humans become as gods, as Jung would see it, both in their assumption of a power previously thought by unindividuated people to reside only in a transcendent God, and also in their exercise of an all-important creative impulse that Jung argues is crucial to individuation.

Second, in biographical terms, the trough remarked on by Bell, seen together with the complaint of God to Jeremiah, recalls work of the TVA, of which McCarthy's father played a crucial role. The dams hewn from the rocky terrain around Knoxville in *Suttree*, the artificial reservoirs they created, and the usurpation of the power supposedly held only by a transcendent god over "the fountain of living waters"—there the Tennessee River—all point to a powerful father figure in control of both the creative impulse and its use to usurp the power of God.

Third, Bell's emphasis on the craft involved in a human being taking the time to create something "to last ten thousand years" brings both the biblical and the patriarchal power derived from this object under the power of the son of the man who worked for the TVA: Cormac McCarthy. As I have remarked in Chapter Two, McCarthy's regular valuation of skilled manual labor remains central to his vision.[13] Despite some ambiguity embedded in both the language concerning this water trough, and in the language regarding the cistern in Jeremiah, it is possible to imagine that in Bell's admiration for the durability of the trough, we might have a metaphorical recognition of the work McCarthy Sr. helped accomplish (good, as well as bad, for the people in that area) with the TVA. Perhaps. But the enormity of the TVA project, and the lack of individual skilled artisanship in building a cistern more likely comparable to the one that angers God in Jeremiah, seem all to make that unlikely in any direct way. Nonetheless, it might be possible that the metaphor, although perhaps not intentional (or conscious, as Jung would have it), still arises from feelings on the part of the son to make peace with the father—perhaps.

Jung's famous dream of moving a candle through darkness was interpreted by him to mean that we must guard the light of reason and consciousness from the dark storms of the unconscious. The brighter the candle, the deeper the surrounding darkness (*Memories* 87–90). But unlike Freud, Jung acknowledged that the demands of the unconscious cannot be overcome. Hard necessity—such as running from Anton Chigurh—can relieve you from the burden of demands arising from the unconscious. But Bell avoids hard necessity. Indeed, he lives a relatively slow life, which for Jung opens him up to the neurotic obsessions we hear in his ruminations on evil threatening his community from without, evil being purchased from within his community, and evil being adopted by his community's children as they live lives of increasing leisure.

In this last worry, Bell actually doesn't go far enough: it is not in the lack of "Sir" and "Mam" that children run astray, but in an almost total lack of hard necessity in the lives of even many underprivileged children. If Bell wanted to make a difference there, he would open a horse riding camp and get them all busy from an early age. He might learn, and then teach these children, the craft of hewing stone. He would in this sense realize the father archetype that is still outside him, figured only in his dreams of his literal father leading the way. Despite having lost a child, he would become an active father in his community.

But this is not that story. And indeed, Bell's severe limitations—he has no creative outlet, no craft nor art, and he seems amazed even at the idea of working on something "maybe just a hour or two after supper"—confound him. Whatever the assorted overlaps may be between Bell's politics and McCarthy's, this sheriff is in no resonant way the writer, whose devotion to craft and creativity is continually established on his pages, and whose habits with every hobby he could find have been remarked on in interviews with him and with Knoxville residents and what family will speak to an interviewer.

Bell's limitations here leave him projecting all his potential power for creative and procreative power onto his dead father, until that father disappears behind an inflated archetype. Bell cannot achieve a dialogue with such an archetype, particularly as this one, in the form of Bell's laconic father, remains silent in the dream: he "*never said nothin*" (*NCFOM* 309). Rather than recognize all the various elements of his identity, Bell struggles among them, at times fracturing, such as when he veers wildly from one complaint to another seemingly unrelated one. This means, however, that the power of the silent figure riding before Bell in his dream carries with him more than one element of Bell's desperately various projections.

The father archetype in the dream furthermore resists interpretation into a single identity, for two reasons. First, this father represents not only Bell's father, but all fathers. As a symbol from both Bell's individual unconscious, and as Jung would have it, a collective unconscious as well, the dream's father figure cannot be reduced to an actual figure at all. The situation itself, particularly in the primeval aspect in which Freudian theory would interpret this carrying of a sacred fire, in Jungian terms reaches beyond a literal historical moment, as much as beyond Bell's individual psychology. The scene recalls Jung's;

> *archetypes of transformation.* They are not personalities, but are typical situations, places, ways and means, that symbolize the kind of transformation in question. [...] They are genuine symbols precisely because they are ambiguous, full of half-glimpsed meanings,

and in the last resort inexhaustible. [...] The discriminating intellect naturally keeps on trying to establish their singleness of meaning and thus misses the essential point; for what we can above all establish as the one thing consistent with their nature is their *manifold meaning*, their almost limitless wealth of reference, which makes any unilateral formulation impossible. (*Archetypes* 38, his emphasis)

Bell's obsessions survey a variety of possibilities, unable to settle on a single problem that might explain his general sense of a world gone wrong. Things missing, that he somehow assumes were always there before, worry him: a lack of manners, a lack of discipline in schools, a lack of religion. Meanwhile he continues to fear evil as something that will be smuggled in from the outside, and eagerly adopted by his community's children. *"These old people I talk to, if you could of told em that there would be people on the streets of our Texas towns with green hair and bones in their noses speakin a language they couldn't even understand, well, they just flat out wouldnt of believed you"* (*NCFOM* 295).

This neurotic fixation on the details that somehow indicate to Bell a lack of social codes (rather than an alternative set of them) of course echoes *Blood Meridian*: there *were* such people in *their* Texas towns, and they were scalped and killed or run off. But here Bell's fixations also point back to the inflation of the father archetype: unable to follow his father (feeling guilt for the loss of his child, the abandonment of fellow soldiers, and his departure from his job as sheriff), he is caught between two extremes: the heathen pollutions of his community's children, and the impossible power of the father image that he cannot integrate into himself and thus which he all too easily imagines in ideal terms.

This nostalgic final image of *No Country for Old Men* follows Bell's father, carrying fire in a horn, riding into the darkness of the past. The image returns us to the title. Yeats wrote "Sailing to Byzantium" in 1927 and it appeared in *The Dark Tower* in 1928, three years after he received the Nobel Prize for Literature, but three years after the Free State. "The memory of terrible struggles was fiercely alive [...]," as M. L. Rosenthal recounts. The poems of *The Tower* "report the hopes and disillusionments of those years, and Yeats's feeling of inadequacy for the physical side of the struggle" (xxv). Rosenthal's proof of this is most obvious in "The Road at My Door," and indeed, that tide might work as well for McCarthy's novel.

> An affable Irregular,
> A heavily-built Falstaffian man,
> Comes cracking jokes of civil war

As though to die by gunshot were
The finest play under the sun.
[...]
I count those feathered balls of soot
The moor-hen guides upon the stream,
to silence the envy in my thought;
And turn towards my chamber, caught
In the cold snows of a dream. (113)

Bell ends with a dream, just as McCarthy's narrator did in the enigmatic epilogue to *Cities of the Plain*. This dream follows yet another confession, beginning in the tacked-on phrasing of a guilty afterthought that the speaker cannot allow himself to leave unremarked on. This book knows it has struggled, that indeed many of the previous books have struggled, with something it often refused to directly address: "*The other thing is that I have not said much about my father and I know I have not done him justice*" (*NCFOM* 308). Our West Texas *Hamlet* then ends in two dreams.

The first is the child's dream, quotidian, faint, about money given and lost—exchange value and the power of the father in nearly literal terms. The second is the grown child's inflation of the father to an archetype:

like we was both back in older times and I was on horseback goin through the mountains of a night. Goin through this pass in the mountains. It was cold and there was snow on the ground and he rode past me and kept on goin. Never said nothin. He just rode on past and he had this blanket wrapped around him and he had his head down and when he rode past I seen he was carryin fire in a horn the way people used to do and I could see the horn from the light inside of it. About the color of the moon. (*NCFOM* 309)

This could be Jung himself in *Memories, Dreams, Reflections*. Jung's transformative dream of a candle surrounded by darkness was interpreted by him as the place of consciousness moving forward through the never-ending space of an unconscious too dark to be held away beyond that small sphere of light. "It was night in some unknown place, and I was making slow and painful headway against a mighty wind. Dense fog was flying along everywhere. I had my hands cupped around a tiny light which threatened to go out at any moment. Everything depended on my keeping this little light alive." But Jung sees himself carrying this light, and when he looks back, the "gigantic black figure following" him proves to be a threatening "*vita peracta*"—the life already accomplished, lived, and perhaps ended. Here, the

leading figure is the dreamer, breaking free with every difficult step from that
dark figure that would negate its progress.

> The storm pushing against me was time, ceaselessly flowing
> into the past, [...] It exerts a mighty suction which greedily
> draws everything living into itself; we can only escape from
> it—for a while—by pressing forward. The past is terribly real and
> present, and it catches everyone who cannot save his skin with a
> satisfactory answer. (*Memories* 88)

In Bell's dream, the dreamer has no answers, and is already turning
backwards to follow the vita peracta—in his case, a father archetype moving
backwards—through an already sterile landscape (*through this pass in the
mountains. It was cold and there was snow on the ground and he rode past me
and kept on goin*). Bell has no satisfactory answers to the challenges of life,
and the dark figures of his failings are indistinguishable—despite what he
claims—from the dark future he sees in the soulless eyes of Chigurh, or
the man he visits before his execution. Bell can only register that fear that
swallows up the self and erases all distinctions between inside and outside,
past, present, and future. Beyond melancholia, Bell grasps at the words of
Jeremiah, of his disappointed, jealous, and ineffectual God, of a grumpy old
man's conservative politics, of a Lord Jim somehow carrying a burden of
guilt under his medal, of a father who's only child has died. These problems
overwhelm him, but they are the manifestations of deeper anxieties with
which his conscious mind can grapple while his dreams ride off into the dark
following someone else's light.

Bell has yielded his failed father's position to become again the son.
And the distant father leads him in a way that Bell's father seems not to have
done in life. In Bell's own implicit understanding of the dream, locating it
as he does as a dream specific to his father and himself, the longing here is
strongly conservative, even reactionary, with a pull backward in time to a
selective moment when one might, presumably, with nothing but horse and
fire in a horn, start over. Of course, one still has to wonder how far these two
would get by riding human hopes along like that with no woman in sight. The
father alone seems to be the answer here, with some promise of realigning
values and practices toward a pure direction that can only be indicated by
him. And the nostalgia here hangs on the dreamer's hope that through that
pass in the mountains he will find just the right earlier time—not so early as
to get scalped, but before the fences might hem this father and son into the
narrowing spaces of the West after *Blood Meridian*.

The initial conflicts powering *No Country for Old Men*, then—conflicts
of genre and structure—resolve themselves only by falling out of the way

of a new (older) generational conflict that itself falls away to older fears yet. Bell's dream insists on its interpretation, however much we might go beyond it, that Bell is finally, in this vision, paying some attention to his father, doing "him justice" (*NCFOM* 308). We should return to this level of interpretation because it both extends and reverses McCarthy's ending of *The Border Trilogy*.

With the death of John Grady, we had the slightly older brother figure Billy acting as something of a patriarch. But *No Country for Old Men*'s father wins the book's arguments so overwhelmingly and insistently that many readers will want to throw the thing away, rejecting it as an unredeemable conservative jeremiad. Even if one rejects the hazy but implied politics of Bell's monologues, it would be a mistake to reject out of hand the force of emotion that occasions them. Bell's rants may sound like those of a grumpy old man, but their frustrations center on nostalgia for a world of impossible safety—especially for young people. Behind his regular accusations against the younger generations that, to Bell, have lost their way, his loss of innocence in World War II (deepened with the losses in Vietnam), and the unbearably personal loss of his daughter, Bell's relationship to his father seems to lie deepest toward the root of his individual psychology.[14]

The reactionary call of Bell's dream to follow only the father also stands in contrast to the motherly function of Betty at the end of *Cities of the Plain*, which was to console and forgive. Where Betty essentially tells Billy that he is too hard on himself, the silent father in Bell's dream as much as says *yes, you are right; the world has gone awry. Follow me, as I carry the proper fire of truth into a better future*.

But of course, this dream stretches and strains, as do all conservative visions, to get back to a past where the possibilities remain sufficiently uncorrupted by the chaos of change. In Jungian terms, we can also see that the image of Bell's father presents us with Bell's projection: where he feels he cannot travel, he imagines his father to lead the way—backwards. The paradoxes here suit the solution of *No Country for Old Men*, as the father's solutions to the problems of the son are inevitably conflicted between setting him out to a future incomprehensible to the father, and recalling him to the values already lost in time to the father. Bell's dream says to us *do not go a further step forward*. That's a harsher generational shift to the past than the blind man's mysterious talk with Culla Holme.

But ultimately, to put my original conceit to work in reverse, the fact that the collapse of the jeremiad into Bell's unresolved Jungian vision is not up to starting the novel, but must rather slip into its form when the crime genre collapses, ought to remind us that *No Country for Old Men* says more to us than Bell's dream. It tells us two stories—one hard-boiled and one worn down—and thus eventually it tells us a third story, about the inadequacy of both responses to a world of male violence. After the struggles of several sons (and a few fathers) in eight McCarthy novels, the ninth ends with a vision of the father's most reactionary solution: the older generation wins only in retreat, while Anton Chigurh limps away to future evil.

Notes

1. Whatever the politics of *No Country for Old Men* (which are not only more discernible, but more relevant to us, than those of the author), Bell's worries surprised me with their eventual ability to alter my thoughts. Noting the desperation behind Bell's sentiments reminds me how pain of loss and fear of uncertainty is, after all, a universal condition, reaching beyond binary arguments on whether Bell's particular pains and fears are accurately located by him, or what to do about them. As much as my politics might differ from *this character's*, I must recognize the validity of feelings prompting even those ideas I might find objectionable. Furthermore, this is where aesthetics returns as an important part of reading even a politically-charged novel: to expand on thought and feeling without particular requirements on how that happens, or on what thoughts and feelings are added, seems to me a crucial part of any aesthetic experience, and an authentic value in novels— whatever their more quotidian exchange value.

2. John Grady's self-conscious smoking in the theatre lobby draws the attention of the other patrons to this boy who "rolled a cigarette and stood smoking it with one boot jacked back against the wall behind," dropping his ashes into the jeans he has cuffed for this purpose (*ATPH* 23). The waitress at the first cafe he goes into there assumes he must be in town for the rodeo (*ATPH* 20). In San Antonio, at least, he is a walking anachronism in 1949.

3. Compare this description, for instance, with the one of John Grady "settin" in his grandfather's office (*ATPH* 11), to see how important the masculine quality of wood and metal and leather and stone are to a young man's sense of strength, of family identity, and ultimately of security within a medial position that controls both domestic space and those wilderness spaces outside the young man's immediate surroundings.

4. Wallis Sanborn, and other hunters familiar with that area of Texas, had never heard this word used as a verb.

5. If I were falling for all this without seeing the underlying intent, I could grouse that no cheap motel in that part of Texas would have central air conditioning for innumerable reasons, not the least would be the cost of cooling all rooms somewhat equally, let alone obviating the possibility of any one room having much control over its temperature. But again, realism is beside the point.

6. I am indebted to Wallis Sanborn for confirming this suspicion that despite Llewelyn's experience as a sniper in Vietnam (*NCFOM* 293), Moss is too far from his prey. His shot at the antelope takes an unreasonable risk that he will indeed wound but not kill one of them.

7. Holloway's discussion of the "utopian wish object" (20) might be extended here to argue that narcotics are the ultimate object that has no value except in their ability to fool a user into feeling that he or she has escaped a world of material exchange. If so, then mind-altering drugs become contraband closest to money in their almost purely symbolic value. This makes them different than other exchange goods. I do not believe that John Grady's idealization of horses means he has no meaningful relationship with Redbo. Drugs, by contrast, have no similar value beyond the same degree as money.

8. It might also be argued that in Bell, McCarthy has created a deeply sympathetic portrait of a man preternaturally weak in the knees, who—like most of us, outside of our dreams—simply finds rhetorical justifications of old fears and desires, without the possibility of recognizing how he is thus manipulated away from free will by his—and most of our—simple, non-heroic nature as human beings. Here again it seems ironic to me the combination of sly indulgence and vitriolic condemnation that Bell has received in the majority of the reviews of *No Country for Old Men*. Lester Ballard found more tolerance than this frightened man so old before his time—as if the neighbor who does not vote the way you do poses more of a threat than a murdering necrophiliac.

9. I am indebted to two conference papers here: to Stacey Peebles's "Bean, Bell, and the Efficacy of Texas Lawmen" for historical information on West Texas Sheriffs, and to Meredith Farmer's "Coining a new standard for judgment: Cormac McCarthy's use of Complexity Theory" for seeing the undeniable "ant-on-sugar = Anton Chigurh" connection I could not see. I will return to Farmer's larger argument, which also partially informs this paragraph's sense of subsumptive hierarchy, in my concluding chapter.

10. This scene, between Bell and his uncle, is given in roman type, in the place heretofore reserved for action. This makes some sense inasmuch as this placement provides the uncle with the space of a character; we see him out side, as it were, the stricter confines of Bell's consciousness in the monologues. But the fact that this scene takes up a significant portion of Chapter IX signals the degree to which Bell must take over the book after Moss is killed and the generic elements of the crime novel have dwindled down.

11. Not to conflate Bell with McCarthy, but simply to again examine one connection between the author's life and his creation of a character, we might place this claim of Bell's again McCarthy's in the second interview with Woodward, that McCarthy's six-year-old son is "the best person I know, far better than I am" (104).

12. It must be mentioned that Freud goes on to restrict "woman" with the domestic sphere, as "guardian of the fire which was held captive on the domestic hearth, because her anatomy made it impossible for her to yield to the temptation of this desire." In case it isn't obvious, I find much of Freud's explanation simply bizarre: as often happens, it seems to be the case here that again we have someone thinking about a situation in which they have never been: standing in the cold dark around a communal fire that provides the only warmth and light was not a common pastime in fin-de-siècle Vienna. Freud may have found among his upper-middle class patients "how regularly analytic experience testifies to the connection between ambition, fire, and urethral eroticism" (37). But to put it bluntly, even among the toughest group of homophobic (and thus aggressively homosocial) men on a back-country backpacking trip, the first man to put out a fire if the snatches are lost would not be allowed to think he has won some contest. I regard the irrational sexism (as much as the more outlandish and unlikely imaginative explanations) in both Freud and Jung as weaknesses—even sometimes fundamentally damning weaknesses—in their theories as justifications for the domination of women for nothing but accidental evolutionary reasons that become as oppressive as they do only through their reinforcement in culture. I use both of them here because it seems obvious that McCarthy, through Yeats, is playing with the same material as they were.

13. "They listened with great attention as John Grady answered their questions and they nodded solemnly and they were careful of their demeanor that they not be thought to have opinions on what they heard for like most men skilled at their work they were scornful of any least suggestion of knowing anything not learned at first hand" (*ATPH* 95–96).

14. It is even curious that McCarthy has made Bell's lost child a daughter. This fits with the shift in which Bell insists that his wife is better than him, the best thing to happen

to him, etc. But everything we have as evidence of this remains in Bell simply telling us so—with one exception. Bell returns home from Eagle Pass to his wife Loretta, who has cooked dinner and "put on music, a violin concerto." Outside it is snowing, and Loretta reminds him of "the last time it snowed" there. When Bell finally retrieves the memory, he says, "That's nice," but he means that "music. Supper. Bein home" (*NCFOM* 136–137). The memory recalled by snow remains private: her smile seems not to point to the loss of the daughter but to some moment of intimacy between them. But the snow outside will be reflected in Bell's dream, where, no matter how "nice" it is "[b]ein home," he will ride off behind his father, two men without women. And the connection of snow and memory, especially as the memory's quality (sad or happy) remains mixed to the reader, suggests infertility and death, and recalls Joyce's "The Dead." I am indebted to Dianne Luce for this last point.

WALLIS R. SANBORN III

Animals and Death in The Gardener's Son, The Stonemason, "Bounty," and "The Dark Waters"

The dominant theme in McCarthy's major works, death, can also be found in the author's other texts. In keeping with the subject of animal presentation and death, four works other than the novels must be addressed. These four texts, the drama, *The Stonemason*, the teleplay, *The Gardener's Son*, and two scenes from *The Orchard Keeper* published as titled short stories, "Bounty" and "The Dark Waters," all present animals prominently and are worthy of individual attention and analysis. *The Stonemason* is a bleak drama, which calls attention to the end of the art of stonemasonry and argues the theme of the unceasing mortality of all living things; everyone and everything dies, and the cycle of birth, life and death affects all. The narrative protagonist, Ben Telfair, watches as his family is decimated by death and his father, grandfather, nephew, dog, and others, die off; these deaths are analogous to the death of the trade of stonemasonry; as the practitioners of stonemasonry die, so does the promotion, artistry and practice of stonemasonry. Additionally, the Telfair family dog, Bossy, dies near the end of the drama. In McCarthy's drama of family death, even the dog dies. Bossy dies, and so the canine's importance lies with its position as one of the dead family members. By killing off the dog, McCarthy is including the dog in the Telfair family.

In McCarthy's teleplay, *The Gardener's Son*, the author frames the opening and closing scenes of the text proper with passages in which mule

From *Animals in the Fiction of Cormac McCarthy*, pp. 15–26. © 2006 by Wallis R. Sanborn III.

teams are prominently displayed and play the role of harbinger to human death. In the teleplay, a revisionist account of a nineteenth century murder and subsequent execution, stock mules, teamed on wagons, signify human death. Where mule teams are present, pulling wagons, there is human death, and the mule team as a framing device is analogous to James Gregg's and Robert McEvoy's deaths, as a mule team pulls and carries, literally and symbolically, the body of the dead.

In "Bounty," the first of two passages from *The Orchard Keeper* to be published as a titled short story, a boy finds a wounded sparrowhawk and takes the animal home, thus he takes control of the avian predator and thus takes control of the natural world; after the bird dies, the boy redeems a one dollar chickenhawk bounty on the carcass. The boy uses the bounty as down payment on a set of traps to further his bounty-hunting career. This bounty scene is the seminal scene of a major McCarthy theme, the theme of the bounty-value of dead wild animals, and one of many in the body of work where a dead animal is worth more to man than a live animal. "The Dark Waters" is the second passage from *The Orchard Keeper* to be published as a titled short story. In title, in theme, in action, this short story is a preface of McCarthy's ongoing textual battle between man and the natural world in the constant struggle of biological determinism. In the short story, a boy is taken on a raccoon hunt by his mentor, and what happens during the hunt initiates the boy into manhood. Of course, this coming of age story is also a narrative of the hunt, the deterministic battle between man and coonhound, and wild animal, and as such, is the seminal scene of the ballet of the hunt. Both short stories foretell McCarthy's *oeuvre*-wide fascination with the animal world and man's ceaseless attempts to control the animals in the natural world, and as well, the drama and the teleplay slot well into the author's body of work, in that both texts deal primarily with the theme of death, human and animal.

The theme of death and animal presentation in *The Stonemason* is McCarthy's bleak argument regarding the unceasing mortality of all living things. The action chronicles the deaths that occur in the Telfair family, as a catalog of family members die or are alluded to as dead by the time the textual action is completed. Those chronicled as dead by the close of the text include Ben Telfair's paternal grandmother (6), paternal Uncle Selman (50–1), paternal great Uncle Charles (62), father Big Ben (102), nephew Soldier (120), beloved paternal grandfather Papaw (98–9), and all of Papaw's brothers, sisters and children (94). In fact, early in the text, Ben refers to all of the dead Telfair "ancestors black and white" (32). Additionally, as the drama is family-centric, a majority of the action occurs in the Telfair family kitchen. Those present in the Telfair kitchen or alluded to in the conversations within the Telfair kitchen are members of the Telfair family.

This familial membership even includes the Telfair family dog, Bossy, who not coincidentally, is dead by the close of the text.

Early in the text, in fact in the very opening lines of the textual action, Act one, scene two, McCarthy posits Bossy in the Telfair family kitchen, thus McCarthy includes the dog in the Telfair family. McCarthy uses direction, not character attention and dialogue, in this introduction of Bossy [McCarthy's italics]: "*Early the following morning. The lights are on in the kitchen and outside it is just graying with daylight. Papaw is sitting in his chair by the stove as Ben enters . . . Ben goes to the window and looks out at the yard. There is a small dog sleeping by the stove and it looks up*" (12). As the action of the drama opens, the two protagonists of the text, Ben Telfair and his paternal grandfather Papaw, are present in the family kitchen, the family meeting place. The importance of the two human characters is indicated by their introduction prior to the dialogue in the scene. Introduced immediately thereafter is the Telfair family dog. This immediate placement of the canine within the family, in the family kitchen, indicates that the dog is indeed a member of the Telfair family. Later in the same scene, as Ben and Papaw leave to work stone, the family dog is named, and the beast's advanced age is indicated:

> *Ben opens the door.*
> MAMA: And let Bossy out.
> BEN: (*To the dog*) Let's go.
> *The dog looks at him.*
> BEN: Let's go, I said.
> *The dog climbs slowly out of the box and goes to the door and looks out.*
> BEN: Hit it.
> *The dog goes out. Ben and Papaw turn up their collars and pull on their caps and let down the earflaps. Ben watches the dog out in the snow.*
> BEN: Mama what are you going to do about this dog?
> MAMA: Aint nothin wrong with that dog.
> BEN: He raises his leg to take a pee and then falls over in it.
> MAMA: You dont need to be worryin bout that dog. That dog's just fine [24–5].

In this comic passage, McCarthy names the dog, or more correctly, identifies the Telfair's name for the dog. And as only family have the right to give a name (*Outer Dark* 235–6), Bossy is identified as a Telfair family member—because he has been named by the Telfairs. Though circular in logic, this naming situation has precedent in *Outer Dark*, when the leader of The Three indicates to Culla that the tinker did not have the right to name the infant child, but Culla or Rinthy could have and should have named the doomed child—by right and by duty. Family members are to be named, and as the dog is a member of the Telfair family, the dog receives the inclusive gift of a name. Interesting also, is McCarthy's use of dialogue here. Ben says to the dog, let's go; in doing so, Ben is using a contraction with an inclusive pronoun—let us go. Using a pronoun such as us indicates that the dog is a part of the collective that encompasses the Telfair family. Again, McCarthy has clearly indicated that Bossy is a Telfair. Finally, the canine seems arthritic, or at the least elderly and unable to move about well, for he cannot balance long enough to void without falling into the waste. But Ben's mother indicates that the dog is acting as it should at that point in life, and as such, should be left alone to live comfortably. This acceptance of the creaky dog is the loving maternal acceptance of one who loves an elderly family member. Of course, as the text is McCarthy's, the dog is not going to be just fine, for death waits.

By Act five, scene one, Ben is the Telfair patriarch, for his father, Big Ben, has committed suicide and his beloved grandfather, Papaw, has died of old age. Literally and symbolically, the Telfair family has died, for the family no longer inhabits the same kitchen in the same home. From the stage-left podium, Ben articulates on family and death: "The big elm tree died. The old dog died. Things that you can touch go away forever. I don't know what that means. I don't know what it means that things exist and then exist no more. Trees. Dogs. People" (104). The familial structure of Ben's life has collapsed, and he searches in grief for a graspable, palpable meaning to the deaths that have occurred within his family, for the Telfair family, as a collective unit, is dead. McCarthy's direction indicates the family house is no longer lived in or even livable, while Ben's narrative lists a number of deaths unseen by the audience; the big elm in the front yard has died, as has the Telfair family tree. And as a dead tree must be cut down, the Telfair family has been cut down. The tree, now dead and in scraps or burned, is no longer touchable. The androcentric Telfair family tree has also fallen because the taproot, Papaw is dead, as is the trunk, Big Ben. Consequently, neither father figure is touchable, either. Also included in Ben's lament is Bossy, the now dead canine, for Bossy, as a beloved member of the Telfair family, is also mourned. Like the other dead, the Elm, Big Ben and Papaw, Bossy is now untouchable, and because of this untouchability, Ben mourns the loss of Bossy. Bossy's death is an inclusive act by the author, for the dog's death clarifies the canine's place within the Telfair family. Nowhere in McCarthy's *oeuvre* is a dead dog so lamented and so mourned as is Bossy in *The Stonemason*—a drama ultimately about the death of a family brought about through the deaths of the members of the family.

In McCarthy's teleplay, *The Gardener's Son*, animals and death again are conjoined, as mules are harbingers of human death. In *The Gardener's Son*, the author frames the opening and closing scenes of the text proper with passages in which stock mule teams play the role of harbinger to human death. As such, stock mules, teamed on wagons, signify human death. Consequently, where teams of stock mules are found in the text, human death is to follow. This theme is not unlike the stock animal as harbinger to human death theme found in *Outer Dark*, a text where the swine is the harbinger to human death. But *The Gardener's Son*, like *The Stonemason*, deals with human death and the destruction of the family, but unlike the drama, the teleplay incorporates violence and nineteenth century class schism into the nexus of familial destruction. In the teleplay, a catalog of family members from the wealthy Gregg family and the poverty struck McEvoy family die, but the focus of the action revolves around the murder of James Gregg, scion to mill owner William Gregg, by Robert McEvoy, scion to the mill's gardener, Patrick McEvoy, and Robert's subsequent execution by hanging. Prior to each man's death, mule teams are situated in either the text or the author's direction, signifying the death(s) to come.

In James Gregg's case, the first paragraphs of McCarthy's direction signify James as doomed (italics McCarthy's):

> *Series of old still shots of the town of Graniteville* [South Carolina] *and of the people. . . . They comprise an overture to the story to follow, being shots of the characters in the film in situations from the film itself, so that they sketch the story out in miniature to the last shot of an old wooden coffin being loaded into a mule-drawn wagon and a shot of the town.*
>
> *Freeze frame of the town, the rows of houses. Animate into action. A wagon comes up a street through the mud. Seated in three sets of spring seats are seven or eight stockholders of the Graniteville Company Mill and the son of the mill's founder who is named James Gregg.*
>
> *James Gregg is pointing out various features of the mill village* [5].

By presenting the photograph of the mule team, wagon and coffin as the final photograph of the montage, McCarthy immediately identifies the mule team with human death, and the position of the photograph can hardly be interpreted as an accident. Clearly, the author is developing a textual theme, for he posits the fated James Gregg in the paragraph that follows the opening montage. In this brief passage signifier and signified are quickly identified, and indeed James Gregg is later mortally wounded (56–7) by Robert McEvoy for crimes known and unknown to the reader. In this first example of mule as harbinger to human death, McCarthy introduces the theme of the mule team and human death, and then, the author presents, by name, the character whose death has been tolled.

Quickly caught, tried, found guilty, and condemned, Robert McEvoy is to die by hanging on 13 June 1876 (68–9). Regardless that the verdict comes before the mule, so to speak, McCarthy sees fit to continue to place the mule team in the text for the purpose of signifying human death, in this case, Robert McEvoy's death; again, the author uses direction to posit the mule team in the text:

> Exterior. Jail. Two men arrive on a wagon in front of the doors and one climbs down and taps at the door with the butt of his whip. The door opens and the jailer looks out. The teamster nods toward the wagon and they talk and the jailer nods and the teamster goes back to the wagon and the two teamsters slide a black wooden coffin off the tailboard and carry it in [83].

In this paragraph of direction, the mule team, identified by the fact that the drovers are teamsters, delivers the condemned man's coffin, McEvoy's black wooden box. In this example, as with the example with the mule team and James Gregg, the signifying mule team is easily identified with the signified. McEvoy is hanged at 1313 hours on Friday the 13th, June 1876 (84–5). To make the mule and human death conjugation even more explicit, McCarthy hauls McEvoy's coffined corpse off in a wagon pulled by a mule:

> Exterior. Long shot of jail and an empty wagon standing in the front with Patrick McEvoy waiting. The doors open and the men come out with the coffin and load it into the back of the wagon. The sheriff approaches McEvoy with a paper and gets him to sign it. The other men stand around somewhat uneasily. McEvoy looks at them and then turns and takes up the reins and chucks up the mule and they start off [86–7].

Here, no longer harbinger of Robert's death, the mule nonetheless signifies Robert's death. For the third time in this short text, McCarthy has conjoined the wagon-pulling mule with human death. The first time the theme is used, James Gregg is to be murdered; the second time the theme is used, Robert McEvoy is to be hanged; the third time the theme is used, McCarthy is presenting the death of the McEvoy family, as the only McEvoy son is now dead; there will be no more McEvoy scions. And the fourth and final time the theme of mule and human death is used in the text, McCarthy is presenting the death of the Gregg family, for James Gregg was the only remaining living Gregg son; there will be no more Gregg scions.

In the final directorial passage that contains the theme of the mule and human death, a team of mules removes the Gregg family plots and tomb-monument, prior to Mrs. Gregg's return to Charleston, her ancestral home:

> *Exterior. Day. The Graniteville cemetery. A scaffolding of poles is erected over the monument of William Gregg and the monument is being hoisted with a block and tackle. A heavy freight wagon with an eight-mule team is waiting to be backed under and receive the monument. A crew of gravediggers wait on with shovels. Teamsters back the mules and the stone is lowered into the bed of the wagon and the diggers come forth with their picks and shovels and proceed to exhume the bodies of the Gregg family. Mrs. Gregg in her carriage waits on in the distance. It is a quiet and sunny scene* [87].

In a lonely scene, not unlike the above scene with Mr. McEvoy, a lone remaining parent retrieves the dead for burial, or in this case, reburial. In each example, a mule team labors, carrying the weight of human death. Mrs. Gregg's material wealth means nothing, because her family has been destroyed, and she is without husband (18) and sons (15, 59), and she is as broken spiritually as is Mr. McEvoy, who has lost his son (85) and his wife (36). McCarthy's nexus to all of this human death is the mule team, for in *The Gardener's Son*, where mule teams are found pulling wagons, human death abounds, and the mule team as a framing device is specifically analogous to James Gregg's death and Robert McEvoy's death, as a mule team pulls and carries, literally and symbolically, the body of the dead.

In "Bounty," the first excerpt from *The Orchard Keeper* (77–85) published as a short story (*The Yale Review* 54.3), McCarthy offers the first scene that contains the theme of the bounty-value of dead wild animals. This bounty-value, of course, means that a dead wild animal is worth more to man than a live one. The bounty-value theme is a major theme in McCarthy's body of work, and is to be found, in some manner, in all nine of the novel length works of fiction. As man places bounty-value on specific animals, man kills said valued animals, and thus, controls the prey through killing. This act of controlling an animal through killing is one that man often repeats in McCarthy's fiction; using force, man controls the wild animals he can, and man kills the animals he cannot control. Either way, man seeks and gains control over the natural world. "Bounty" contains another important McCarthy theme as well, the theme of man's attempts to control flying animals. Flight symbolizes a freedom and a power that man does not possess. As such, man seeks to control avian freedom and power through controlling avians, often resorting to killing the flying animals, namely birds and the flying mammals, bats. All of McCarthy's novel length works except *Outer Dark* contain scenes of man explicitly attempting to control avians. Clearly, "Bounty" is an important work because the titled short story foreshadows the dominant, *oeuvre*-wide themes of bounty-value of a wild animal and control of the natural world—with attention here to a doomed sparrowhawk—through killing. And of course, bounty-value and control through killing are subthemes of McCarthy's omnipresent theme of death.

In "Bounty," an unnamed boy finds a wounded sparrowhawk, and he takes the little avian home. Thus the boy takes control of the natural world through control and capture, but the little bird dies in captivity:

> It was in August that he found the sparrowhawk on the mountain road, crouched in the dust with one small falcon wing fanned and limp, eyeing him without malice or fear—something hard there, implacable and unforgiving.... He carried it home and put it in a box in the loft and fed it meat and grasshoppers for three days and then it died [368].

This passage, excerpted from the first published paragraph of McCarthy's adult work, identifies McCarthy's naturalist bent, while additionally, the passage includes the theme of death and the theme of man controlling the natural world, specifically here, man controlling the flying wild animals of the natural world. The boy captures the wild bird, and he boxes the animal; the flying animal, no longer free, dies in captivity, for a broken wing is not necessarily a mortal wound, and a sparrowhawk, a master predator, is not meant to eat pieces of meat and insects from the hand of a boy. This idea that wild animals are not suited for captivity is also an important idea in McCarthy's later works, especially *The Crossing*. In McCarthy's body of work, wild animals do not do well in captivity. However, a dead wild animal still has value, bounty-value.

The boy still has use for the dead sparrowhawk, for there exists in the county, a chickenhawk bounty of one dollar, and the boy goes into town and to the courthouse to redeem his bounty:

> There was a woman at a small desk just inside the door.... He stood for a few minutes looking around the hall and reading the signs over the doors and finally she asked him what it was he needed.
> He held the bag up. Hawk bounty, he said.
> Oh, she said. I think you go in yonder [369].

For the first time, the author presents the *oeuvre*-wide theme of the bounty-value of a wild animal; certain wild animals are worth more to man, dead than alive. The boy commences to the second clerk, and she asks if the dead bird is a chickenhawk. The boy replies in the affirmative and states that the dead bird is not yet full grown. The boy tells a lie, for the baby chickenhawk is actually a sparrowhawk, but the bounty is not for sparrowhawks; it is for chickenhawks. Chickenhawks prey upon chickens, and man invests time, money and energy raising chickens for eggs, meat, and feathers, and financial gain. As such, a wild animal that hurts man's profit must be controlled. One way to control the wild animals in the natural world is to kill the wild animals. One way to promote the killing of specific wild animals is to place a monetary bounty-value on the specific wild animal, in this case, the poultry ravaging chickenhawk. Subsequently, a wild animal's value to man increases after death, and so the boy lies about the type of hawk he possesses, for a dollar is a large sum to the boy, and the boy has a preplanned use for the bounty money.

After leaving the courthouse, the boy goes through town and arrives at a general store, where he gazes in the window and sees what he wants hanging from the wall. Concurrently, McCarthy continues his bounty motif. After entering the store, the boy is helped by an elderly gentleman:

Can I help ye, son? He said.
How much are they . . . your traps there.
The man turned. Traps? Steel traps.
Yessir.
. . . what size?
Them. He pointed. Number ones [373].

The boy is going to invest in traps and enter the bounty-hunting business, for the boy understands bounty-value, in theory and in practice, and as such, believes that collecting bounty money is quite easy. The boy uses his bounty dollar to contract for twelve traps, four of which the boy receives at the time of the transaction. McCarthy dates the action, as well, as the traps are to be paid for in full by the first of January 1941 (374). As this scene is set in August, it becomes clear that the year of the scene is 1940. Returning to the traps and the themes of bounty-value and death in the text, typical of man in McCarthy's work, the boy seeks control of the natural world through the killing of wild animals; additionally, the boy understands the concept of bounty-value, and as such, seeks material gain through the trapping and killing of bounty-valued wild animals. Finally, the bounty-value concept is discovered when the boy captures and controls an avian, thus taking from the bird its freedom and its life. This seminal short story is an important work, regardless that it is an excerpt, because McCarthy's *oeuvre*-wide themes of death, control of the natural world, control through killing, and bounty-value are present from the first paragraph of the work. "The Dark Waters," also contains the dominant themes of the McCarthy body of work.

"The Dark Waters" is, in title, in theme, in action, a preface of McCarthy's ongoing textual conflict between man and coonhound, and wild animal, in a biologically deterministic world. In this titled short story (*The Sewanee Review* 73.2), also an excerpt from *The Orchard Keeper* (119–27), man, devolved to the point that he needs aid in hunting, uses coonhounds to hunt wild prey. As this titled short story is McCarthy's first published narrative of the hunt, it is also the seminal scene of the ballet of the hunt— man and coonhound hunting in an unseen balance, which is the product of more than five thousand years of canine domestication and training (see Chapter 9). This narrative of the ballet of the hunt is also a coming of age story, where a boy is taken on a raccoon hunt by his mentor, and the boy passes an initiation right into manhood. Of course, as this story focuses on the hunt, the theme of death is omnipresent through the narrative. So, as with "Bounty," "The Dark Waters" is a primer into the dominant themes in McCarthy's body of work.

The story opens with the ballet of the hunt as a man communicates with a coonhound, sight unseen, secondary to the pattern and direction of the canine's calls:

> Her first high yelp was thin and clear as the air itself, its tenuous and diminishing echoes sounding out the coves and hollows, trebling to a high ring like the last fading note of a chime glass. . . .
>
> The strung-out ringing yelps came like riflefire. The boy was on his feet. Has she treed yet? he asked.
>
> No. She's jest hit now. Then he added: She's close though, hot [210].

In this scene, the coonhound and the man communicate; she bays, and he follows. As well, the man can ascertain how close she is to the wild animal and whether or not the canine has treed the prey animal. This is the balance between man and coonhound, each chasing the prey, but separately, not in geographic proximity. Easily understood by the reader is the boy's secondary position in the hunt; the boy is obviously green, and his questions and mannerisms indicate his freshness as a hunter. The man is a willing mentor, and this relationship of paternal-mentor/male student is one that McCarthy will use again and again in the fiction.

As the action continues, the boy and the man race through the winter woods, above and parallel to a rushing, but freezing creek. The time is winter, and the hunting pack and prey are ominously approaching the water. Here, McCarthy is introducing a major motif, the drowning motif, for many, if not all of the later texts contain scenes of animals drowning, and clearly the author understands the deadly power of water over mammals human and nonhuman. Additionally, the winter setting increases the deadly power of water, for hypothermia increases the risk of drowning. The man and the boy continue their pursuit running "down" (211) toward the creek as they can hear the "rush" (211) of the freezing water of the creek, swollen from recent rain, which rumbles like a "freight" (211) train passing in the distance. McCarthy increases the danger of the water through the direction of the chase, downward, and the fact that rain has recently fallen; the water in the creek is rushing, not standing. Finally, McCarthy uses a simile of force and power and mass and density, the freight train, to evoke the mighty power of the water. The man, the boy, the coonhounds, and the prey animal must converge at the creek:

> ... Lady's clear voice was joined by another, lower and less insistent.... He could follow her progress.... Then she stopped.
> There was a moment of silence; then the other dog yapped once. Sounds of brush crashing. Two wild yelps just off to his right and then a concussion of water. A low voice at his side said: He's got her in the creek.... [211].

The boy and the man race to the creek, and find the raccoon drowning the lead coonhound: "The oval of the flashbeam ... came to rest on the combatants clinching in the icy water.... They could see Lady's ear sticking out from under the coon's front leg" (212–3). After the raccoon is spooked off, Lady is swept down the creek and is again in great danger of drowning. It is at this point that the boy risks his own life and leaps into the frigid, rushing water and, and after some struggle, saves the drowning coonhound (213–4). The boy proves himself adept at life and death, while he also impresses the seasoned hunters with his physical courage. This convergence at the creek, of hunter and hunted, wild and domestic, boy and man, is thematically indicative of the McCarthy body of work. The domestic canine attempts to hunt the wild raccoon in a deterministic battle, and in this case, the wild trumps the domestic, and but for the boy's actions, the domestic would have died through drowning. Concurrently, man attempts to control the natural world through killing, and the thematic and textual ballet of the hunt is born. Of course, the theme of death is the unifying force of the narrative, as it is in all of McCarthy's body of work.

McCarthy's lesser-studied works are important because these works contain the major themes, motifs and action that dominate McCarthy's major works. Both of the short stories, "Bounty" and The Dark Waters," foretell McCarthy's *oeuvre*-wide fascination with the animal world and man's ceaseless attempts to control the animals in the natural world—very often through the killing of the wild animals of the natural world for bounty-value. Additionally, "The Dark Waters" contains a deterministic battle for survival between Lady, the coonhound, and the male raccoon, and the theme of the ballet of the hunt, and "Bounty" is the seminal scene of McCarthy's bounty motif. As well, both *The Stonemason* and *The Gardener's Son* offer prominent thematic and textual displays of both human and animal death, with the former using the family dog in the cycle of life and inevitable death, and the latter using mules as harbingers of human death. In theme, text and action, all four of the lesser-known works bear the McCarthy imprimatur, and as such, fit quite well into the *oeuvre*.

Chapter 2 will be an analysis of the feline hierarchy present in *The Orchard Keeper*, Cormac McCarthy's first novel. In the text, a feline hierarchy exists, by which felines, domestic, feral, legendary, and wild, can be posited according to the animal's proximity to and dependence upon man. That is, the closer a feline is to man, the more dependent a feline is upon man, the lower the feline is on the feline hierarchy. A domestic kitten, utterly dependent upon man, exists at the abject position on the hierarchy, and a panther, a wild animal independent from man, exists at the apex of the hierarchy. In between the abject and the apex are felines in various states of existence.

JOHN CANT

The Road

> When your dreams are of some world that never was or of some world
> that never will be and you are happy again then you will have given up.
> Do you understand? And you cant give up. I wont let you.

The Road is Cormac McCarthy's tenth novel.[1] Its appearance has been
greeted with acclaim by all and sundry, especially those who were less than
impressed by *No Country for Old Men*. Press reaction has been enthusiastic
and opinion in academic circles similarly positive, albeit only available in
unpublished form at the time of writing. It is the only one of McCarthy's
books to have been received with uniform approval. In every case this approval
focuses on the book's stylistic qualities; McCarthy scholars read in it a return
to the unapologetically rich and poetic rhetoric of *Suttree* and *Blood Meridian*;
and to the author's willingness to address fundamental philosophical questions
in a manner generally out of fashion in a culture that has lost faith in the very
notion of the grand narrative. The Grand Narrative of Western culture may
he considered to have been McCarthy's concern all along, focused in the main
on that variant known as American Exceptionalism, but always presenting
that variant within its broader cultural context, and also identifying it as a
product of changing historical circumstances.[2] My reading of the novel is
that it is indeed a return, but not simply to a former daringly ambitious style,
since it would be an exaggeration to claim that McCarthy ever completely

From *Cormac McCarthy and the Myth of American Exceptionalism*, pp. 266–280. © 2008 by
Taylor & Francis.

abandoned this mode of writing. In my view *The Road* is a literary return, a retrospective on the author's own previous works, a re-viewing of his own work that offers a different perspective to that of the young man whose vision was structured by the oedipal paradigm that we find in the aforementioned *Suttree* and *Blood Meridian*.[3] In this respect it continues the development that I have identified in *No Country for Old Men*, but in this latest case the author's eclecticism, so marked in that novel, has sources closer to home. The "other books" out of which McCarthy constructs *The Road* are his own; the road is that which he has trodden himself.[4]

I have already remarked on McCarthy's habit of structuring his texts in different ways, to the extent that no two of his novels have the same form. *The Road* is no exception; it consists of a continuous sequence of discrete paragraphs, some only a few lines in length, none occupying much more than a single page. There are no chapters; paragraphs are separated by spaces that would occupy three lines of text: occasionally a pause is hinted by the indication of an ellipsis at the beginning or end of a page.[5] This structure is clearly intended to reflect the nature of the journey that constitutes the action of the book. The journey itself is of a piece, a series of short stages, entirely on foot, and comprising a continuous whole. The movement of the travellers and the movement of the text are one.[6] The long, painful journey is punctuated by infrequent intervals of rest and shelter or by rare but violent encounters with other travellers. Such a form creates for the writer the problem of maintaining the reader's engagement with the text. McCarthy's way of dealing with this gives him ample opportunity to express in rich language that metaphysical profundity that so many commentators have enjoyed. His descriptions of place and landscape are characteristically eidetic, an effect that is produced by sentences that are rich in nouns but devoid of verbs. But the paragraphs tend to feature a double style of a kind I mention in previous chapters and the sparse descriptions tend to lead up to final passages that are linguistically and philosophically ambitious. This creates an inner rhythm that carries the reader forward, buoyed up by the pleasures of the text. For example:

> He tried to think of something to say but he could not. He'd had this feeling before, beyond the numbness and the dull despair. the world shrinking down about a raw core of parsible entities. The names of things slowly following those things into oblivion. Colors. The names of birds. Things to eat. Finally the names of things one believed to be true. More fragile than he would have thought. How much was gone already? *The sacred idiom shorn of its referents and so of its reality. Drawing down like something trying to preserve heat. In time to wink out forever.*[7] (My italics)

Passages like this cause the reader to pause, reflect, perhaps re-read. They contrast markedly with the headlong pace and action that so compels the reader through *No Country for Old Men*. The passage also illustrates another characteristic of the text: it is initially a representation of the inner voice of the main protagonist, but as the train of thought develops it seems to segue into that of the author. In this way McCarthy manages to imbue the text with a sense of his own presence without departing from the technique designed to elide it. A further passage illustrates the same point:

> He walked out in the gray light and stood and he saw for a brief moment the absolute truth of the world. The cold relentless circling of the intestate earth. Darkness implacable. The blind dogs of the sun in their running. The crushing black vacuum of the universe. And somewhere two hunted animals trembling like ground-foxes in their cover. Borrowed time and borrowed world and borrowed eyes with which to sorrow it.[8]

The sense of man's insignificance in a godless universe, one of McCarthy's constant themes, is powerfully conveyed here. The theme is addressed directly and the author's characteristic answer to the existential question is provided in the working out of the tale.

Both these passages convey the atmosphere of the novel as a whole. The "two hunted animals" are a father and son, cast adrift in a world in which civilization and its concomitants have been destroyed. Most commentators refer to this setting as post-apocalyptic and one can readily see why. A few brief passages are drawn from the father's memory; one of them would seem to describe a nuclear attack:

> The clock's stopped at 1:17. A long shear of light and then a series of low concussions. He got up and went to the window. What is it? she said. He didn't answer. He went into the bathroom and threw a lightswitch but the power was already gone. A dull rose glow in the windowglass.[9]

Given the reference to the atomic bomb in *The Crossing* (and possibly *The Orchard Keeper* and *Cities of the Plain*) this is, on the face of it, a not unreasonable interpretation. But the general scale of the destruction of not only a large area of the United States, but of the world as a whole, suggests the need for a more considered interpretation. There are no birds or animals left alive in this world. Most of the trees and many of the buildings have been burned. The air is filled with ash which necessitates the wearing of face masks in order to filter what is breathed in. This ash is present at all times despite the fact that it rains with great frequency; at the same time, "The weeds they forded turned to dust about them."[10]

Only human beings remain, and those few in number. Murderous feral gangs roam the country killing and eating their fellows, such is the reduced state of their being. Infants are roasted on spits and captives are locked in a cellar that is in effect a larder. These monstrous happenings signal to us that we are present in another of McCarthy's allegorical worlds. The impression is strengthened by the fact that neither father nor son is given a name. If this was a post-nuclear holocaust world then ubiquitous radioactivity, especially in the ash and dust, would have long since killed everybody, the "event" whatever it may have been, having occurred some years prior to the main action of the text. None of the characters encountered in the novel have any of the symptoms of radiation sickness. In this case the "nuclear holocaust" is itself a metaphorical explanation for the state of the world that McCarthy creates as his wider metaphor for the condition of man in the realisation of his cosmic insignificance, powerfully signified in quotation (8) above.

The image of the waste land is one that has recurred throughout McCarthy's previous novels and is an intertexual reference to Eliot. In *The Road*, this image is reasserted more powerfully than ever before. The ash, the dust, the ubiquity of death, especially the death of nature, all contribute to this image: "He . . . looked out over the wasted country."[11] Ash and dust recall the words of the funeral service. The imagery of the poem reverberates through the novel: "I will show you fear in a handful of dust." "I had not thought death had undone so many, . . ." "He who was living is now dead— We who were living are now dying."[12]

The Road is replete with passages that express the same deathly sterility:

> The city was mostly burned. No sign of life. Cars in the street caked with ash, everything covered with ash and dust. Fossil tracks in the dried sludge. A corpse in a doorway dried to leather. Grimacing at the day. He pulled the boy closer. Just remember that the things you put in your head are there for ever, he said. You might want to think about that.
>
> You forget some things, don't you?
>
> Yes. You forget what you want to remember and you remember what you want to forget.[13]

The father's reason for the journey—"They were moving south. There'd be no surviving another winter here"[14] echoes "I read, much of the night, and go south in the winter."[15] The ultimate challenge of cosmic insignificance arises in the contemplation of death. It is this challenge that the Professor fails to meet in *The Sunset Limited*. Suttree was a young man; he conquered the fear of death but fled death itself. Sheriff Bell was wise enough not to challenge the unchallengeable. But the father in *The Road* is marked for death; he knows it and so do we. "... he stood bent with his hands on his knees, coughing. He raised up and stood with weeping eyes. On the gray snow a fine mist of blood."[16] This signifier of the father's doom is encountered at an early stage of the journey and we know that the question the novel must answer is not what will happen to the father, but to the son? and how are they to confront the waste land and what I suggest it signifies? McCarthy's favoured answer, expressed in each of his texts to a greater or lesser extent, is that of the inherent vitality of the ardenthearted, for whom the significance of life is asserted existentially and in defiance of mere reason alone. So it is in *The Road*. At various points of the text and journey the pair speak of "carrying the fire;" one thinks of Sheriff Bell's dream of his father carrying fire in a horn at the end of *No Country for Old Men*, the fire that I suggest signifies civilization being passed from father to son. Here civilization is no more and this pair carry no fire in any literal sense; but the literal is not McCarthy's concern. At first we can only guess at the meaning of this image:

We're going to be okay, aren't we Papa?

Yes. We are.

And nothing bad is going to happen to us.

That's right.

Because we're carrying the fire.

Yes. Because we're carrying the fire.[17]

The phrase is repeated on page 109 and again on page 182, but it is not until we are almost at the end of the father's journey and his life that we learn its meaning. The father realises that the son must go on without him:

I want to be with you.

You cant.

Please.

You cant. You have to carry the fire.

I don't know how to.

Yes you do.

Is it real? The fire?

Yes it is.

Where is it? I don't know where it is.

Yes you do. It's inside you. It was always there. I can see it.[18]

The fire signifies that vitality that burns within the ardent heart, the mystery that is the spark of life itself and that needs no reason to exist. McCarthy reinforces this idea in the last passage in which the dying father's inner voice becomes that of the author: "In that cold corridor they had reached the point of no return which was measured from the first by the light they carried with them."[19] I have argued that the oedipal character of McCarthy's early and middle period works is notably diminished in *No Country for Old Men*. *The Road* reverses the oedipal theme completely and it is this reversal that gives the text a unique place in the author's *oeuvre*. The entire novel is devoted to a journey motivated by the father's heroic quest for a place in which his young son can survive. And this quest, undertaken in the certainty of his own impending death, is motivated by paternal love, a love that the son returns:

> He held the boy close to him. So thin. My heart, he said. My heart. But he knew that if he were a good father still it might well be as she had said. That the boy was all that stood between him and death.[20]

His own tenuous hold on life means nothing when the boy's own life is threatened by sickness: "You have to stay near, he said. You have to be quick. So you can be with him. Hold him close. Last day of the earth."[21] Nothing could be further from the anguished conflict between father and son implied in *Suttree* and *Blood Meridian*. I have interpreted the oedipal trope in McCarthy's work in terms of his raising of his own voice against that of the literary fathers—Faulkner, Melville, Eliot; many more have fed his eclecticism. How then to account for this reversal? The eclecticism was so apparent in *No Country for Old Men* that I suggested it was no longer a cause for "the anxiety of influence," no longer an "ugly fact."[22] Jay Ellis suggests that McCarthy's latest work is indicative of his changed familial circumstances, his third marriage and his joy in his young and growing son.[23] One can well imagine that this might be the case. Indeed McCarthy mentions his son John in his second Woodward interview, describing him as: "the best person I know, far better than I am."[24] This idealisation of the child is reflected in *The Road*: the father's determined pragmatism in the face of potential danger is constantly challenged by the boy's assertion of the claims of conscience. When the father reclaims their belongings from the thief on the beach and leaves him naked and bereft of any chance of survival, the boy weeps, not only for pity of the doomed man, but also for what his father has become:

> Let's go, he said. And they set out along the road south with the boy crying and looking back at the nude and slatlike creature standing there in the road shivering and hugging himself. Oh Papa, he sobbed.[25]

As his death approaches McCarthy gives the father words close to those quoted by Woodward: "You have my whole heart. You always did. You're the best guy. You always were."[26]

However, the evident allegorical nature of the text suggests a further, more generalised and literary interpretation, best approached by a consideration of the novel's location in fairly specific geographical spaces and the previous literary texts with which McCarthy himself has associated those spaces. The tropes of location, landscape and movement have been interpreted in previous chapters in relation to both individual novels and groups thereof. The "journey" of McCarthy's work, commenting as I suggest it does on the United States' sense of its own identity, has traced the path of the mythic representation of that identity, a path that has led from east to west. The road followed by father and son in this latest novel runs to the south however and its starting point is located in an area of woods and mountains where the winters are too cold to survive without shelter. As they journey they encounter features that gradually convey a sense of identifiable place:

> What is that Papa?
>
> It's a dam.
>
> What's it for?
>
> It made the lake. Before they built the dam that was just a river down there. The dam used the water that ran through it to turn big turbines that would generate electricity.[27]

This immediately suggests Appalachian East Tennessee as a possible location, a suggestion strengthened by "A log barn in a field with an advertisement in faded ten foot-letters across the roofscape. See Rock City."[28] Such advertisements are not uncommon in East Tennessee. They refer to a tourist feature associated with Lookout Mountain, near Chattanooga, in the Great Smoky Mountains, part of the Appalachian range. Any remaining doubts as to the generalised location of the start of this journey are soon dispelled:

> Three nights later in the foothills of the eastern mountains he woke in the darkness to hear something coming. He lay with his hands at either side of him. The ground was trembling. . . . It was an earthquake.[29]

This area of East Tennessee is the location of frequent earthquakes. McCarthy's latest novel features a journey that commences where his own literary journey began, together with oblique reminders of those early texts. On the very first page the father wakes with his son beside him, just as Culla Holme wakes beside his sister in *Outer Dark*. Like Culla, he has had a nightmare:

> In the dream from which he'd wakened he had wandered in a cave where the child led him by the hand. Their light playing over the wet flowstone walls. Like pilgrims in a fable swallowed up and lost among the inward parts of some granitic beast. Deep stones where the water dripped and sang. Tolling in the silence the minutes of the earth and the hours and the days of it and the years without cease.[30]

We are at once in the McCarthy world of Appalachian allegory: father and son are indeed "pilgrims in a fable," their progress will be the substance of this tale. The dreamer's cave recalls Lester Ballard's womb-like underworld in *Child of God*. When the father lies in the dark, deliberately waking so as not to dream of ". . . a flowering wood where birds flew before them . . . with the uncanny taste of a peach from some phantom orchard fading in his mouth,"[31] we recall the worlds of *Wake for Susan* and *The Orchard Keeper*. The image of idyllic boyhood is recalled by the father standing on a bridge over a stream, "Where once he'd watched trout swaying in the current, tracking their perfect shadows on the stones beneath."[32] The small boy of *A Drowning Incident* watched minnows in such a stream. The more horrific images of *The Road* recall the later works, those set in the southwest:

> People sitting on the sidewalk in the dawn half immolate and smoking in their clothes. Like failed sectarian suicides. Others

would come to help them. Within a year there were fires on the ridges and deranged chanting. The screams of the murdered. By day the dead impaled on spikes along the road.[33]

In *Blood Meridian* we read that,

The way narrowed through rocks and by and by they came to a bush that was hung with dead babies. . . . In the afternoon they came upon a village in the plain where smoke still rose from the ruins and all were gone to death.[34]

As my epigraph for my chapter on *The Crossing* I quote Billy Parham's vain assertion "Yo no soy un hombre del camino."[35] In this latest text father and son are "men of the road" in more senses than one.

I have already noted the way in which the author's own voice seems to speak through that of the father in *The Road*. This trope is also reinforced by other aspects of the novel. East Tennessee is indeed the area in which McCarthy grew up and the father revisits his own boyhood places. "What is this place Papa? It's the house where I grew up."[36] The dam mentioned above would have been created by the TVA.[37] Thus in this novel there is a complex imbrication of previous work revisited, fictional and authorial voices and the author's own distant past. If the last two of these must remain speculative to some degree the literary intertextuality seems clear. And like all such intertextuality, the interest lies not only in the similarities between texts, but in the differences—the re-visions. I wish to conclude my analysis by considering both differences and similarities, for although the former are radical the latter remain of fundamental significance.

Certain characteristic McCarthy tropes are to be found in *The Road* and these maintain a sense of continuity with his previous work. I have already mentioned the use of poetic language and the expression of profound ideas, often in the form of a coda to a descriptive passage. Detailed and precise descriptions of activities requiring skill occur in all the texts, expressive of the value the author places on work well done—an attitude that he surely adopts regarding his own literary work. In such a passage we read of the father's efforts to repair the trolley's wheel mount:

They collected some old boxes and built a fire in the floor and he found some tools and emptied out the cart and sat working on the wheel. He pulled the bolt and bored out the collet with a hand drill and resleeved it with a section of pipe he'd cut to length with a hacksaw. Then he bolted it all back together and

stood the cart upright and wheeled it around the floor. It ran
fairly true. The boy sat watching everything.[38]

This passage comprises one of the separate paragraphs of which the text
is comprised. The care with which the actions are described matches the
care taken over the actions themselves, a characteristic matching of style
and meaning. The wording is technical and accurate; there are no missing
verbs. The effect of the passage is to divert the reader's mind from the anxiety
generated through identification with the protagonists in the extremity of
their plight, just as it diverts the minds of the characters themselves to be
absorbed in practical activity. A further level of meaning is added by the final
phrase. The watching boy is learning both practical and moral lessons by
observing his father's endeavours. The moral value that McCarthy associates
with well-made things is asserted with painful irony when the father seeks
salvage on the beached boat, itself ironically named "Pájaro de Esperanza"
(Bird of Hope):

> Inside [the box] was a brass sextant, possibly a hundred years old.
> He lifted it from the fitted case and held it in his hand. Struck
> by the beauty of it. The brass was dull and there were patches of
> green on it that took the form of another hand that had once
> held it but otherwise it was perfect. He wiped the verdigris from
> the plate at the base. Hazzaninth, London. He held it to his eye
> and turned the wheel. It was the first thing he'd seen in a long
> time that stirred him. He held it in his hand and then he fitted
> it back into the blue baize lining of the case and closed the lid
> and snapped the latches shut and set it back in the locker and
> closed the door.[39]

That the father feels that he can only return the beautiful object to its case
conveys a sense of poignancy that is intensified by the realisation that this
is another action that signifies cultural demise, a further sinking towards
that cultural entropy that the text identifies as the waste land. In the novels
of the *Border Trilogy* McCarthy discourses on the question of maps. His
general refusal to assign psychological motivation to his characters, who
are for the most part types, is of a piece with his refusal of gnosis. His
characters tend to assert that maps are false, simplifications that cannot
signify the full complexity and variation of the changing world, fixed in
time, representations of space, myths which lead astray those who think
that they can be read. In *The Road* the case is otherwise: the travellers have a
road map, fallen into pieces but still representing a world that is no longer.
This map signifies not much less than exists in the world, but now much

more. It is the world that will not suffice. Thus there is a profound sense of irony in the use of the map:

> Long days. Open country with the ash blowing over the road. The boy sat by the fire at night with the pieces of the map across his knees. He had the names of towns and rivers by heart and he measured their progress daily.[40]

In my reading the fragmented map, signifying a world that once was but is no more, can be seen as a metaphor for those texts that constitute McCarthy's own literary past, his former works now revisited.

I have consistently identified the overriding theme of McCarthy's work as a critique of American Exceptionalism in particular and Western gnosis in general. This trope is expressed in the father's reaction to books:

> Years later he'd stood in the charred ruins of a library where blackened books lay in pools of water. Shelves tipped over. Some rage at the lies arranged in their thousands row on row. He picked up one of the books and thumbed through the heavy bloated pages. He'd not have thought the value of the smallest thing predicated on a world to come. It surprised him. That the space which these things occupied was itself an expectation. He let the book fall and took a last look around and made his way out into the cold gray light.[41]

The books contain the "lies" that have led to this cultural demise and the faith in the future on which they based their validity has proved illusory. In this respect books and maps are alike.

One of the ways in which McCarthy draws attention to his narrative style is by employing occasional changes of voice. I have pointed this out in *Suttree* when the eponymous hero suddenly speaks of his "father's letter" in the narrative voice.[42] The same technique is used in *The Road*: the pair make camp in the woods:

> He held the child and after a while the child stopped shivering and after a while he slept.
>
> . . .
>
> The dog that he remembers followed us for two days. I tried to coax it to come but it would not. I made a noose of wire to catch it. There were three cartridges in the pistol. None to spare. She

walked away down the road. The boy looked after her and then he looked at me and then he looked at the dog and he began to cry and to beg for the dog's life and I promised I would not hurt the dog.[43]

This quite radical departure from consistent technique seems to intensify the poignancy of the scene as the father's emotion can be more powerfully imagined as he tells his own story. The affective quality of the passage is heightened when one considers the significance of dogs in McCarthy's works generally: they are frequently associated with friendship, family ties and affectionate relationships in general.

It is abundantly clear that the great difference between *The Road* and earlier texts lies in the loving nature of the relationship between father and son, the complete reversal of the oedipal structure found previously. If I am correct in interpreting this as McCarthy's assertion of his own voice against that of the literary fathers and that his late departure from the paradigm is evidence of his final confidence that his own voice can now be heard, then it is not surprising that he should turn his critical attention to his own work. Given his declared concern to write of death, it must also be the case that he considers the possibility of the end of his authorial career.[44] This also must cause such a thoughtful and self-aware writer to look back at his own work and perhaps see some of it in a different light, or perhaps through different eyes, eyes made less pitiless by late experiences of love. The work on which I wish to focus in this respect is both the most allegorical of the earlier texts and also that which most directly relates to the myth of Oedipus, namely *Outer Dark*. The parallels between the two texts are clear enough. Each novel features a father and son; the father travels the road on a quest that will end in a death. Violence and murder punctuate the action which takes place in an identifiable but non-specific Appalachian mountain setting. The father of the earlier text betrays a complete indifference to the fate of his infant son, the son he abandoned at birth in the woods in the hope that he would die. In what is surely McCarthy's most shocking and horrific literary moment Culla Holme remains an impassive spectator:

The man took hold of the child and lifted it up. It was watching the fire. Holme saw the blade wink in the light like a long cat's eye slant and malevolent and a dark smile erupted on the child's throat and went all broken down the front of it. The child made no sound. It hung there with its one eye glazing over like a wet stone and the black blood pumping down its naked belly. The mute one knelt forward. He was drooling and making little whimpering noises in his throat. He knelt with his hands

outstretched and his nostrils rimpled delicately. The man handed
him the child and he seized it up, looked once at Holme with
witless eyes, and buried his moaning face in its throat.[45]

There is cannibalism in *The Road* also but the loving father tries to comfort
the son and the passage strikes a more restrained note:

> He was standing [there] checking the perimeter when the boy
> turned and buried his face against him. He looked quickly to
> see what had happened. What is it? he said. What is it? The boy
> shook his head. Oh Papa, he said. He turned and looked again.
> What the boy had seen was a charred human infant headless and
> gutted and blackened on a spit. He bent and picked the boy up
> and started for the road with him, holding him close. I'm sorry,
> he whispered. I'm sorry.[46]

The comparison is completed, similarity and difference, when the boy's life
is truly imperilled:

> He was a big man but he was very quick. He dove and grabbed
> the boy and rolled and came up holding him against his chest
> with the knife at his throat. The man had already dropped to
> the ground and he swung with him and levelled the pistol and
> fired from a two-handed position balanced on both knees at
> a distance of six feet. The man fell back instantly and lay with
> blood bubbling from a hole in his forehead.
>
> . . . He . . . put the boy down in the ashes and leaves. He wiped the
> blood from his face and held him. It's OK, he said. It's OK.[47]

The similarity between the two texts is further emphasised in the
person of the tinker, Deitch in *Outer Dark*. I find in him a parallel with the
Wandering Jew of Christian mythology.[48] In the later novel father and son
encounter an ancient man, "A small figure distant on the road, bent and
shuffling."[49] Deitch, having spent a "lifetime . . . strapped in front of a cart
. . . couldn't stand straight to be hung."[50] He says his name is Ely—the only
character in the novel to be given a name although he later says that the
name is false. He it is who announces that "There is no God and we are his
prophets."[51] Like Deitch, the old man has penetrating things to say:

> Where men cant live gods fare no better. You'll see. It's better to
> be alone. So I hope that's not true what you said because to be on

the road with the last god would be a terrible thing so I hope its not true. Things will be better when everybody's gone.

... When we're all gone at last then there'll be nobody here but death and his days will be numbered too. He'll be out in the road there with nothing to do and nobody to do it to. He'll say: Where did everybody go? And that's how it will be. What's wrong with that?[52]

The old man expresses the notion that when man goes his culture, capable of personifying death as McCarthy does in the person of Chigurh in *No Country for Old Men*, goes with him, the extreme of cultural entropy encountered in the passage related to note 7 above. The relation of this old man to Deitch is reinforced in our final view of him:

When he looked back the old man had set out with his cane, tapping his way, dwindling slowly on the road behind them like some storybook peddler from an antique time, dark and spider thin and soon to vanish forever.[53]

Deitch was a "storybook peddler" and Rinthy Holme was associated with "an old dead time."[54] The relation between *The Road* and *Outer Dark* seems clear and intentional. The effect of the intertextuality is to confirm McCarthy's rejection of the intensely oedipal nature of his earlier work. Although the mythic image of the American waste land is taken to a new, all-encompassing extreme, this is done to provide a space in which a more individual, and perhaps personal eschatology is traced out. Although individual death must come at the end, collective continuity remains a possibility if the generations can pass on that ardenthearted vitality which is the inherent motor of life. Just as Eliot's "Waste Land" ends on a note of hope quite out of keeping with what has gone before, so McCarthy's Road runs not "from dark to dark"[55] but to a regaining of the lost female and the sense that the dead father's quest has been fulfilled, that the son will survive:

The woman when she saw him put her arms around him and held him. Oh, she said, I am so glad to see you. She would talk to him sometimes about God. He tried to talk to God but the best thing was to talk to his father and he did talk to him and he didn't forget. The woman said that was all right. She said that the breath of God was his breath yet though it pass from man to man through all of time.[56]

The question that the text leaves unanswered is that of the need for that revolt, oedipal or otherwise. If the oedipal paradigm passes with the patriarchal culture that generated it, what will take its place and how will the revolt of those who wish to make books, inevitably "out of other books," express itself in a mythic form that will carry the new writers against the voices of Fathers and Mothers alike? The authorial voice expresses the passing of the oedipal turn in a late interjected paragraph: "Do you think that your fathers are watching? That they weigh you in their ledgerbook? Against what? There is no book and your fathers are dead in the ground."[57] *The Road* expresses a sense of the passing of a culture. It contains no intimation of what might take its place.

Ultimately the novel goes beyond all of the above and expresses what we all know: that in the long end all things will pass and the pattern of movement that was set in being aeons ago will one day cease and days will be no more since there will be no-one to measure their passing. Or as *The Road*'s final paragraph has it:

> Once there were brook trout in the streams in the mountains. You could see them standing in the amber current where the white edges of their fins wimpled softly in the flow. They smelled of moss in your hand. Polished and muscular and torsional. On their backs were vermiculite patterns that were maps of the world in its becoming. Maps and mazes. Of a thing which could not be put back. Not be made right again. In the deep glens where they lived all things were older than man and they hummed of mystery.[58]

The mystery hums in the ardent heart but not forever.

The Road expresses that paradox that lies at the heart of all serious pessimistic literature: its literary passion defies the very emptiness that it proclaims. It declares the inevitability of cultural entropy, but is itself an example of cultural vitality.

NOTES

1. Despite the author's claim I am not counting *The Sunset Limited* as a novel. Among the more considered, but still laudatory reviews of *The Road* is that of Steven Kellman who concludes that, Beckett-like, "... McCarthy offers a clear-eyed guide to how, though we can't go on. We go on. It is, despite everything, a bracing potion, one for the road." ("Cormac McCarthy Imagines the End"—Review of *The Road* for *The Texas Observer*, Oct. 20th. 2006.) Adam Mars-Jones writes, "*The Road* ... [is] a thought and feeling experiment, bleak, exhilarating (in fact endurable) only because of its integrity, its wholeness of seeing." ("Life After Armageddon." Review of *The Road* in *The Observer*, 26/11/2006.)

2. McCarthy's willingness to address 'ultimate' questions is exemplified in the old man's declaration that "There is no God and we are his prophets." (p. 143) This is surely a characteristic McCarthy inversion of the Islamist claim "There is no God but Allah and Muhammad is his messenger," Muhammad being the Prophet of course. The apocalyptic tone of the novel reflects the mood of America following the destruction of the World Trade Centre (if not its religiosity), just as (I argue) *Blood Meridian* reflected the mood generated by the Vietnam War. See also note 33.

3. Together with all the other texts to a greater or lesser extent as I have argued in preceding chapters; up to but not including *No Country for Old Men*.

4. I am referring here to the quote from Woodward that I have mentioned several times in previous chapters. See for example p. 283, Note 4, above.

5. These occur in a central position thus:

. . .

6. This relation between language and movement is explored in Eva-Lynn A. Jagoe's essay "Pace and the Pampas in Argentine Travel Narratives" in which she analyses the way in which narrative style reflects the motion that is described and also reveals ideologies inherent in the attitudes of the writers of the texts.

7. *The Road*, p. 75. In this passage McCarthy expresses some of his habitual concerns; the relation between culture and the material world; the way in which signifiers become unreadable when the world that generated them disappears—the dependence of the signifier on the signified. What the passage describes is the onset of a cultural entropy against which McCarthy himself seems to fight ardentheartedly in his texts, especially in ambitious passages such as these.

8. Ibid. p. 110. Faulkner uses the same technique to place in the consciousness of unsophisticated characters thoughts that they would not realistically be able to harbour. The father is not without sophistication but the narrative voice does seem to go beyond what he might possess in these metaphysical passages. McCarthy suggests that it is he himself who has "borrowed eyes" from his characters in order to "sorrow" the pain of the world.

9. Ibid. p. 45. The wife and mother is driven to despair at the destruction of her world. To avoid her inevitable fate, as she sees it, as a victim of rape, murder and cannibalism, she commits suicide. The father's love for the son prevents him from joining her: his quest to enable his son to survive results in the recovery of the female at the tale's end. This is consistent with the structure of myths of the redemption of nature and the conquest of death to which both "The Waste Land" and *The Road* conform. The same trope is found in *Cities of the Plain*.

10. Ibid. p. 6. The "Post Apocalyptic" can be regarded as a genre of its own. I have referred to its cinematic representations in Chapter 11 with respect to *Blood Meridian*, namely the "Mad Max" movies of the 1980s. (p. 307) A contemporary example is Alfonso Cuaron's *Children of Men*, itself an allegory of contemporary British paranoia regarding "otherness." The text itself extends the cinematic reference: "We're not survivors. We're the walking dead in a horror film." One thinks of Romero's *Night of the Living Dead*, a satire on contemporary consumerism, given added relevance by the traveller's use of a supermarket trolley to transport their meagre belongings.

Extreme images are also conjured by very real fears concerning global warming and climate change: the effects of Hurricane Katrina on New Orleans provided the USA with images drawn from everyday reality that were apocalyptic indeed. The war in Iraq is also such a source, not to mention the horrors associated with Abu Ghraib and Guantanamo Bay. I have mentioned the attacks on the World Trade Centre in note 1 above. *The Road* seems to reflect the mood of fear that has permeated the Western mind in the first decade of the twenty-first century.

11. Ibid. p. 5.

12. "The Waste Land" ll. 30, 63, 328–9.

13. *The Road*, p. 11.

14. Ibid. p. 4.

15. "The Waste Land" l. 18.

16. *The Road*, p. 26.

17. Ibid. p. 70.

18. Ibid. p. 234.

19. Ibid. p. 236.

20. Ibid. p. 25.

21. Ibid. p. 210.

22. I have mentioned McCarthy's first Woodward interview and his reference to the "ugly fact that books are made out of other books" on a number of occasions (eg p. 5). I have also referred to Harold Bloom's well known treatise on "influence." (p. 15)

23. I mentioned the importance Ellis attached to McCarthy's personal circumstances in the previous appendix. See p. 330, note 26.

24. "Cormac Country" in *Vanity Fair*, August 2005, p. 104.

25. *The Road*, p. 217.

26. Ibid. p. 235.

27. Ibid. p. 17.

28. "Seerockcity" is the tag of a website that advertises the location to the world at large.

29. Ibid. p. 23–4.

30. Ibid. p. 3.

31. Ibid. p. 15–6.

32. Ibid. p. 25.

33. Ibid. p. 28. The reference to "failed sectarian suicides" is a further intimation of the text's association of an apocalyptic consciousness with current political violence. See also note 2.

34. *Blood Meridian*, p. 57.

35. "I am not a man of the road." *The Crossing*, p. 414 (and p. 211 above).

36. *The Road*, p. 21. His boyhood is also recalled in quote 32.

37. As noted previously McCarthy Senior was chief counsel for the Tennessee Valley Authority.

38. Ibid. p. 14.

39. Ibid. p. 192.

40. Ibid. p. 181.

41. Ibid. p. 157–8.

42. See p. 159 above.

43. *The Road*, p. 73–4.

44. There are rumours of another novel; they remain rumours only at the time of writing.

45. *Outer Dark*, p. 236. In chapter 6 I interpret this as a parody of the mass. (p. 87 above.)

46. *The Road*, p. 167.

47. Ibid. p. 56.

48. See p. 83 above.

49. *The Road*, p. 136.

50. *Outer Dark*, p. 192.

51. *The Road*, p. 143. "Ely" has Jewish connotations.

52. Ibid. 145–6. The old man paints a portrait of Anton Chigurh out of a job.

53. Ibid. p. 147.

54. *Outer Dark*, p. 98.

55. *The Road*, p. 220.

56. Ibid. p. 241.

57. Ibid. p. 165.

58. Ibid. p. 241. This final poetic passage marks McCarthy out as quite unlike anyone else writing today. As I claimed at the start of this book, he insists that literature must dare to address the serious questions. The reiterated image of the trout (see quote 32 above) once again recalls the boyhood scene of *A Drowning Incident*, linking the text's closing lyrical passage to McCarthy's earliest world and works. "Maps and mazes" are what he has been tracing in a writing career that has drawn on the culture of the USA and had its roots in the mountains and glens of East Tennessee.

Chronology

1933	Born in Providence, Rhode Island, on July 20, the third of six children, to Charles Joseph and Gladys McGrail McCarthy.
1951–52	Attends the University of Tennessee as a liberal arts major.
1953	Joins U.S. Air Force and serves for four years.
1957–59	Returns to the University of Tennessee.
1961	Marries Lee Holleman, who had been a student at the University of Tennessee; they have a son and later divorce.
1965	*The Orchard Keeper* is published.
1966	Marries Anne DeLisle in England.
1968	*Outer Dark* is published.
1973	*Child of God* is published.
1976	Separates from wife; divorces later.
1977	*The Gardener's Son*, a screenplay, premieres on public television.
1979	*Suttree* is published.
1985	*Blood Meridian, or The Evening Redness in the West* is published.
1992	*All the Pretty Horses* is published; wins National Book Award for fiction and the National Book Critics Circle Award.
1994	*The Stonemason*, a play, is published. *The Crossing* is published.

1998	*Cities of the Plain* is published. Marries Jennifer Winkley; later has a son.
2005	*No Country for Old Men* is published.
2006	*The Sunset Limited: A Novel in Dramatic Form* and *The Road* are published.
2007	*The Road* wins the Pulitzer Prize.

Contributors

HAROLD BLOOM is Sterling Professor of the Humanities at Yale University. He is the author of 30 books, including *Shelley's Mythmaking, The Visionary Company, Blake's Apocalypse, Yeats, A Map of Misreading, Kabbalah and Criticism, Agon: Toward a Theory of Revisionism, The American Religion, The Western Canon,* and *Omens of Millennium: The Gnosis of Angels, Dreams, and Resurrection. The Anxiety of Influence* sets forth Professor Bloom's provocative theory of the literary relationships between the great writers and their predecessors. His most recent books include *Shakespeare: The Invention of the Human,* a 1998 National Book Award finalist, *How to Read and Why, Genius: A Mosaic of One Hundred Exemplary Creative Minds, Hamlet: Poem Unlimited, Where Shall Wisdom Be Found?,* and *Jesus and Yahweh: The Names Divine.* In 1999, Professor Bloom received the prestigious American Academy of Arts and Letters Gold Medal for Criticism. He has also received the International Prize of Catalonia, the Alfonso Reyes Prize of Mexico, and the Hans Christian Andersen Bicentennial Prize of Denmark.

STEVEN SHAVIRO is a professor at Wayne State University. He is the author of *Doom Patrols: A Theoretical Fiction About Postmodernism* and *The Cinematic Body,* among other work.

TERRI WITEK is a professor at Stetson University, where she is also director of the Sullivan Creative Writing Program. She is the author of a book on Robert Lowell and also has published other titles such as *The Shipwreck Dress.*

JOHN WEGNER is an associate professor of English at Angelo State University and was editor of *The Cormac McCarthy Journal Online*. He has published articles on McCarthy, Hawthorne, Ellen Glasgow, and other subjects.

GEORG GUILLEMIN is the author of *The Pastoral Vision of Cormac McCarthy*. He is a translator and interpreter.

VINCE BREWTON is an associate professor at the University of North Alabama, where he also is director of the honors program.

SARA L. SPURGEON is an assistant professor at Texas Tech University. She is coauthor of *Writing the Southwest*. She serves on the advisory board of the Western Writers Series and the editorial board of the journal *Western American Literature*.

JAMES R. GILES teaches at Northern Illinois University. He has written *Violence in the Contemporary American Novel* and *Confronting the Horror: The Novels of Nelson Algren*.

JAY ELLIS teaches in the writing and rhetoric program at the University of Colorado. He is the author of *No Place for Home: Spatial Constraint and Character Flight in the Novels of Cormac McCarthy*.

WALLIS R. SANBORN III has taught at the University of Texas. His work has appeared in *The Cormac McCarthy Journal* and other publications.

JOHN CANT is the author of *Cormac McCarthy and the Myth of American Exceptionalism*. His work has also appeared in *The Cormac McCarthy Journal*.

Bibliography

Ambrosiano, Jason. "Blood in the Tracks: Catholic Postmodernism in *The Crossing*." *Southwestern American Literature* 25 (1999): 83–91.

Arnold, Edwin T. "Blood and Grace: The Fiction of Cormac McCarthy," *Commonweal*, (November 4, 1994).

———. "Cormac McCarthy's Frontier Humor." From *The Enduring Legacy of Old Southwest Humor*, edited by Ed Piacentino, 190–209. Baton Rouge: Louisiana State University Press, 2006.

———. "Cormac McCarthy's *The Stonemason*: The Unmaking of a Play." *Southern Quarterly* 33, nos. 2–3 (Winter–Spring 1995): 117–29.

———. "Cormac McCarthy's Whales and Men." From Cormac McCarthy: Uncharted Territories/Territoires Inconnus, edited by Christine Chollier, pp. 17–30. Reims, France: PU de Reims; 2003.

———. "'Go to sleep': Dreams and Visions in the Border Trilogy." *Southern Quarterly* 38, no. 3 (Spring 2000): 34–58.

Arnold, Edwin T., and Dianne C. Luce, ed. *A Cormac McCarthy Companion: The Border Trilogy*. Jackson: University Press of Mississippi, 2001.

Bailey, Charles. "'Doomed Enterprises' and Faith: The Structure of Cormac McCarthy's *The Crossing*." *Southwestern American Literature* 20 (1994): 57–67.

———. "The Last Stage of the Hero's Evolution: Cormac McCarthy's *Cities of the Plain*." *Southwestern American Literature* 25, no. 1 (Fall 1999): 74–82.

Beck, John. "Filibusterers and Fundamentalists: *Blood Meridian* and the New Right." In *Polemics: Essays in American Literary and Cultural Criticism*, edited by David Holloway, 13–26. Vol. 1. Sheffield, England: Black Rock Press, 2004.

———. *The Second European Conference on Cormac McCarthy*. Manchester: University of Manchester, England, June 2000.

Bell, Vereen M. *The Achievement of Cormac McCarthy*. Baton Rouge: Louisiana State University Press, 1988.

Berry, K. Wesley. "The Lay of the Land in Cormac McCarthy's *The Orchard Keeper* and *Child of God.*" *Southern Quarterly* 38, no. 4 (Summer 2000): 61–77.

Bingham, Arthur. "Syntactic Complexity and Iconicity in Cormac McCarthy's *Blood Meridian.*" *Language and Literature* 20 (1995): 19–33.

Bloom, Harold, ed. *Cormac McCarthy's* All the Pretty Horses. Philadelphia, Pa. : Chelsea House, 2004.

Bowers, James. *Reading Cormac McCarthy's* Blood Meridian. Boise, Idaho: Boise State University, 1999.

Brickman, Barbara Jane. "Imposition and Resistance in Cormac McCarthy's *The Orchard Keeper.*" *Southern Quarterly* 38, no. 2 (Winter 2000): 123–34.

Campbell, Neil. "'Beyond Reckoning': Cormac McCarthy's Version of the West in *Blood Meridian or The Evening Redness in the West.*" *Critique* 39, no. 1(1997): 55–64.

Canfield, J. Douglas. "The Border of Becoming: Theodicy in *Blood Meridian.*" In *Mavericks on the Border: The Early Southwest in Historical Fiction and Film*, 37–48. Lexington: University Press of Kentucky, 2001.

———. "The Dawning of the Age of Aquarius: Abjection, Identity, and the Carnivalesque in Cormac McCarthy's *Suttree*. *Contemporary Literature* 44, no. 4 (2003): 664–96.

Ciuba, Gary M. *Desire, Violence & Divinity in Modern Southern Fiction: Katherine Anne Porter, Flannery O'Connor, Cormac McCarthy, Walker Percy*. Baton Rouge: Louisiana State University Press, 2007.

Combest, Ashley. "Lester Ballard as Savior? Representations of Christ in Cormac McCarthy's *Child of God.*" *Publications of the Mississippi Philological Association* (2003): 14–17.

Cremean, David. "For Whom the Bell Tolls: Conservatism and Change in Cormac McCarthy's Sheriff from *No Country for Old Men.*" *Cormac McCarthy Journal* 5 (2006): 42–61.

Cutchins, Dennis. "*All the Pretty Horses*: Cormac McCarthy's Reading of *For Whom the Bell Tolls*." *Western American Literature* 41, no. 3 (2006): 267–99.

Eaton, Mark A. "Dis(re)membered Bodies: Cormac McCarthy's Border Fiction." *Modern Fiction Studies* 49, no. 1 (2003): 155–80.

Frye, Steven. "Cormac McCarthy's 'World in Its Making': Romantic Naturalism in *The Crossing*." *Studies in American Naturalism* 2, no. 1 (2007): 46–65.

———. "Yeats' 'Sailing to Byzantium' and McCarthy's *No Country for Old Men*: Art and Artifice in the New Novel." *Cormac McCarthy Journal* 5 (2006): 27–41.

———. "Shamans and Savages: History, Historiography, and the Figure of the Mexican in Cormac McCarthy's The Border Trilogy." *Journal of Indo-American Studies* 1 (2002): 140–56.

Giles, James R. "Violence and the Immanence of the 'Thing Unknown': Cormac McCarthy's *Suttree*." In *Violence in the Contemporary American Novel: An End to Innocence*, 84–99. Columbia: University of South Carolina Press, 2000.

Hall, Wade, and Rick Wallach, eds. *Sacred Violence: A Reader's Companion to Cormac McCarthy*. El Paso: University of Texas Press, 1995.

Holloway, David. *The Late Modernism of Cormac McCarthy*. Westport, Conn.: Greenwood Press, 2002.

———. "Modernism, Nature, and Utopia: Another Look at 'Optical Democracy' in Cormac McCarthy's Western Quartet." *Southern Quarterly* 38, no. 3 (Spring 2000): 186–205.

———, ed. *Proceedings of the First European Conference on Cormac McCarthy*. Miami, Fla.: Cormac McCarthy Society, 1999.

Jarrett, Robert L. *Cormac McCarthy*. New York: Twayne Publishers ; London: Prentice Hall International, 1997.

Josyph, Peter. "Older Professions: The Fourth Wall of *The Stonemason*." *Southern Quarterly* 36, no. 1 (Fall 1997): 137–44.

Lilley, James D., ed. *Cormac McCarthy: New Directions*. Albuquerque: University of New Mexico Press, 2002.

Madden, David. *Touching the Web of Southern Novelists*. Knoxville, Tenn.: University of Tennessee Press, 2006.

Owens, Barcley. *Cormac McCarthy's Western Novels*. Tucson: University of Arizona Press, 2000.

Rothfork, John. "Language and the Dance of Time in Cormac McCarthy's *Blood Meridian.*"*Southwestern American Literature* 30, no. 1 (Fall 2004): 23–36.

———. "Redemption as Language in Cormac McCarthy's *Suttree.*" *Christianity and Literature* 53 (2004): 385–97.

Spencer, William C. "Altered States of Consciousness in *Suttree.*" *Southern Quarterly* 35, no. 2 (Winter 1997): 87–92.

Tebbetts, Terrell. "Sanctuary Redux: Faulkner's Logical Pattern of Evil in McCarthy's *No Country for Old Men.*" *Philological Review* 32, no. 1 (Spring 2006): 69–81.

Wegner, John. "Whose Story Is It?: History and Fiction in Cormac McCarthy's *All the Pretty Horses.*" *Southern Quarterly* 36, no. 2 (Winter 1998): 103–110.

Acknowledgments

Steven Shaviro, " 'The Very Life of Darkness' ": A Reading of *Blood Meridian*. From *The Southern Quarterly*, v. 30 (Summer 1992). Copyright © 1992 by The University of Southern Mississippi. Reproduced by permission.

Terri Witek, "Reeds and Hides: Cormac McCarthy's Domestic Spaces." From *The Southern Review* 30, no. 1 (January 1994): 136–142. © 1994 by Louisiana State University. Reprinted by permission of the author.

John Wegner, "Wars and Rumors of Wars' in Cormac McCarthy's Border Trilogy." From *The Southern Quarterly*, v. 38 (Spring 2000). Copyright © 2000 by The University of Southern Mississippi. Reproduced by permission.

Georg Guillemin, "Introduction: The Prototypical *Suttree.*" From *The Pastoral Vision of Cormac McCarthy*, 3–17. © 2004 by Georg Guillemin. Reprinted by permission.

Vince Brewton, "The Changing Landscape of Violence in Cormac McCarthy's Early Novels and the Border Trilogy." From *Southern Literary Journal* 37, no. 1 (Fall 2004): 121–43. © 2004 by University of North Carolina Press. Reprinted by permission.

Sara L. Spurgeon, "Foundation of Empire: The Sacred Hunter and the Eucharist of the Wilderness in Cormac McCarthy's *Blood Meridian.*" From *Exploding the Western: Myths of Empire on the Postmodern Frontier*, 19–40. © 2005 by Sara L. Spurgeon. Reprinted by permission.

James R. Giles, "Discovering Fourthspace in Appalachia: Cormac McCarthy's *Outer Dark* and *Child of God.*" From *Spaces of Violence* by James R. Giles. Copyright 2006 by University of Alabama Press. Reproduced with permission of University of Alabama Press in the format other book via Copyright Clearance Center.

Jay Ellis, "Fetish and Collapse in *No Country for Old Men.*" From *No Place for Home: Spatial Constraint and Character Flight in the Novels of Cormac McCarthy* by Jay Ellis. Copyright 2006 by Taylor & Francis Group LLC—Books. Reproduced with permission of Taylor & Francis Group LLC—Books in the format other book via Copyright Clearance Center.

Wallis R. Sanborn III, "Animals and Death in *The Gardener's Son, The Stonemason,* "Bounty," and "The Dark Waters." From *Animals in the Fiction of Cormac McCarthy.* © 2006 Wallis R. Sanborn III by permission of McFarland & Company, Inc., Box 611, Jefferson NC 28640. www.mcfarlandpub.com

John Cant, *"The Road."* From *Cormac McCarthy and the Myth of American Exceptionalism* by John Cant. Copyright 2007 by Taylor & Francis Group LLC—Books. Reproduced with permission of Taylor & Francis Group LLC—Books in the format other book via Copyright Clearance Center.

Index

Characters in literary works are indexed by first name (if any), followed by the name of the work in parentheses